Grammar Links 3

A Theme-Based Course for Reference and Practice

Volume B

SECOND EDITION

Janis van Zante

Debra Daise
University of Colorado,
International English Center

Charl Norloff
University of Colorado,
International English Center

Randee Falk

M. Kathleen Mahnke
Series Editor
Saint Michael's College

Houghton Mifflin Company Boston New York

Publisher: Patricia A. Coryell
Director of ESL: Susan Maguire
Senior Development Editor: Kathleen Sands Boehmer
Editorial Assistant: Evangeline Bermas
Senior Project Editor: Margaret Park Bridges
Senior Manufacturing Coordinator: Marie Barnes
Marketing Manager: Annamarie Rice
Marketing Associate: Laura Hemrika

Cover image: Stock Illustration Source © 2003 David Ridley, *Multicultural Figures*

Photo credits: p. 221: © Bettman/Corbis; p. 222 top left: Andrew Wakeford/Getty Images; p. 222 middle left: Jacobs Stock Photography/Getty Images; p. 222 bottom left: Teri Dixon/Getty Images; p. 222 top right: Elke Selzle/Getty Images; p. 222 middle right: SW Productions/Getty Images; p. 222 bottom right: Ryan McVay/Getty Images; p. 229: Stock Montage Inc.; p. 250: Courtesy of Lucasfilm Ltd. Raiders of the Lost Ark © 1981 Lucasfilm Ltd. & TM. All rights reserved. Used under authorization. Unauthorized duplication is a violation of applicable law.; p. 254: © Raymond Gehman/Corbis; p. 257: Stewart Cohen/Getty Images; p. 291: © Robbie Jack/Corbis; p. 295: Lambert/Getty Images; p. 297 left: © Shepard Sherbell/Corbis Saba; p. 297 middle: Amy Neunsinger/Getty Images; p. 297 right: Lisette Le Bon/SuperStock; p. 309: Phil Stevens Photography; p. 318 left: © 2003 Rich Clarkson and Associates; p. 318 right: John Edwards/Getty Images; p. 330 top: AP/Wide World Photos/Scott Audette; p. 330 middle: AP/Wide World Photos/Charlie Bennett; p. 330 bottom: AP/Wide World Photos/Uwe Lein; p. 343: Rob Atkins/Getty Images; p. 344 top left: Don Farrall/Getty Images; pp. 344 bottom left and top right, 364, 371: AP/Wide World Photos; p. 344 bottom right: AP/Wide World Photos/Anchorage Times/Joe Rychetnik; p. 356: National Oceanic and Atmospheric Administration/Department of Commerce; p. 367: AP/Wide World Photos/David Zalubowski; p. 377:© Warren Faidley/Weatherstock; p. 385: © Attar Maher/Corbis Sygma; p. 425: Laurent Delhourme/Getty Images; p. 434: Life Stock Photos; p. 447: BananaStock/SuperStock; p. 452: © Michael S. Yamashita/Corbis

Printed in the U.S.A.

Library of Congress Control Number: 2003115026

ISBN: 0-618-27420-0

123456789-HES-08 07 06 05 04

Contents

Introduction

WELCOME TO *GRAMMAR LINKS*!

Grammar Links is a comprehensive five-level grammar reference and practice series for students of English as a second or foreign language. The series meets the needs of students from the beginning through advanced levels:

- *Grammar Links Basic*: beginning
- *Grammar Links, Book 1*: high beginning
- *Grammar Links, Book 2*: intermediate
- *Grammar Links, Book 3*: high intermediate
- *Grammar Links, Book 4*: advanced

Available with each *Grammar Links* student text are an audio program and printable Web-based teacher's notes; the teacher's notes are accompanied by the answer key and tapescripts for each book. Tests and other materials are also available on the Houghton Mifflin Website and are described below. In addition, *Grammar Links 1–4* feature workbooks for further practice of all grammar points introduced in the student books.

NEW IN THIS EDITION

- A fresh, new design with eye-catching art, realia, and a focus on ease of use
- Streamlined, easy-to-read grammar charts showing structures at a glance
- Succinct explanations of grammar points for easy understanding
- Simplified content coverage accompanied by vocabulary glosses to let students focus on grammar while learning about topics of interest
- An even greater number and variety of activities than before, now signaled with icons for easy reference:

 **Listening activities** for receptive practice of grammar structures in oral English

 **Communicative activities** that lead to fluent use of grammar in everyday speaking

 **Writing activities** for productive practice of targeted structures in extended written discourse

 **Links to the World Wide Web** for:

- Model paragraphs for writing assignments
- Practice tests, both self-check tests for student use and achievement tests for teacher use
- Links to interesting sites related to unit themes for further reading and discussion
- Vocabulary flashcards for review of the content-related vocabulary that is used in text readings and exercises
- Much more! See for yourself at www.hmco.com/college/esl.

TO THE TEACHER

Series Approach

Recent research in applied linguistics tells us that when a well-designed communicative approach is coupled with a systematic treatment of grammatical form, the combination is a powerful pedagogical tool.

Grammar Links is such a tool. The grammar explanations in *Grammar Links* are clear, accurate, and carefully sequenced. All points that are introduced are practiced in exercises, and coverage is comprehensive and systematic. In addition, each grammar point is carefully recycled in a variety of contexts.

The communicative framework of *Grammar Links* is that of the theme-based approach to language learning. Unlike other approaches, theme-based models promote the development of both communicative and linguistic abilities through in-depth contextualization of language in extended discourse. The importance of this type of contextualization to grammar acquisition is now well documented. In *Grammar Links*, content serves as a backdrop for communication; high-interest topics are presented and developed along with the grammar of each chapter. As a result, *Grammar Links* exercises and activities are content-driven as well as grammar-driven. While learning about adjective clauses in Book 3, for example, students explore various aspects of the discipline of psychology. While they are practicing gerunds and infinitives in Book 2, they read about successful American entrepreneurs. And while practicing the simple present tense in Book 1, students learn about and discuss North American festivals and other celebrations. Throughout the series, students communicate about meaningful content, transferring their grammatical training to the English they need in their daily lives.

Complementing the communicative theme-based approach of the *Grammar Links* series is the inclusion of a range of successful methodological options for exercises and activities. In addition to more traditional, explicit rule presentation and practice, we have incorporated a number of less explicit, more inductive techniques. Foremost among these are our discovery exercises and activities, in which students are asked to notice general and specific grammatical features and think about them on their own, sometimes formulating their own hypotheses about how these features work and why they work the way they do. Discovery exercises are included in each unit opener. They are frequently used in chapter openers as well and are interspersed throughout the *Grammar Practice* sections, particularly at the higher levels.

In short, the *Grammar Links* approach provides students with the best of all possible language learning environments—a comprehensive, systematic treatment of grammar that employs a variety of methods for grammar learning within a communicative theme-based framework.

About the Books

Each book in the *Grammar Links* series is divided into approximately 10 units. Each unit looks at a well-defined area of grammar, and each unit has an overall theme. The chapters within a unit each focus on some part of the targeted unit grammar, and each chapter develops some specific aspect of the unit theme. In this way, chapters in a unit are linked in terms of both grammar coverage and theme, providing a highly contextualized base on which students can build and refine their grammatical skills.

Grammar coverage has been carefully designed to spiral across levels. Structures that are introduced in one book are recycled and built upon in the next. Students not only learn increasingly sophisticated information about the structures but also practice these structures in increasingly challenging contexts. Themes show a similar progression across levels, from less academic in Books 1 and 2 to more academic in Books 3 and 4.

Grammar Links is flexible in many ways and can be easily adapted to the particular needs of users. Although its careful spiraling makes it ideal as a series, the comprehensive grammar coverage at each level means that the individual books can also stand alone. The comprehensiveness and careful organization also make it possible for students to use their text as a reference after they have completed a course. The units in a book can be used in the order given or can be rearranged to fit the teacher's curriculum. Books can be used in their entirety or in part. In addition, the inclusion of ample practice allows teachers to be selective when choosing exercises and activities. All exercises are labeled for grammatical content, so structures can be practiced more or less extensively, depending on class and individual needs.

Unit and Chapter Components

- **Unit Objectives.** Each unit begins with a list of unit objectives so that teachers and students can preview the major grammar points covered in the unit. Objectives are accompanied by example sentences, which highlight the relevant structures.
- **Unit Introduction.** To illustrate grammar use in extended discourse, a reading and listening selection introduces both the unit grammar and the unit theme in a unit opener section entitled *Grammar in Action.* This material is followed by a grammar consciousness-raising or "noticing" task, *Think About Grammar.* In *Think About Grammar* tasks, students figure out some aspect of grammar by looking at words and sentences from the *Grammar in Action* selection, often working together to answer questions about them. Students induce grammatical rules themselves before having those rules given to them. *Think About Grammar* thus helps students to become independent grammar learners by promoting critical thinking and discussion about grammar.
- **Chapter Introduction.** Each chapter opens with a task. This task involves students in working receptively with the structures that are treated in the chapter and gives them the opportunity to begin thinking about the chapter theme.
- ***Grammar Briefings.*** The grammar is presented in *Grammar Briefings.* Chapters generally have three or four *Grammar Briefings* so that information is given in manageable chunks. The core of each *Grammar Briefing* is its **form** and **function** charts. In these charts, the form (the *what* of grammar) and the function (the *how, when,* and *why*) are presented in logical segments. These segments are manageable but large enough that students can see connections between related grammar points. Form and function are presented in separate charts when appropriate but together when the two are essentially inseparable. All grammatical descriptions in the form and function charts are comprehensive, concise, and clear. Sample sentences illustrate each point.
- ***Grammar Hotspots.*** *Grammar Hotspots* are a special feature of *Grammar Links.* They occur at one or more strategic points in each chapter. *Grammar Hotspots* focus on aspects of grammar that students are likely to find particularly troublesome. Some hotspots contain reminders about material that has already been presented in the form and function charts; others go beyond the charts.
- ***Talking the Talk.*** *Talking the Talk* is another special feature of the *Grammar Links* series. Our choice of grammar is often determined by our audience, whether we are writing or speaking, the situations in which we find ourselves, and other sociocultural factors. *Talking the Talk* treats these factors. Students become aware of differences between formal and informal English, between written and spoken English.

- ***Grammar Practice.*** Each *Grammar Briefing* is followed by comprehensive and systematic practice of all grammar points introduced. The general progression within each *Grammar Practice* is from more controlled to less controlled, from easier to more difficult, and often from more receptive to more productive and/or more structured to more communicative. A wide variety of innovative exercise types is included in each of the four skill areas: listening, speaking, reading, and writing. The exercise types that are used are appropriate to the particular grammar points being practiced. For example, more drill-like exercises are often used for practice with form. More open-ended exercises often focus on function.

  In many cases, drill-like practice of a particular grammar point is followed by open-ended communicative practice of the same point, often as pair or group work. Thus, a number of exercises have two parts.

  The majority of exercises within each *Grammar Practice* section are related to the theme of the unit. However, some exercises depart from the theme to ensure that each grammar point is practiced in the most effective way.
- **Unit Wrap-Ups.** Each unit ends with a series of activities that pull the unit grammar together and enable students to test, further practice, and apply what they have learned. These activities include an error correction task, which covers the errors students most commonly make in using the structures presented in the unit, as well as a series of innovative open-ended communicative tasks, which build on and go beyond the individual chapters.
- **Appendixes.** Extensive appendixes supplement the grammar presented in the *Grammar Briefings.* They provide students with word lists, spelling and pronunciation rules, and other supplemental rules related to the structures that have been taught. The appendixes are a rich resource for students as they work through exercises and activities.
- **Grammar Glossary.** A grammar glossary provides students and teachers with definitions of the grammar terms used in *Grammar Links* as well as example sentences to aid in understanding the meaning of each term.

Other Components

- **Audio Program.** All *Grammar Links* listening exercises and all unit introductions are recorded on audio CDs and cassettes. The symbol 🎧 appears next to the title of each recorded segment.
- **Workbook.** *Grammar Links 1–4* student texts are each accompanied by a workbook. The four workbooks contain a wide variety of exercise types, including paragraph and essay writing, and they provide extensive supplemental self-study practice of each grammar point presented in the student texts. Student self-tests with TOEFL® practice questions are also included in the workbooks.
- **Teacher's Notes.** The *Grammar Links* teacher's notes for each student text can be downloaded from www.hmco.com/college/esl. Each contains an introduction to the series and some general and specific teaching guidelines.
- **Tapescript and Answer Keys.** The tapescript and the answer key for the student text and the answer key for the workbook are also available at the *Grammar Links* Website.
- **Links to the World Wide Web.** As was discussed above, the *Grammar Links* Website www.hmco.com/college/esl has been expanded for the second edition to include student and teacher tests, teacher notes, model writing assignments, content Web links and activities, and other material. Links are updated frequently to ensure that students and teachers can access the best information available on the Web.

TO THE STUDENT

Grammar Links is a five-level series that gives you all the rules and practice you need to learn and use English grammar. Each unit in this book focuses on an area of grammar. Each unit also develops a theme—for example, business or travel. Units are divided into two or three chapters.

Grammar Links has many special features that will help you to learn the grammar and to use it in speaking, listening, reading, and writing.

FEATURE	BENEFIT
Interesting Themes	Help you link grammar to the real world—the world of everyday English
Introductory Reading and Listening Selections	Introduce you to the theme and the grammar of the unit
Think About Grammar Activities	Help you to become an independent grammar learner
Chapter Opener Tasks	Get you started using the grammar
Grammar Briefings	Give you clear grammar rules in easy-to-read charts, with helpful example sentences
Grammar Hotspots	Focus on especially difficult grammar points for learners of English—points on which you might want to spend extra time
Talking the Talk	Helps you to understand the differences between formal and informal English and between written and spoken English
Grammar Practice	Gives you lots of practice, through listening, speaking, reading, and writing exercises and activities
Unit Wrap-Up Tasks	Provide you with interesting communicative activities that cover everything you have learned in the unit
Vocabulary Glosses	Define key words in readings and exercises so that you can concentrate on your grammar practice while still learning about interesting content
Grammar Glossary	Gives you definitions and example sentences for the most common words used to talk about English grammar—a handy reference for now and for later
Websites	Guide you to more information about topics of interest Provide you with self-tests with immediate correction and feedback, vocabulary flashcards for extra practice with words that might be new to you, models for writing assignments, and extra practice exercises

All of these features combine to make *Grammar Links* interesting and rewarding—and, I hope, FUN!

M. Kathleen Mahnke, Series Editor
Saint Michael's College
Colchester, VT USA

ACKNOWLEDGMENTS

Series Editor Acknowledgments

This edition of *Grammar Links* would not have been possible without the thoughtful and enthusiastic feedback of teachers and students. Many thanks to you all!

I would also like to thank all of the *Grammar Links* authors, from whom I continue to learn so much every day. Many thanks as well to the dedicated staff at Houghton Mifflin: Joann Kozyrev, Evangeline Bermas, and Annamarie Rice.

A very special thanks to Kathy Sands Boehmer and to Susan Maguire for their vision, their sense of humor, their faith in all of us, their flexibility, their undying tenacity, and their willingness to take risks in order to move from the mundane to the truly inspirational.

M. Kathleen Mahnke, Series Editor

Author Acknowledgments

Many people made valuable contributions to this book. We would like to acknowledge and thank the following:

The staff at Houghton Mifflin, for their constant patience and encouragement

Each other and the other *Grammar Links* authors, for inspiration, advice, and continued friendship throughout the writing and production process

Our students, for their willingness to test the material

Linda Butler, author of *Grammar Links Basic* and *Grammar Links 1*, for her many valuable insights based on her classroom experience with the first edition of this book

Michael Masyn, of the International English Center at the University of Colorado, for his experience and suggestions

Bob Jasperson, Director of the International English Center, for his support

Len Neufeld, for ensuring that the *Grammar Briefings* were presented in the clearest and best possible way.

In addition, we thank the following reviewers:

Brian McClung, North Lake College
Janet Selitto, Valencia Community College

Finally, we are immensely grateful for the support, encouragement, and patience of our close friends and families, especially Lakhdar Benkobi, Len Neufeld, Richard, Jonathan, and Joshua Norloff, and Peter van Zante.

Debra Daise, Randee Falk, Charl Norloff, and Janis van Zante

Unit **Six**

Gerunds and Infinitives

TOPIC FOCUS
Entertainment

UNIT OBJECTIVES

- **gerunds**
  (*Singing* is her profession.)
- **infinitives**
  (It's fun *to watch* television.)
- **verbs that take gerunds or infinitives or both**
  (Jeff *enjoys listening* to music. He *wants to go* to the concert. He *remembered reading* about it. He *remembered to get* the tickets.)
- **performers of the actions of gerunds and infinitives**
  (Leila didn't understand *their liking* horror movies. She asked *them to tell* her the reason.)
- **verbs followed by base forms**
  (Our parents *let* us *go* to the concert. We *heard* the band *play*.)

Grammar in Action

Reading and Listening: A Popular Export?

Read and listen to this article.

A Popular Export?

The United States's biggest export is its popular culture. Popular culture includes forms of entertainment that appeal to large numbers of people—for example, television programs, movies, and popular music. These American entertainment products are extremely popular internationally, but they also cause controversy. Here are some opinions from people in various countries:

A: "I like **to listen** to American music because there are so many different styles. **Listening** to it gives me the opportunity **to experience** the cultural diversity of the United States. I'm studying English in order **to understand** the songs better."

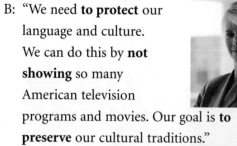

B: "We need **to protect** our language and culture. We can do this by **not showing** so many American television programs and movies. Our goal is **to preserve** our cultural traditions."

C: "I dislike **having** so much American entertainment in this country and throughout the world. It's the same everywhere, so it's causing cultural differences among countries **to disappear**. It's important for the world **not to lose** cultural diversity."

D: "I like **watching** Hollywood movies. The movie-makers are good at **telling** enjoyable stories that appeal to lots of different people. American movies have been popular internationally since the 1920s. I don't think we've lost our cultural identity as a result of **watching** them."

E: "My everyday life is pretty boring. **To escape** is a pleasure for me. So my favorite free-time activity is **watching** action-adventure movies. I can dream of **being** a hero."

F: "It's easy **to blame** American television programs and movies for **bringing** violence to this country. But the United States isn't the only source of the violent images we see."

export = something that is sent to another country for sale there. *controversy* = disagreement. *diversity* = quality of having differences, variety.

Think About Grammar

Work with a partner to complete the tasks.

A. In the article, the boldfaced words are

gerunds (the base form of a verb + *-ing*), e.g., *listening*, and

infinitives (*to* + the base form of a verb), e.g., to *listen.*

Look at the article, and underline the gerunds and circle the infinitives.

B. Gerunds and infinitives are similar in some uses but differ in others. Look at each of the gerunds and infinitives you marked in the article. When you find a use, check it off. Check each use off only once; leave a blank where you did not find a gerund or infinitive for a use.

Use	**Gerund**	**Infinitive**
1. subject of sentence	✓	✓
2. object of verb (i.e., verb + ______)	______	______
3. following an adjective (adjective + ______)	______	______
4. object of preposition (preposition + ______)	______	______
5. following a noun (noun + ______)	______	______

Chapter 12

Gerunds and Infinitives

Introductory Task: A Good Decision?

A. Some verbs can be followed by infinitives (e.g., *to watch*), and some can be followed by gerunds (e.g., *watching*). Read the conversation between two roommates. Circle the forms that you think are correct. If you're not sure, try to guess. You will be able to check your answers in Part B.

Gil: It's almost eight o'clock. Do you **want** to watch / watching (1) *Bulletproof*?

Ken: That's a police drama, isn't it? I don't really **enjoy** to watch / watching (2) those kinds of programs. Besides, I **need** to do / doing (3) some more homework.

Gil: I just **finished** to do / doing (4) the math assignment. Have you finished it yet?

Ken: Yes, I have. I **plan** to study / studying (5) English next.

Gil: There's a situation comedy called *Buddies* on at eight, too. Let's watch it.

Ken: Gil, I'm sorry, but I refuse to watch / watching (6) TV tonight. My education comes first. I'm going to **keep** to study / studying (7).

Gil: Television can be educational. My teacher often **recommends** to watch / watching (8) *Washington Affairs* for information about the government and current events.

Ken: Does your teacher **suggest** to watch / watching (9) situation comedies, too?

Gil: I'm not sure, but I think there are good reasons for us to watch them. For example, by listening to the conversations, we can improve our comprehension skills.

Ken: Turn on the TV! I've **decided** to study / studying (10) English by watching *Buddies*.

B. Listen to the conversation. Check your answers in Part A.

C. Look at the boldfaced verbs in the conversation. Complete the lists:

Verbs that are followed by an infinitive:

want ______ ______ ______ ______

Verbs that are followed by a gerund:

______ ______ ______ ______ ______

situation comedy = a humorous television series with a regular cast of characters.

GRAMMAR BRIEFING 1

Gerunds

FORM

A. Forming Gerunds

1. Gerunds are formed from verbs. Use the base form of the verb + *-ing*. (See Appendix 3 for spelling rules for verbs + *-ing*.)	I enjoy **swimming.**
2. For negative gerunds, use *not* before the base form of the verb + *-ing*.	Thank you for **not smoking**.

B. Gerund Phrases

Gerunds can occur as part of a phrase.	Victor likes **running** in marathons. **Finding** a good job isn't easy.

FUNCTION

A. Gerunds as Subjects and Subject Complements

1. Gerunds are often used as subjects of sentences. When a gerund is the subject, use a singular verb.	**Planning** a party **takes** lots of time and effort.
2. Gerunds can also be subject complements.	My hobby is **singing.**

(continued on next page)

B. Gerunds as Objects

1. Certain verbs can have gerunds as their objects.

   These verbs include:

appreciate	deny	enjoy	mention	postpone	recommend	understand
avoid	discuss	finish	mind	quit	resent	
delay	dislike	keep	miss	recall	suggest	

(For a more complete list, see Appendix 18. For verbs that can also take infinitives, see Chapter 13, Grammar Briefing 1, page 241.)

He **suggested not staying out** late.

The whole family **enjoys skiing**.

2. Gerunds can also be objects of certain phrasal verbs (e.g., *give up, put off*).

   (See Appendix 8 for common phrasal verbs that take objects.)

He's **given up looking** for a new apartment.

I **put off telling** him the bad news.

C. Gerunds as Objects of Prepositions

1. Gerunds can be objects of prepositions.

I gave him some tips **about studying**.

2. They can therefore occur after:

   - Verb + preposition combinations (e.g., *look into, talk about, worry about*).

     (See Appendixes 9 and 10 for common verb/phrasal verb + preposition combinations.)

I'm **thinking about buying** tickets.

   - *Be* (or a similar verb) + adjective + preposition combinations (e.g., *be afraid of, be good at, be happy about*).

     (See Appendix 17 for common *be* + adjective + preposition combinations.)

They **are interested in seeing** the concert.

He **seems nervous about taking** the test.

D. Expressions with Gerunds

1. Use *by* + gerund to tell how something is done.

You get tickets **by calling** the theater.

They celebrated **by going** out to dinner.

2. Use *go* + gerund to talk about doing recreational activities. Gerunds used with *go* include *bicycling, camping, dancing, fishing, hiking, jogging, running, shopping, skiing,* and *swimming*.

Let's **go camping** this weekend.

We **went dancing** last night.

(continued on next page)

D. Expressions with Gerunds (continued)

3. Gerunds are also used in other common expressions.

We **had fun skiing.**

It's no use complaining.

Don't just **stand there doing** nothing.

I **waste all my money eating** in restaurants.

These expressions include:

be busy	have fun (trouble/a problem/ problems/a good time, etc.)	sit/stand/lie + there
can't help	it's no use	spend/waste + time/money

GRAMMAR HOTSPOT!

Don't confuse gerunds with the present participle of verbs in the progressive tenses.

My hobby is **singing.** (gerund *singing* as subject complement)

Susan **is singing** in the rain. (present progressive of verb *sing*)

GRAMMAR PRACTICE 1

Gerunds

1 Identifying Gerunds and Present Participles: Culture Shock?

In the following text, underline the gerunds and present participles. Mark the gerunds *G* and the present participles *PP.*

I'm an American student, and I'm taking (PP) my first trip outside the United States. Before I started traveling (G), I'd been looking forward to experiencing a completely different culture. But not all the experiences that I'm having are new and different. For example, at the moment, I'm listening to the radio. Willie Nelson is singing, "On the road again . . . The life I love is making music with my friends." I don't mind listening to country-and-western music at home, but hearing it in this country seems very strange. Watching television here is a surprise, too—many of the programs come from the United States. I'm experiencing a weird kind of culture shock!

2 Gerunds as Subjects and Subject Complements: Thinking About Entertainment

Complete the sentences with gerunds (single words or phrases). Use your ideas about different forms of entertainment.

1. Dancing OR Playing the guitar ______ is a lot of fun.
2. A form of entertainment that I don't enjoy very much is ______.
3. ______ is a good way to escape from everyday life.
4. ______ is usually a waste of time.
5. An activity that is both educational and entertaining is ______.
6. My favorite entertainment is ______.

3 Gerunds as Objects of Verbs: Matching Up

A. American students starting college often live in dormitories. To find roommates who get along, colleges ask students to describe themselves. Complete the sentences with a gerund formed from the verb in parentheses.

Although my teachers recommend not waiting (1 (not, wait)) *to do assignments, I usually postpone* ______ (2 (study)) *until late at night. I'm not very tidy, and I don't mind* ______ (3 (live)) *in a messy room. I dislike* ______ (4 (watch)) *most kinds of TV shows, except for science fiction dramas. I've never missed* ______ (5 (see)) *an episode of Star Trek. I don't like rock music at all, but I really enjoy* ______ (6 (listen)) *to my CDs of Broadway show tunes. I suggest* ______ (7 (not, pair)) *me with a roommate who likes rock and doesn't like show tunes.*

B. Write a statement like the one in Part A about your preferences in studying, keeping your room, television, and music. Use at least six verbs followed by a gerund, for example: *avoid, can't imagine, dislike,* (*not*) *enjoy, finish, keep,* (*not*) *mind, miss, postpone, resent.*

See the *Grammar Links* Website for another model statement for this assignment.

C. Read your statements to the class. Try to decide which students would get along best as roommates. (Hint: Colleges have discovered that music preferences matter the most.)

4 **Gerunds as Objects of Prepositions:** The Roots of Rock and Roll

Complete the sentences with an appropriate preposition and a gerund formed from the verb in parentheses. (If necessary, look in Appendixes 9 and 17 for help with prepositions.)

In the 1950s, television and Elvis Presley were responsible ___for making___ (1 make) rock and roll popular. Elvis's voice had a special quality, and he was known ______________ (2 move) in a unique way while he sang and played the guitar. Although some people strongly disapproved of his style, many others were enthusiastic ______________ (3 see) his performances. All over the country, people talked ______________ (4 watch) him on TV. Elvis succeeded ______________ (5 attract) huge audiences.

How did Elvis create his style of rock and roll? One influence was rhythm-and-blues music, developed by African-American musicians. He was interested ______________ (6 play) like those musicians did. Another influence was country-and-western music—the traditional music of the South, which Elvis was used ______________ (7 hear). Both rhythm-and-blues music and country-and-western music are good ______________ (8 express) common experiences and feelings. Here are examples of lyrics from country-and-western songs: "I'm afraid ______________ (9 lose) you." "Don't you ever get tired ______________ (10 hurt) me?"

Check out the *Grammar Links* Website for information about Elvis Presley and links to song lyrics.

5 *By* + Gerund: Entertainment Challenges

A. Work with a partner. Think of at least two ways to answer the each of the following questions. Use *by* + gerund in your answers.

1. How can you play the guitar without using your hands?

   You can play the guitar by plucking the strings with your teeth or toes.
   You can do it by asking someone else to play it for you.
2. How can you find out when a TV program will be on if you don't have a schedule?
3. How can you operate a CD player without touching it with your fingers?
4. How can you get into a concert if all the tickets have already been sold?
5. How can you become more physically fit while watching TV?

B. As a class, compare answers. For each question, choose your favorite solution.

6 Gerunds with *Go* and in Other Expressions: Popular Culture in Two Generations

Use the words in parentheses and the expressions in the box above each paragraph to complete the sentences. Use each expression once.

be busy	~~go~~	~~having a hard time~~	sits around	spends too much time	wastes his money

Parent: I'm having a hard time living (1 live) with my teenage son these days. He used to go bicycling (2 bicycle) with his friends, but now he just ________ (3 listen to) loud, aggressive music. He ________ (4 buy) CDs by rappers and metal bands. And he ________ (5 go) to concerts when he should ________ (6 do) his homework.

can't help	go	have a good time	have problems	it's no use

Son: My parents ________ (7 understand) my interest in gangsta rap and hard rock music, and ________ (8 explain) it to them. They ________ (9 listen) to music that was popular before I was born. My mom and dad ________ (10 dance) sometimes. My mom's favorite is disco music by the Bee Gees. I guess they ________ (11 like) that old stuff.

7 Using Gerunds: The Music That We Keep Listening To

A. Work in a small group.

1. Read the following information.

   A researcher, Robert M. Sapolsky, wondered why some people like listening to new kinds of music but others don't. He conducted a survey and concluded that age is the explanation: If you are over 35 when a style of popular music is introduced, you probably won't like it. Most people continue listening to styles of music that they first heard when they were 20 or younger.

2. Use the words and expressions in the box to talk about your own music preferences and those of people who are older or younger than you.

   Verb: *appreciate, avoid, enjoy, (dis)like, don't mind, keep, miss, understand, quit*
   Verb–Preposition: *care about, (dis)approve of, talk about, insist on*
   Be **+ Adjective + Preposition**: *be accustomed to, be fond of, be interested in, be enthusiastic about, be used to*
   Other Expressions: *can't help, have trouble, have problems, spend time, it's no use*

   Example: I'm interested in trying new music, but my parents keep listening to music that was popular when they were young. They sometimes talk about not liking the music I listen to.

3. Decide whether you agree or disagree with the researcher's conclusions.

B. Use the words and expressions in the box to write sentences with gerunds.

1. Write three sentences about music preferences that you have in common with other members of your family or with friends.

   Example: My mother and I both enjoy playing old Beatles records.

2. Write three sentences about differences of opinion about music that you have with other members of your family or with friends.

   Example: I dislike hearing the music that my teenage children like, but it's no use complaining about it.

GRAMMAR BRIEFING 2

Infinitives I

FORM

A. Forming Infinitives

1. To form infinitives, use *to* + the base form of a verb.	I want **to dance**.
2. For negative infinitives, use *not* before *to* + the base form of the verb.	I must ask you **not to smoke**.

(continued on next page)

B. Infinitive Phrases

Infinitives can occur as part of a phrase.	I want **to dance** a tango.

FUNCTION

A. Infinitives as Subjects and Subject Complements

1. Infinitives can be subjects. However, usually *it* is put in subject position and the infinitive is put at the end of the sentence. The meaning is the same.	**To dance** professionally became her dream. = **It** became her dream **to dance** professionally.
2. Infinitives can also be subject complements.	His preference was **to go** to a movie instead of a play.

B. Infinitives as Objects

Certain verbs can have infinitives as their objects. These verbs fall into three groups:*

- Verb + infinitive

  Some verbs are followed directly by an infinitive. They include:

  He **agreed to sing.**

agree	can/can't afford	intend	offer	seem	wait
appear	decide	learn	plan	tend	

- Verb + noun phrase + infinitive

  Some verbs are followed by a noun phrase and then an infinitive. They include:

  She **convinced John to sing**.

cause	force	invite	persuade	teach	trust
convince	hire	order	remind	tell	warn

- Verb (+ noun phrase) + infinitive

  Some verbs can be followed directly by an infinitive or can have a noun phrase before the infinitive. They include:

  She **asked to sing.**

  She **asked him to sing.**

ask	choose	get	want
beg	expect	need	would like

*See Appendix 19 for more complete lists of these groups of verbs. For verbs that can also take gerunds, see Chapter 13, Grammar Briefing 1, page 241.

GRAMMAR **HOT**SPOT!

1. Infinitives cannot be objects of prepositions. Use gerunds instead.	I'm thinking **about buying tickets**. **NOT**: I'm thinking about ~~to buy tickets~~.
2. *To* is part of some phrasal verb–preposition, verb–preposition, and *be* + adjective + preposition combinations (e.g., *look forward to, be used to*). This *to* is a preposition, not part of an infinitive, and it is followed by a gerund.	**I'll look forward to seeing** you again. **NOT**: I'll look forward to ~~see~~ you again. We **were used to singing** in a group. **NOT**: We were used to ~~sing~~ in a group.

GRAMMAR PRACTICE 2

Infinitives I

8 Infinitive as Subject; *It* + Infinitive: Is It Your Dream to Be a Rock Star?

Restate each sentence in two ways using an infinitive phrase.

1. Becoming a rock star isn't easy.

   To become a rock star isn't easy.
   It isn't easy to become a rock star.
2. Becoming a successful rock musician takes hard work and creativity.
3. Developing a unique style is necessary.
4. Being able to compose music is essential.
5. Writing expressive song lyrics is important.
6. Creating artistic videos is a great challenge.

9 Verb + Infinitive Patterns: Our Band

Complete the sentences with *her*, [0], or *her*/[0].

1. a. We agreed [0] to play in the band.
   b. We invited her to play in the band.
   c. We wanted her/[0] to play in the band.
   d. We hoped ________ to play in the band.
2. a. I told ________ to practice often.
   b. I expected ________ to practice often.
   c. I planned ________ to practice often.
   d. I persuaded ________ to practice often.

3. a. Ben offered ________________ to sing the new song.

   b. Ben taught ________________ to sing the new song.

   c. Ben would like ________________ to sing the new song.

   d. Ben chose ________________ to sing the new song.

4. a. We decided ________________ to record the song.

   b. We asked ________________ to record the song.

   c. We convinced ________________ to record the song.

   d. We needed ________________ to record the song.

10 Verb + Infinitive Patterns: An Interview on the Music Channel

Complete the sentences with an infinitive or an appropriate pronoun and infinitive.

A: Lucie, your latest video seems __to be__ (1 be) very popular with our viewers all over the world. I want __you to know__ (2 know) how happy I am that you are here tonight.

B: I would like ________________ (3 thank) you for inviting me.

A: First of all, I want ________________ (4 know) more about your background.

B: Well, my mother is a classical pianist, and she taught ________________ (5 play) the piano. And I learned ________________ (6 write) songs by being around my father, who's a poet. My parents expected ________________ (7 continue) with classical music, but I chose ________________ (8 not, do) it. I needed ________________ (9 develop) my own style.

A: What's next? Do you intend ________________ (10 go) on another concert tour?

B: I've decided ________________ (11 not, perform) for a while because I want to experiment with new forms of music.

A: As one of your greatest fans, I would like ________________ (12 know) how much I'm looking forward to hearing your new music.

11 Using Verbs with Infinitives: I Want (You) to Tell What's Going On

A. Work with a partner. Look at these scenes from four common types of television shows. Discuss what the characters might be doing. Use your imagination. Then write about three of the scenes. For each description, use at least three of the verbs given followed by infinitives (alone or as phrases).

1. Police Drama

warn, want, tell, offer, attempt, ask

Example: The police officer is warning her not to go into the house. She wants to know what happened. . . .

2. Situation Comedy

would like, tell, refuse, persuade, pretend, beg

3. Cooking Program

would like, teach, learn, invite, hope, ask

4. Hospital Drama

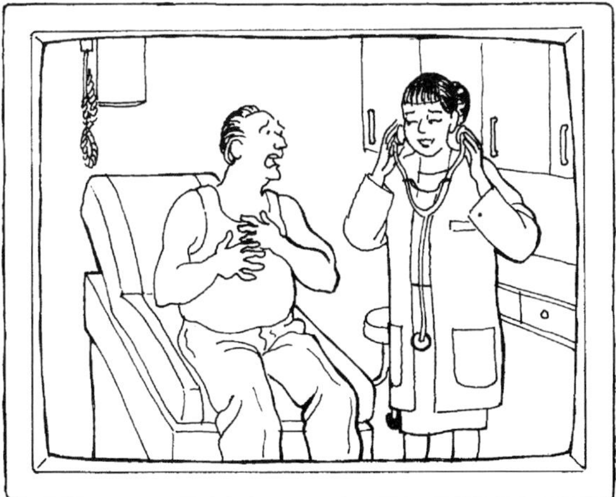

trust, tell, seem, need, expect, agree

B. Tell the class your description of one of the scenes.

GRAMMAR BRIEFING 3

Infinitives II

FUNCTION

A. Adjective + Infinitive

Certain adjectives can be followed by infinitives. Many of these adjectives describe feelings or attitudes.

He is **eager to help out.**

We were **lucky to get** tickets.

These adjectives include:

afraid	ashamed	determined	fortunate	hesitant	prepared	relieved	shocked
amazed	careful	disappointed	glad	lucky	proud	reluctant	sorry
anxious	delighted	eager	happy	pleased	ready	sad	willing

B. *In Order* + Infinitive

In order + infinitive expresses purpose. *In order* can be omitted with no change in meaning.

We're meeting next week (**in order**) **to discuss** the project.

(**In order**) **to get** the discount, you have to be a student.

C. *Too* and *Enough* with Infinitives

Infinitives are used with *too* and *enough* + adjective, adverb, and/or noun. This use of infinitives also expresses purpose. Use them as follows:

- *Too* + adjective/adverb + infinitive.

  (**Note**: *Too* often implies a negative feeling or situation.)

  The children are **too old to get in** for half price.

  We're walking **too slowly to catch up** with them.

- Adjective/adverb + *enough* + infinitive.

  The children are **young enough to get in** for half price.

  He plays **well enough to get on** the team.

- *Enough* + noun + infinitive.

  (**Note**: *Enough* often implies a positive feeling or situation.)

  I have **enough money to buy** tickets for everyone.

D. Infinitives as Noun Modifiers

Infinitives can modify a noun. An infinitive follows the noun that it modifies.

I heard about an easy **way to learn** languages.

GRAMMAR **HOT**SPOT!

Use the infinitive to express purpose. Do not use *for* + gerund.	We're here (**in order**) **to do** business. **NOT**: We're here ~~for doing~~ business.

TALKING THE TALK

In speech and informal writing, infinitives are often shortened to *to* when the meaning is clear.	I've never visited Russia, but I'd like **to**. (*to* = to visit Russia) *A*: Have you ever sung with a band? *B*: No, I'm too lazy **to**. (*to* = to sing with a band)

GRAMMAR PRACTICE 3

Infinitives II

12 Adjectives + Infinitives: Soap Opera Scenes

Complete the sentences with an appropriate infinitive.

1. Warren told Nicola that his brother had been killed by a shark. Ever since then, he has been afraid __to swim__ in the ocean. Nicola thought that Warren's brother was still alive, so she was surprised ________________ the story.

2. Danielle was frantic because she had lost her wedding ring. She was relieved ________________ it in her purse, and she put it on. She didn't want Phillip to know that she'd taken her ring off, so she was reluctant ________________ him what had happened.

3. Candace was ready ________________ to a party with Shawn, but her father refused to let her go. Candace became determined ________________ her parents' house and live on her own.

4. After his terrible accident, Griff was fortunate ________________ alive. His girlfriend Trista was anxious ________________ to the doctor about Griff's condition and their future together.

soap opera = kind of daytime TV drama with strong emotions and conflicts between characters.

13 Infinitive of Purpose: Why Did They Do It?

A. Complete the sentences with an appropriate infinitive of purpose.

1. Wendy turned on Channel 8 (in order) to see the news.
2. Brian switched to the weather channel ______________________________.
3. Before Mike started watching TV, he went into the kitchen ______________________________.
4. Luis got bored with the program he was watching, so he picked up the remote control ______________________________.
5. While Zella was driving, she turned on the radio ______________________________.
6. Instead of watching TV, Elina went to the library ______________________________.

B. Work with a partner.

1. Make a list of the types of TV programs (e.g., situation comedies, talk shows, sports events) that you, your friends, and members of your family watch.
2. Tell your partner why you, your friends, or your family members watch each type of program you listed. Use infinitives of purpose to state the reasons.

Example: My dad watches baseball games in order to relax.
I watch situation comedies in order to laugh/to see my favorite actors.

14 Infinitives with *Too* and *Enough*: Changing Channels

Complete the sentences with *too* or *enough*, as appropriate, and an infinitive. Use the words in parentheses.

The Sports Show

Dan: Casey, I'd like your prediction on tonight's game. Will the Blues win?

Casey: The Blues are good enough to beat (1 (good, beat)) any team. But they may be ______________ (2 (weak, win)) tonight. Harris has been injured. He doesn't have ______________ (3 (strength, play)) many minutes.

Dan: I've heard that Mihalic may join the Blues soon. Is he very talented?

Casey: Yes, he's ______________ (4 (talented, be)) a top player. But it's ______________ (5 (soon, know)) if he'll live up to his talent. It would be great to have him on the team, though. I hope he can join ______________ (6 (soon, help)) the Blues this season.

Police Drama

Captain: Have you talked to the victim's wife?

Detective: Not yet. She's ______________ (1 (upset, talk about)) what happened.

Captain: Do you have a suspect?

Detective: Yeah, but I hope that it isn't ______________ (2 (late, catch)) him. He stole a lot of money. He has ______________ (3 (money, live on)) for a long time.

Captain: Then we need to find him soon. I hope you're ______________ (4 (smart, figure out)) how to do it.

15 Infinitives as Noun Modifiers: The Value of Television

Television has both positive and negative aspects. Think of some positive aspects of television and different television programs. Write sentences with each of the following nouns + infinitive phrases: *ability, chance, opportunity, way.*

Example: Television gives people a chance to learn about new and different things. OR
Watching Moneyline is a good way to get information about business.

16 Using Infinitives; Infinitives Shortened to *To*: Your Own Talk Show

A. Imagine that you are the host of a television talk show. Your next guest will be a person who is well known in the world of entertainment—for example, a television or music star. Decide who the guest will be. What do you want to ask her or him? Complete the following *yes/no* questions with infinitive phrases.

1. Can you afford to buy a Rolls-Royce?
2. Have you ever wanted ______________?
3. Are you afraid ______________?
4. Do you feel fortunate ______________?
5. Are you too ______________?
6. Do you have enough ______________?
7. Have you had an opportunity ______________?
8. Would you like ______________?

B. Work with a partner. Ask your partner the questions you wrote in Part A. Your partner plays the part of the star and uses his or her imagination to answer the questions. The answers should include some infinitives shortened to *to*. Then reverse roles. Present your interviews to the class.

Example: Student A: Can you afford to buy a Rolls-Royce?
Student B: Yes, I can afford to. OR Yes, I can afford to, but I don't want to.

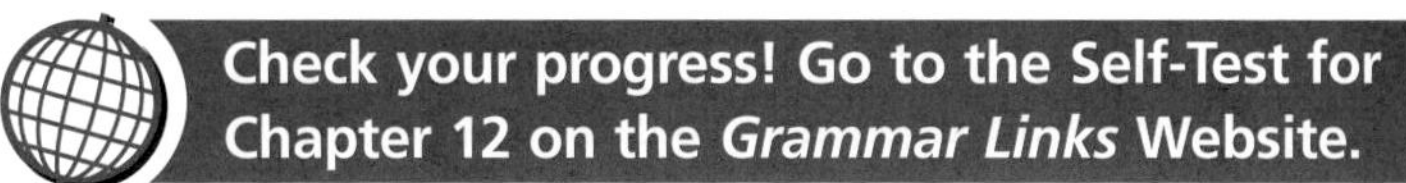

Check your progress! Go to the Self-Test for Chapter 12 on the *Grammar Links* Website.

Chapter 13

More About Gerunds and Infinitives

Introductory Task: A Crime Movie

A. Work with a partner. The sentences describe what happened in a crime movie. In each sentence, look at the boldfaced verb + infinitive or gerund. Decide which happened first—the action expressed by the verb or the action expressed by the infinitive or gerund. Mark the action that happened first with ***1*** and mark the action that happened second with ***2*** (e.g., in sentence 1, planning comes first, then stealing). If both actions happened at the same time, mark both with ***1***.

1. A group of thieves **planned** (1) **to steal** (2) some jewels from a museum in Greece.
2. A burglar alarm was connected to the floor of the museum, so they **decided to enter** from the roof.
3. A witness ran to the police station and **reported seeing** someone on the roof.
4. The thieves **kept lifting** jewels out of the building.
5. They **wanted to finish** the job.
6. They **intended to sell** the jewels to a man in Amsterdam.
7. The police caught them several days later, but they **denied stealing** anything.
8. While they were in jail, the thieves got into an argument, and finally one of them **admitted stealing** the jewels.

burglar alarm = a device that warns if thieves enter a building. *witness* = someone who sees a crime occur.

B. Complete the sentences with *gerund* or *infinitive*.

1. The action expressed by the ______________ tends to occur after the action expressed by the verb.
2. The action expressed by the ______________ tends to occur before or at the same time as the action expressed by the verb.

GRAMMAR BRIEFING 1

Verbs + Gerunds and Infinitives

FUNCTION

A. Verbs That Take Only Gerunds or Only Infinitives

1. Some verbs take only gerunds or only infinitives. (See Chapter 12 and Appendixes 18 and 19 for these verbs.)	I **finished studying.** **NOT**: I finished ~~to study~~. I **planned to study.** **NOT**: I planned ~~studying~~.
2. There is often a difference between verbs that take only gerunds and verbs that take only infinitives. Sometimes this difference can help you figure out whether to use a gerund or an infinitive:	
• Gerunds often follow verbs that indicate that an action is happening or has happened. That is, the action of the gerund happens before the action of the verb or at the same time.	I **miss** (2nd) **jogging** (1st). (The jogging happens first, then I miss it.) We **enjoy cooking** (same time). (The cooking and our enjoyment happen at the same time.)
• Infinitives often follow verbs that indicate that an action will or can happen. That is, the action of the infinitive happens after the action of the verb.	They **convinced** (1st) Dave **to jog** (2nd). (First they convinced him, then he jogged.) I **want** (1st) **to cook** (2nd) tomorrow. (First I want to, then I cook.)

(continued on next page)

B. Verbs That Take Gerunds and Infinitives

1. Some verbs can take a gerund or an infinitive.

   I **hate studying.** = I **hate to study.**

   They **continued working.** = They **continued to work.**

   These verbs include:

begin	hate	love	start
continue	like	prefer	

2. Some verbs can take a gerund or a noun phrase + infinitive. If the infinitive is used with a general noun phrase (e.g., *people*), the sentence has the same meaning as the sentence with the gerund.

   We **advise not driving.** = We **advise people not to drive.**

   We **advised John not to drive.**

   These verbs include:

advise	encourage	require
allow	permit	urge

C. Verbs That Take Gerunds and Infinitives but with a Difference in Meaning

Some verbs take gerunds or infinitives but with a difference in meaning. The difference in meaning is related to the difference discussed in section A. These verbs include:

- *Remember*:

  Remember + gerund—the action of the gerund comes before the action of remembering.

  2nd 1st
  I **remember rehearsing** for the play. (I rehearsed in the past; I remember now.)

  Remember + infinitive—the action of remembering comes before the action of the infinitive.

  1st 2nd
  I always **remember to go** to rehearsals. (First I remember, i.e., think of going; then I go.)

(continued on next page)

C. Verbs That Take Gerunds and Infinitives but with a Difference in Meaning (continued)

- *Forget*:

Forget + gerund—the action of the gerund comes first.	2nd 1st I'll never **forget meeting** you for the first time. (I met you in the past; I won't forget this event.)
Forget + infinitive—the action of forgetting comes first, so the action of the infinitive doesn't happen.	1st 2nd I'm sorry I **forgot to meet** you this morning. (First I forgot, so I didn't meet you.)

- *Stop*:

Stop + gerund—the action of the gerund happens first and then stops.	2nd 1st She **stopped smoking**. (She smoked in the past but then stopped.)
Stop + infinitive—some other action stops and then the action of the infinitive happens.	1st 2nd She **stopped to smoke**. (She stopped what she was doing in order to then smoke.)

- *Try*:

Try + gerund—the attempted action, expressed by the gerund, occurred.	I **tried calling** you, but you weren't home. (I did actually call.)
Try + infinitive—the attempted action, expressed by the infinitive, did not occur.	I **tried to call** you, but I couldn't find a phone. (I wanted to call but couldn't.)

GRAMMAR PRACTICE 1

Verbs + Gerunds and Infinitives

1 Verbs That Take Only Gerunds or Only Infinitives: A Film Festival

A. Use the words in parentheses to complete the sentences with an infinitive or gerund. (Hint: Does the action come after the action of the verb? Or does the action come before or at the same time as the action of the verb?)

1. The university film festival is going to show some famous Hollywood movies. I want <u>to see</u> (see) all of them.
2. I saw several classic movies at the festival last year. I really enjoyed <u>watching</u> (watch) them.
3. We're staying at the library until nine tonight. Then we're going to quit ________ (study) and go to *Citizen Kane*.

4. A classmate and I were talking about *The Godfather*, and I promised ______________ (go) to it with her. It starts at seven tonight.

5. I went to *Close Encounters of the Third Kind* last night. When I finished ______________ (watch) it, I believed that aliens really had visited Earth.

6. I'm looking forward to *Some Like It Hot*. I've been working hard all week, and I need ______________ (see) a funny movie.

7. I haven't seen *North by Northwest* yet, but I've read about it. I expect ______________ (like) it a lot.

8. Have you seen *Gone with the Wind*? While you're watching it, you can imagine ______________ (live) in the South during the time of the Civil War.

9. The film festival is great. I appreciate ______________ (have) this chance to escape into a fantasy world.

10. I can't go to this festival, but I hope ______________ (attend) it next year. It sounds like fun.

B. Work with a partner. Write answers to the following questions. In each sentence, include an infinitive phrase or gerund phrase and one of these verbs: *appreciate, can imagine, enjoy, hope, need, want.*

1. People watch movies for many different reasons. What are three reasons that they watch them?

   Example: They enjoy escaping from reality.

2. Choose three of the following types of movies: action-adventure movies, animated movies, comedies, crime movies, disaster movies, horror movies, musicals, romances, science fiction, thrillers, Westerns. What is a reason that people like watching each type of movie?

   Example: comedies—They enjoy seeing other people in embarrassing situations.

2 Using Verbs That Take Gerunds and Infinitives: What's Your Opinion?

A. Work with a partner. American movies are popular all over the world, but they also cause controversy in many places (see page 222). What kinds of reactions do people in other countries have to American movies? Are their preferences going to change in the future? Write four sentences with gerunds and infinitives using the following verbs: (*not*) *like*, *love*, *prefer*, *hate*, *begin*, *continue*.

Example: People like watching American movies because they like to see something new and different. OR In many countries people don't like having so many American movies in their theaters. They won't continue going to them.

B. Read your sentences to the class. As a class, discuss your opinions about this topic.

3 Verbs That Take Gerunds and Noun Phrase + Infinitives: Entertainment and More

A. Use the words in parentheses to complete the sentences with a gerund or an infinitive.

1. Seeing movies allows you to experience (experience) other cultures.
2. Some people advise ________ (go) to movies for education as well as entertainment.
3. Teachers sometimes encourage their students ________ (watch) movies to improve their listening skills.
4. Getting information from a movie doesn't require ________ (understand) all the words.
5. There are some very good old movies that I advise you ________ (rent) at the video store.
6. For example, I urge you ________ (see) *Breaking Away*. It's funny, and you can get a sense of life in an American college town in the 1970s.

B. Work alone and then with a partner.

1. Think of two movies you would advise your partner to see. For each movie write two sentences, giving your advice and the reason for it. Use *advise* (or *encourage* or *urge*) with an infinitive. Then tell your partner what you have written.

   Example: I advise you to see *2001: A Space Odyssey*. It has great special effects, and you can imagine being in another world.

2. Decide on two movies that you and your partner both like. Give advice to the class about them. Use *advise* with a gerund.

   Example: We advise seeing *Casablanca*. It has romance and suspense.

To find out more about old movies, check out the *Grammar Links* Website.

4 ***Remember, Forget, Stop,* and *Try*: Slapstick Comedy**

A. Stan Laurel and Oliver (Ollie) Hardy were famous slapstick comedians. Listen to the descriptions of typical slapstick situations involving Stan and Ollie. Then listen again and circle the correct answers.

1. Did Ollie put his hat on his head? (Yes) / No
2. Did Stan take the cake off the seat of the car? Yes / No
3. Did Stan leave the roller skate at the top of the stairs? Yes / No
4. Did Ollie turn on the water? Yes / No
5. Did Stan leave the ladder leaning against the house? Yes / No
6. Did Ollie and Stan carry the sofa? Yes / No
7. Did Ollie and Stan put up the sail? Yes / No
8. Did Ollie go out with Stan now? Yes / No
9. Did Stan go out with his wife now? Yes / No

B. Listen again. This time you will hear an explanation of what happened. Check your answers in Part A.

> *slapstick* = type of comedy with lots of silly mistakes, collisions, falls, and arguments.

5 *Remember, Forget, Stop,* and *Try*: The Hughes Brothers

Use the words in parentheses to complete the sentences with gerunds or infinitives.

Background: *Rollo and Lucky Hughes's neighbor Mrs. Gray is an elderly widow. She deposited $5,000 in the bank, but the bank made a mistake and didn't credit her account. Now she can't pay her bills and is desperate. Rollo and Lucky have decided to rob the bank to get her money back.*

Scene I: *The living room in Rollo and Lucky's small house*

Rollo: Stop watching (1 watch) TV, Lucky. It's time to go. Did you remember to put (2 put) gas in the car?

Lucky: Yeah, I did. I was going to wash the car, too, but I forgot ________ (3 do) it.

Rollo: That's not important now. Where's my comb? It was here earlier. I remember ________ (4 see) it on the table.

(Lucky leaves for a moment and returns.)

Lucky: I tried ________ (5 look) for it in the bathroom, and it's not there.

Rollo: Never mind. We'll stop ________ (6 buy) one on the way to the bank.

Lucky: Your hair looks okay. Why do you need a comb?

Rollo: Don't you remember ________ (7 plan) the robbery? I'm going to have a comb in my pocket and pretend it's a gun.

Lucky: Oh, now I remember. Then the teller will give us the money.

Scene II: *At the bank*

Lucky: I'm really nervous about doing this, Rollo. I can't stop ________ (8 shake).

Rollo: Don't worry. Just remember ________ (9 hand) the note to the teller. . . .

(Lucky hands the teller a note that says, "Give us $5,000 and nobody will get hurt.")

Teller: I recognize you. You're Lucky Hughes! You were in my class in high school. I'll never forget ________ (10 go) to school with you.

Lucky: Please don't call the police! We're only trying ________ (11 help) poor Mrs. Gray.

Teller: You haven't gotten any smarter, have you? I know you mean well, but you need to learn: Crime never pays.

6 **Using Gerunds and Infinitives:** Your Movie Script

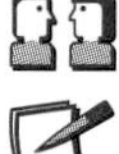

A. Work in small groups. Write a short script for a scene from any kind of movie (e.g., action-adventure, comedy, disaster, horror, romance, science fiction). There should be a role for each person in the group. In your script, use at least three of these verbs followed by a gerund or by an infinitive: *forget, remember, stop,* and *try*. Also, use at least two verbs that are followed only by gerunds and at least two that are followed only by infinitives. You can choose from the following list or use any others: *admit, agree, deny, enjoy, finish, hope, intend, keep, need,* and *plan*.

B. Perform your movie scene for the class.

See the *Grammar Links* Website for a model script for this assignment.

GRAMMAR BRIEFING 2

Performers of the Actions of Gerunds and Infinitives

FORM and FUNCTION

A. Performers of the Actions of Gerunds

1. In the sentences we've seen so far, the action of the gerund is performed by:	
• The subject of the sentence.	**I** hate **taking** the keys. (I perform the action of taking the keys.) **The assistant** finished **setting up** the cameras. (The assistant performs the action of setting up the cameras.)
• People in general, rather than specific performers.	**Swimming** is a lot of fun. (People in general perform the action of swimming and find it fun.) I can't understand **giving up** without trying. (I can't understand when people in general perform the action of giving up.)
2. Sometimes, however, there is a specific performer that is **not** the subject of the sentence. This performer of the gerund action is expressed by a possessive noun or possessive determiner.	I hate **my brother's/his taking** the keys. (My brother performs the action of taking the keys.) I can't understand **Megan's/her giving up** without trying. (Megan performs the action of giving up.)

(continued on next page)

B. Performers of the Actions of Infinitives

1. In the sentences we've seen so far, the action of the infinitive is performed by:	
• The subject of the sentence.	**Barbara** plans **to cook** dinner for you. (Barbara performs the action of cooking.) **Phil** is always eager **to please** people. (Phil performs the action of pleasing.)
• The people or things in the noun phrase that comes before the infinitive (with verbs that take noun phrase + infinitive).	I convinced **John to go** to the party. (John performs the action of going.) I expect **them to help** us. (They perform the action of helping.)
• People in general.	These days, it isn't easy **to find** a job. (for people in general)
2. Sometimes there is no noun phrase and the performer of the infinitive action is not the sentence subject or people in general. In such cases, the performer is expressed with *for* + noun phrase.	I'll wait **for Jack/him to come** home. (Jack performs the action of coming home.) These days it isn't easy **for recent graduates to find** a job. (Recent graduates perform the action of finding jobs.)

TALKING THE TALK

In speech, the performer of the gerund action is often indicated by a nonpossessive noun or an object pronoun, instead of by possessive forms.	I really appreciate **Don/him** doing that for me. *Compare*: I really appreciate Don's/his doing that for me. (more formal)

GRAMMAR PRACTICE 2

Performers of the Actions of Gerunds and Infinitives

7 Performers of Gerunds: Indiana's Adventures

A. *Raiders of the Lost Ark* and the other Indiana Jones movies are among the most popular action-adventure movies ever made. Combine the sentences. Replace the boldfaced word in the second sentence with a gerund phrase based on the first sentence. In combining, change the first sentence in any way needed. Include a possessive form for the performer of the gerund where needed.

1. Indiana went to find the lost Ark of the Covenant. Indiana was excited about **this.**
   Indiana was excited about going to find the lost Ark of the Covenant.
2. Indiana found his former girlfriend Marion in Nepal. Marion didn't appreciate **this.**
   Marion didn't appreciate Indiana's/his finding her in Nepal.
3. Marion disappeared in Cairo. Indiana was upset about **this.**
4. Indiana found her in a tent where she had been tied up. Indiana was happy about **this.**
5. He didn't untie her. She resented **this.**
6. Indiana dropped into a pit full of poisonous snakes. Indiana hated **this.**
7. The villains pushed Marion into the pit, too. Marion was terrified by **this.**
8. Indiana found the lost ark. **This** made the villains very angry.
9. They captured Marion. **This** infuriated Indiana.
10. Indiana told her not to look at the evil spirits coming from the ark. Indiana saved Marion's life by **this.**

Ark of the Covenant = an ancient religious object. *pit* = a deep hole. *villain* = an evil person. *infuriate* = make extremely angry.

B. Work with a partner. Use the sentences you wrote in Part A to tell each other about *Raiders of the Lost Ark.* Use nonpossessive forms.

Example: Marion didn't appreciate Indiana [OR him] finding her in Nepal.

8 Performers of Infinitives: Remaking King Kong

A. Use the information in the first sentence to complete the second sentence. Use *for* with a noun phrase when necessary.

1. The director asked Adam, "Will you act in the movie?" The director asked
   Adam to act in the movie ________________.
2. Adam asked the director, "Can I play the leading role?" Adam asked
   to play the leading role ________________.

3. The director said to Adam, "If you'll play the leading role, I'll be happy." The director will be happy *for Adam to play the leading role* ______.

4. Adam said, "If I play the leading role, I'll be happy." Adam will be happy ______.

5. Then the director talked to Adam for a long time, and finally Adam said, "Okay. I'll wear a gorilla costume." The director persuaded ______.

6. Then the director said to Adam, "You're going to climb to the top of the Empire State Building." The director planned ______.

7. Adam said, "No problem. I'll climb to the top of the building." Adam wasn't afraid ______.

8. Adam's girlfriend Suki said to him, "Adam, please don't climb to the top!" Suki was afraid ______.

9. Adam said, "I'm going to win an Academy Award." Adam intended ______.

10. Suki said to Adam, "In that case, you can do it!" Suki was willing ______.

B. Imagine that you're going to direct a movie in which your classmates play roles. Write six sentences about your plans. Include at least two sentences with *for* + noun or pronoun. Use any of the following verbs: *expect, persuade, plan, want, would like*. Use *be* + *eager, happy, pleased*, or other adjectives.

Example: *I want to make a science-fiction movie. I'm eager for Lena to play the part of an alien. I'm going to ask her to pilot the alien space ship.*

GRAMMAR BRIEFING 3

Verbs Followed by Base Forms

FORM

A. *Have, Make, Let*

Have, *make*, and *let* are causative verbs. That is, their meaning relates to causing (in the case of *let*, allowing) someone to do something.	V NP base form **I'll have my assistant call** you.
These verbs are always followed by noun phrase + base form of verb. Do **not** use an infinitive after these verbs.	V NP base form I **made them leave**, so I could be alone. V NP base form The boss **let us leave** early, because it's Friday.

(continued on next page)

B. Verbs of Perception

1. *Hear, notice, observe, see,* and *watch* are verbs of perception. These verbs are followed by a noun phrase + the base form of a verb. Do **not** use the infinitive.	V NP base form I **heard Professor Smith give** a talk on French poetry. V NP base form We **saw them perform.**
2. These verbs can also be followed by a noun phrase + the *-ing* form. Do not use a possessive before the *-ing* form.	V NP *-ing* form I **heard Professor Smith giving** a talk on French poetry. V NP *-ing* form We **saw them performing.** **NOT:** We saw ~~their~~ performing.

GRAMMAR HOTSPOT!

The verb *help* can take an infinitive or a base form. In speech the base form is more common. *Help* can occur with or without a noun phrase.	I **helped** (**them**) **to clean up** after the party. OR I **helped** (**them**) **clean up** after the party.

GRAMMAR PRACTICE 3

Verbs Followed by Base Forms

9 Forms Following Causative Verbs, Verbs of Perception, and Other Verbs: The Wizard of Oz

The following is a summary of *The Wizard of Oz*, a movie classic from 1939.* Complete the sentences with the base, infinitive, or *-ing* forms of the verbs in parentheses. If two forms are correct, show both forms.

At the beginning of the movie, we hear Dorothy singing/sing (1 sing) "Somewhere Over the Rainbow." She is at home in Kansas with her little dog, Toto. A sudden tornado comes, and Dorothy and Toto are carried over the rainbow into the land of the Munchkins. Dorothy watches the little Munchkins ______ (2 dance). Soon she wants ______ (3 go)

*The summary is in the simple present, a tense often used in telling stories.

back to Kansas. The Good Witch gives her a pair of red slippers and tells her ________________ [4 (follow)] a yellow brick road to the Emerald City, where she will find the Wizard of Oz. The Wizard will help her ________________ [5 (find)] her way back home. Soon after she starts down the road, Dorothy discovers the Scarecrow. She has him ________________ [6 (come)] with her so that he can ask the Wizard ________________ [7 (give)] him a brain. Next, they find the Tin Man, who is rusty. Dorothy helps him ________________ [8 (move)] again by oiling him. She lets the Tin Man ________________ [9 (join)] them on their journey, because he hopes ________________ [10 (get)] a heart. They meet the Cowardly Lion and allow him ________________ [11 (come)], too. He wants the Wizard ________________ [12 (give)] him courage. After the Wizard finally lets them ________________ [13 (enter)] the Emerald City, they tell him why they are there. The Wizard makes them ________________ [14 (go)] to the castle of the Wicked Witch. When the Witch sets fire to the Scarecrow, Dorothy throws water at the flames. The water kills the witch. We hear her ________________ [15 (scream)] and see her ________________ [16 (melt)]. Later the Good Witch reappears. She tells Dorothy and her friends that they always had what they were looking for, but that they had to find it out for themselves. She has Dorothy ________________ [17 (click)] the heels of her slippers three times, and Dorothy and Toto are back in Kansas.

tornado = a violent windstorm.

Learn more about *The Wizard of Oz* by going to the *Grammar Links* Website.

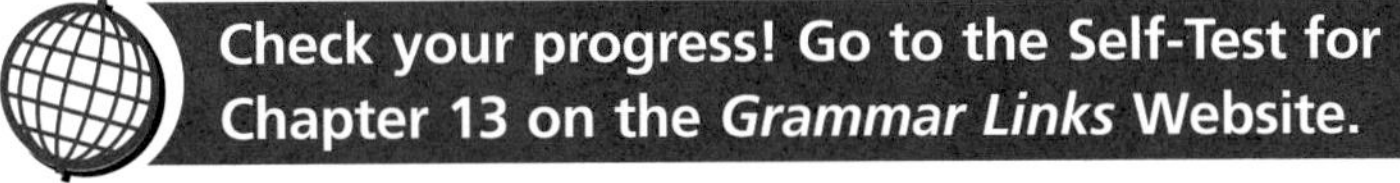

Check your progress! Go to the Self-Test for Chapter 13 on the *Grammar Links* Website.

Wrap-up Activities

1 Going to Graceland: EDITING

Correct the 10 errors in the passage. There are errors in gerunds and infinitives and related forms. Some errors can be corrected in more than one way. The first error is corrected for you.

Every year, thousands of people from all over the world travel to Memphis, Tennessee, ~~for visiting~~ *to visit* Graceland, Elvis Presley's home. I've never been to Graceland, but I want going there. I look forward to do it someday because Elvis has a very important place in the history of American popular culture. I wasn't enough old to see Elvis when he was alive, but I'll never forget to hear "Love Me Tender" for the first time. I've watched his movies, and I've talked to people who saw his performing in the 1950s. People who are my age sometimes have problems to understand why he shocked people so much.

Elvis's home, Graceland

I think that Elvis was an example of the American dream—a poor boy who became successful by using his talent and energy. When he was young, he dreamed about to be rich someday. But later it was difficult for him to deal with his success. He was very generous, and he often went to the store for buying Cadillacs and other expensive gifts for people. Being so generous caused him to have financial problems, though. He started taking too many pills, and he became famous for eating lots of fried food. Now we are used to think of Elvis as a troubled person who lost control of his life—an American tragedy. But I prefer to keep remembering his musical achievements.

2 A Game Show Pre-Test: WRITING

Step 1 Work in small groups. Imagine that you work for a cable television channel, English Language Learning Network. You produce a game show called *Grammar Challenge.* Many people would like to be contestants on the show. In order to select the best contestants, you have decided to test their ability to use gerunds and infinitives and to use verbs that take base forms. Write a fill-in-the-blanks test with 10 items.

Example:

1. I tried ______________ (scream) for help, but no one heard me.
2. That car is too expensive for me ______________ (buy).

Step 2 After your teacher has checked your test, make copies of it for the other students in the class. After they have completed it, check their answers.

3 A Fan Letter: WRITING

Write a letter to an actor or singer whom you admire. Include at least five of the following:

a verb + gerund	an adjective + infinitive
a verb + preposition + gerund	a noun modified by an infinitive
a verb + infinitive	an infinitive of purpose
a verb + NP + base or *-ing* form	*too* or *enough* + infinitive

Example:
Dear Bob,
I'm writing to express my admiration for your singing. I had a chance to hear your latest album recently, and I want you to know how much I liked listening to it. . . .

See the *Grammar Links* Website for a complete model letter for this assignment.

4 What's Your Opinion? SPEAKING/WRITING

Step 1 Work in small groups. Read the following statement:

American entertainment products—especially music, television programs, and movies—will continue to be popular and successful internationally for many years.

Step 2 Discuss whether you agree or disagree with the statement and why. In your discussion, use some of the words listed in sentences with gerunds and infinitives.

Verbs: *appreciate, (dis)approve of, avoid, continue, enjoy, keep, like, love, need, prefer, refuse, start, stop, try, would like*

Expressions: *have fun, spend time*

***Be* + Adjective + Preposition**: *concerned about, critical of, enthusiastic about, interested in, responsible for*

Example: I agree. People prefer to watch American television programs, and they will continue watching them. OR I disagree. People are going to become more enthusiastic about seeing programs from their own countries, and they're going to stop watching so many American programs.

Step 3 Write a paragraph explaining why you agree or disagree with the statement. Use at least six sentences with gerunds and infinitives.

Example:
American entertainment products will continue to be popular and successful internationally for several reasons. First, for some small countries, producing their own TV programs costs too much. But not making their own programs isn't a problem, because they can get American programs that people enjoy watching. . . .

See the *Grammar Links* Website for a complete model paragraph for this assignment.

Unit **Seven**

Modals

TOPIC FOCUS
Courtship and Marriage

UNIT OBJECTIVES

- **modals of ability**
  (A typical three-year-old ***can*** talk.)
- **belief modals used to talk about the present and future**
  (She has *MD* after her name, so she ***must*** be a doctor. She ***will*** probably be happy to meet him.)
- **social modals**
  (***May*** I help you? What ***should*** I wear to the wedding?)
- **perfect modals**
  (Things ***might have*** gone better for them.)
- **belief modals used to talk about the past**
  (They ***must have*** been married for a long time.)
- **social modals used to talk about the past**
  (You ***could have*** found Mr. Right long ago.)

Grammar in Action

Reading and Listening: In Class

Read and listen to this discussion from a cultural anthropology class.

Teacher: Before class ends, I want to remind you that the midterm exam is next week. You **should** read the information that I've written on the blackboard about it. **Can** everyone see the blackboard?

Student A: **Is** the exam **going to** be difficult?

Teacher: It **shouldn't be** too difficult. Students who have come to every class and done all the reading **should** do well on it. Of course, you **must** review the material. A review is always necessary. And I have a suggestion: You **might** work together in study groups.

Student B: **May** I ask one more question? **Could** you repeat the definition of *courtship*?

Teacher: Of course. Courtship is part of the process of choosing a mate, that is, a husband or wife. Courtship refers to social activities between males and females that **might** lead to marriage. Dating **can** be a part of courtship, as it often is in this country, but it **doesn't have to** be—courtship customs are different in different cultures. And the ways of choosing a mate differ, too. There are various possibilities. For example, the individuals themselves **may** find their mates. Or their family members **could** be the ones who find suitable mates for them. Or they **might** ask a matchmaker, or go-between, to identify potential mates. But even if families or matchmakers arrange an introduction, this doesn't necessarily mean that the individuals **must** marry one another. In most cases, the individuals **are allowed** to make the final decision.

Student C: In this culture, most people think that a decision to marry **ought to** be based on romantic love—that you **shouldn't** marry someone unless you're strongly attracted to them. How important is romantic love as a basis for choosing a mate in other cultures?

Teacher: Well, cultural anthropologists who have done research on this topic believe that romantic love **must** be nearly universal. That is, they're certain that it occurs almost everywhere. But they have found it isn't universally important as a basis of marriage. In many cultures, family considerations are more important. I know you're interested in this topic, so we **will** discuss it more next week, but we've run out of time. You **may** go now.

cultural anthropology = the study of humans' beliefs, patterns of behavior, and customs.

Think About Grammar

The boldfaced words in the discussion are one-word modals, phrasal modals, and modal-like expressions. Modals are used to express belief that something is certain, likely, or just possible. They are also used to express ability and to do other things like give advice or permission and to make requests or suggestions. Most modals have more than one use.

Work with a partner. In each of the following pairs of sentences from the discussion, a modal occurs as a belief modal and in another use. Complete the sentence that follows the pair with *a* and *b*. (If you need help in deciding how a modal is used, go back to the discussion and read the sentence in its context.)

1. a. You **should** read the information that I've written on the blackboard.
   b. Students who have come to every class and done all the reading **should** do well on the exam.

   Should is used to say that something is likely in __b__ and to give someone advice in __a__.

2. a. **Can** everyone see the blackboard?
   b. Dating **can** be a part of courtship.

   Can is used to say that something is possible in ______ and to ask about ability in ______.

3. a. **Could** you repeat the definition of *courtship*?
   b. Their family members **could** be the ones who find suitable mates for them.

   Could is used to say that something is possible in ______ and to make a request for someone to do something in ______.

4. a. Individuals themselves **may** find their mates.
   b. You **may** go now.

   May is used to say that something is possible in ______ and to give someone permission to do something in ______.

5. a. Courtship refers to social activities that **might** lead to marriage.
   b. You **might** work together in study groups.

   Might is used to say that something is possible in ______ and to make a suggestion to someone in ______.

6. a. You **must** review the material.
   b. Cultural anthropologists believe that romantic love **must** be nearly universal.

   Must is used to say that something is certain in ______ and to express the necessity for someone to do something in ______.

Chapter 14

Modals

Introductory Task: How Certain Is She?

Work with a partner. Read each group of statements made by Andrea and answer the questions.

1. a. Theresa **is** married. She introduced me to her husband.
   b. Dale **might be** married. It's possible that he is, but I really don't know.
   c. Brian **must be** married. He wears a wedding ring.
   d. Dana **could be** married. Maybe she is, maybe she isn't.

   Which boldfaced verb or modal + verb combination(s) did Andrea use when she was

   fully certain about the situation? is ________________

   very certain about the situation? ________________

   not very certain about the situation? ________________ ________________

2. a. Tamika **might not be** married. It's possible that she isn't, but I don't have any way of knowing for sure.
   b. Elliot **must not be** married. I've seen him at movies and restaurants with several different women.
   c. Sheila **isn't** married. I know for a fact that she is single.
   d. Marco **couldn't be** married. He's only 16, and he lives with his parents.

   Which boldfaced verb or modal + verb combination(s) did Andrea use when she was

   fully certain about the situation? ________________

   very certain about the situation? ________________ ________________

   not very certain about the situation? ________________

3. The sentences in 1 are affirmative sentences. The sentences in 2 are negative sentences. One modal expresses a different degree of certainty in negative sentences than it does in affirmative sentences.

   Circle the modal: could might must

GRAMMAR BRIEFING 1

Overview of Modals

One-Word Modals

FORM

A. Overview

Modals are auxiliary verbs.

Unlike auxiliary verbs *have* and *be*, one-word modals don't change form and are followed by the base form of the verb.

One-word modals include *can, could, may, might, must, should, will,* and *would*.

They **should be** home now.

He **can help** you, and we **can help**, too.

B. Affirmative Statements

SUBJECT	MODAL	BASE FORM OF VERB	
I	**can**	**speak**	English.
He	**should**	**call**	her.

C. Negative Statements

SUBJECT	MODAL + *NOT**	BASE FORM OF VERB	
Lauren	**cannot**	**go**.	
They	**will not**	**listen**	to me.

D. *Yes/No* Questions and Short Answers

QUESTIONS	SHORT ANSWERS
Should they **come**?	Yes, they **should**.
Will he **be** there?	No, he **won't**.

E. *Wh-* Questions

WH- QUESTIONS ABOUT THE SUBJECT	OTHER *WH-* QUESTIONS
Who might come?	**What can** he **do**?

*CONTRACTIONS

can + not → can't
could + not → couldn't
might + not → mightn't
must + not → mustn't
should + not → shouldn't
will + not → won't
would + not → wouldn't

(continued on next page)

Phrasal Modals

FORM

A. Overview

Phrasal modals begin with *be* or *have* and end with *to*. The *be* and *have* change form. Phrasal modals are followed by the base form of the verb.	She **was supposed to go** yesterday, and **I'm supposed to go** today. He **has to leave** now, and we **have to leave**, too.
Phrasal modals include *be able to*, *be allowed to*, *be going to*, *be supposed to*, *be to*, *have to*, and *have got to*.	

B. Affirmative Statements

SUBJECT	PHRASAL MODAL	BASE FORM OF VERB	
She	**is able to**	**speak**	English.
He	**has to**	**leave**	now.

C. Negative Statements

SUBJECT	PHRASAL MODAL + *NOT**	BASE FORM OF VERB	
They	**were not to**	**be**	here.
She	**does not have to**	**go**	home.

D. *Yes/No* Questions and Short Answers

QUESTIONS	SHORT ANSWERS
Are we **supposed to study** now?	Yes, you **are**.
Do they **have to leave** yet?	No, they **don't**.

E. *Wh-* Questions

WH- QUESTIONS ABOUT THE SUBJECT	OTHER *WH-* QUESTIONS
Who is supposed to come?	**What do** we **have to bring**?

*For contractions with *be* and *do*, see Chapter 1, Grammar Briefing 1, page 5.

One-Word Modals and Phrasal Modals

FUNCTION

A. Overview

1. Most modals have more than one meaning.	He **could** swim well. (past ability) The phone **could** be busy. (present possibility)
2. Different modals often express similar meanings.	He **could** be here. = He **might** be here. = He **may** be here.

(continued on next page)

B. Combining Modal Meanings

To express two modal meanings, use a one-word modal + a phrasal modal or use two phrasal modals. (One-word modals cannot be used together.)

You **must be able to** swim in order to go. OR
You **have to be able to** swim in order to go.
NOT: You ~~must can~~ swim in order to go.

Modal-like Expressions

FORM and FUNCTION

Overview

1. In this unit, the term *modal* includes modal-like expressions *ought to* and *had better.* Modal-like expressions are similar to modals in meaning and use. They are followed by the base form of the verb. Like one-word modals, they don't change form.

   You **ought to go**, and he **ought to go**, too.

   You **had better be** careful, and he **had better be** careful, too.

2. *Ought to* and *had better* are used in affirmative statements. *Ought to* is not usually used in negatives. *Ought to* and *had better* are not usually used in questions.

   He **ought to tell/had better tell** someone.

   He **had better not** tell anyone.

GRAMMAR **HOT**SPOT!

1. One-word modals:
   - *Can + not* is written as one word even if not contracted.

     She **cannot/can't** go.
   - *May + not* is not contracted.

     You **may not** smoke in here.
     NOT: You ~~mayn't~~ smoke in here.

2. Phrasal modals:
   - *Have to* does not contract with the subject.

     I **have to** study.
     NOT: ~~I've to~~ study.
   - *Have to* occurs with *do* in negatives and questions. *Have got to* doesn't occur in negatives and questions.

     Do I **have to** study?
     NOT: ~~Have I to/Have I got to~~ study?

     I **don't have to** study tonight.
     NOT: I ~~haven't to/haven't got to~~ study tonight.

GRAMMAR PRACTICE 1

Overview of Modals

1 Identifying One-Word Modals, Phrasal Modals, and Modal-like Expressions: A Study Group

Work with a partner. Read the exchange of instant messages between two students. Underline the modals and circle the verbs that follow them. Including the example, there are 16 modals.

Instant Message with "Bo23"

Bo23

Last message received at:

Bo23: Hi, Darryl. We ought to (meet) soon. The midterm exam is going to include questions about marriage customs in other cultures, so we have to review that topic. We've got to review the definitions of the terms in the textbook, too.

DK: I have everything in my notes. For example, in most cultures men must not have more than one wife at a time. It's prohibited. But there are a few cultures in which men are allowed to have more than one wife. That's called *polygyny*.

Bo23: Could I borrow your notes?

DK: Of course. I can bring them to the study group. Do you want to meet at eight tomorrow night?

Bo23: I haven't made any other plans, so I should be able to meet at eight. I'm not sure about Andre, though. He might not be free then. We'd better check with him before we decide for sure.

DK: He isn't available now. When is he supposed to be home?

Bo23: He had to work tonight, so he may not be home until later. I will send you a message after I talk to him. Bye for now.

2 One-Word Modals, Phrasal Modals, and Modal-like Expressions—Form: A Student–Teacher Conference

Complete the sentences using the correct form of the words in parentheses. Use contractions where possible.

S: I'm sorry that I couldn't come (1 could / not / come) to class last Friday.

I ________ (2 have to / stay) home because I was sick.

________ (3 I / may / ask) you some questions?

T: Yes, of course.

S: When ________ (4 we / have to / turn in) our term papers?

T: Everyone ________ (5 be supposed to / turn in) their papers by the day of the final exam. Students ________ (6 can / give) them to me earlier, but they ________ (7 may / not / turn them in) after the exam.

S: ________ (8 we / be allowed to / choose) any topic related to courtship?

T: Yes, you are, but you ________ (9 ought to / think about) it carefully. Your paper ________ (10 have got to / include) examples to illustrate your ideas, but it ________ (11 must / not / be) too long, so choose a topic that's not too broad. But don't pick a topic that you ________ (12 can / not / find) enough information about.

S: I'm interested in personality characteristics that attract people when they're choosing a mate.

T: You ________ (13 might / be able to / find) some interesting information on that in the library.

S: I'll go look now, since I ________ (14 have to / not / go) to class yet. Thanks very much.

GRAMMAR BRIEFING 2

Modals of Ability

FORM and FUNCTION

A. *Can*

Use *can* to express ability in the present or in general.	I **can** hear the TV in the other room. Dogs **can** hear sounds that humans **can't** hear.

B. *Could*

Use *could* to express past ability (but see C2).	When I was younger, I **could** stay up all night without feeling tired.

C. *Be Able To*

1. Because *be* changes form, you can use *be able to* to express ability:	
• In the present or in general.	I can't speak Spanish, but I'**m able to** understand it.
• In the past.	I couldn't speak Spanish when I was young, but I **was able to** understand it.
• In the future.	After I go to Mexico, I'**ll be able to** understand Spanish.
• With other tenses, such as the present perfect. (Do not use *could.*)	I'**ve been able to** swim since I was six. **NOT**: I ~~could~~ swim since I was six.
2. To talk about **past ability connected to single events**, use *be able to*, not *could.*	Last night, the police **were able to** catch the thief. **NOT**: Last night, the police ~~could~~ catch the thief.
However, if the sentence is negative, either *be able to* or *could* can be used.	Last night, the police **weren't able to** catch the thief. OR Last night the police **couldn't** catch the thief.

GRAMMAR PRACTICE 2

Modals of Ability

3 Present, Past, and Future Ability: Developing Survival Skills

Complete the sentences with an appropriate form of *be able to.* Where *can* or *could* is possible, write it as well. Use negatives where indicated. Use contractions with *not.*

1. When people are choosing a mate, they want someone that they can/are able to (a) get along with well. There might be a special reason for this: Children can't/aren't able to (b (not)) survive without a great deal of attention. Of course, a mother may ______ (c) take care of her children on her own. But children might have an easier time when they grow up with two parents who ______ (d) get along well and cooperate in raising them.

2. Eli is a four-year-old child. His parents are very proud of his rapid development. For example, when he was 18 months old, he ______ (a) speak in complete sentences. When he was three, although he ______ (b (not)) write yet, he ______ (c) read simple books. He ______ (d) do simple arithmetic problems since he was three and a half.

3. Eli's parents take turns looking after him. Last Monday, for example, his father stayed home with him, and his mother ______ (a) finish an important project at her office. Yesterday, his father ______ (b (not)) stay home, but his mother stayed with him. She took Eli to the library, and he ______ (c) find some good books to read. Tomorrow his mother might ______ (d) take him to her office.

4. Even though Eli is a very capable child, he ______ (a (not)) take care of himself at any time in the near future. Someday, he ______ (b) survive on his own, but until then he will need his parents' care and cooperation.

4 Present, Past, and Future Ability: Your Skills

Read the following statements. For each one, write a sentence that gives an example of the statement. Use *can, can't, could,* or *couldn't* where possible. Use a form of *be able to* otherwise.

1. Ten years ago, I was able to do things that I'm not able to do now.

   Example: *I could learn to speak foreign languages easily.*
2. Ten years ago, I wasn't able to do things that I'm able to do now.
3. Ten years from now, I'll be able to do things that I'm not able to do now.
4. There are things that I might be able to do soon.
5. There are many things I've been able to do for a long time.
6. I have many useful abilities now.

GRAMMAR BRIEFING 3

Belief Modals Used to Talk About the Present

FORM and FUNCTION

A. Overview

Speakers use belief modals to express different degrees of certainty. The following modals are used to express different degrees of certainty about the present:

DEGREE OF CERTAINTY	MODALS IN AFFIRMATIVE SENTENCES	MODALS IN NEGATIVE SENTENCES
very certain ↓	**must, have to, have got to**	**must not (mustn't), could not (couldn't), cannot (can't)**
	should, ought to	**should not (shouldn't)**
not very certain	**may, might, could**	**may not, might not (mightn't)**

1. Modals in affirmative sentences express degrees of certainty about what is.

   He **must** be here. (= I'm strongly certain that he is here.)
2. Modals in negative sentences express degrees of certainty about what is not.

   He **must not** be here. (= I'm strongly certain that he is not here.)
3. If speakers are entirely certain, they do not use a modal.

   He **is** here. (= I know he is here.)
4. *Could* and *might* are the belief modals used in questions about the present.

   Could/Might they be at the party?

(continued on next page)

B. Expressing Degrees of Certainty in Affirmative Sentences

Must, Have To, Have Got To

1. Use *must, have to,* and *have got to* when you feel that something is almost certainly true—that there are no other real possibilities.	He **must** be on the way. He didn't answer the phone. She**'s got to** be here. Her books are on the desk.

Should, Ought To

1. Use *should* and *ought to* when you feel that something is the most likely possibility.	He **should** be home. He's usually home at this time. The food here **ought to** be good. The restaurant is crowded.
2. *Should* and *ought to* are **not** usually used to express possibilities that are undesirable.	The food here is probably bad. **NOT**: The food here ~~ought to/should~~ be bad.

May, Might, Could

Use *may, might,* and *could* when you feel that a possibility isn't necessarily more likely than other possibilities.	The kids **may** be tired. I don't know. He **might** be at school now. Or he **could** be at work.

C. Expressing Degrees of Certainty in Negative Sentences

In negative sentences, use *must, should, may,* and *might* the same way as in affirmative sentences.	He **mustn't** be there. He didn't answer the phone. He **shouldn't** be home yet. He usually works late. The baseball game **may not/mightn't** be over yet. I don't know.
However:	
• Use *could* and *can* when you are very certain.	He **couldn't/can't** be in Colombia. I saw him yesterday.
In negative sentences *could* and *can* also often express surprise, especially about something that is not pleasant.	The food **couldn't/can't** be gone. The party just started.
• Do not use *have to, have got to,* or *ought to.*	He **mustn't/couldn't/can't** be here yet. **NOT**: He ~~doesn't have to~~ be here yet. He **shouldn't** be home yet. **NOT**: He ~~ought not to~~ be home yet.

(continued on next page)

D. Other Ways of Expressing Degrees of Certainty

You can sometimes use adverbs and adjectives instead of belief modals:	
• Adverbs used in this way include *certainly, probably, possibly,* and *maybe.*	Dinner is **probably** ready now. (= Dinner should be ready now.) **Maybe** dinner is ready now. (= Dinner might be ready now.)
• Adjectives used in this way include *certain, probable, likely,* and *(im)possible.*	They're **certain** to be ready now. (= They must be ready now.) He's **likely** to be home. (= He should be home.)

GRAMMAR HOTSPOT!

Remember! *Can't* is a belief modal, but *can* is not.	The food **can't** be gone. There **may/might/could** be more food in the kitchen. **NOT**: There ~~can~~ be more food in the kitchen.

TALKING THE TALK

Have/has to, have/has got to, and *ought to* are often pronounced "hafta, hasta," "'ve gotta, 's gotta," and "oughta."	"He hasta be tired." "Dinner oughta be ready."

GRAMMAR PRACTICE 3

Belief Modals Used to Talk About the Present

5 Belief Modals About the Present—Form and Meaning: The Family Connection

Chitra's aunts are having a get-together. Complete their sentences with the appropriate form of the choice that is correct or better expresses the meaning. Use contractions where possible.

1. Chitra must __________ (must / might) be interested in getting married. She's asked everyone in the family to help her find a husband.
2. We __________ (must / should) have several friends whose sons would be suitable husbands for her. We have quite a few friends, so I think it's a likely possibility.
3. Jaya's son __________ (have to / may) be interested in meeting Chitra. I haven't asked Jaya, so I'm not very certain.
4. Sonia's son __________ (must / could) be a teacher now. I think it's possible that he is.
5. Rita's son __________ (have to / might) be a lawyer now. He finished law school a couple of years ago, and he works for a law firm.
6. Harry __________ (may + not / could + not) live with his parents now. I'm not certain.
7. Tara __________ (have got to + not / must + not) have any sons. She's never mentioned any to me.
8. Reema has two sons. __________ (Might / May) one of them be ready to get married?
9. The young man in this picture __________ (have got to / ought to) be Anjali's son. I'm very certain because he looks *exactly* like her.
10. It __________ (should + not / ought to + not) be too early to call Shoba. She's usually up by this time.
11. Sanjay __________ (can + not / might + not) be away on a trip. I saw him this morning.

6 Belief Modals about the Present: Making Guesses

Rob has received an e-mail message from a woman he's interested in meeting, but his computer is not working right, and information is missing. Read his thoughts about the message. Use information in the message to complete the sentences with *must*, *have to*, *have got to*, *should*, *ought to*, *may*, *might*, *could*, and, in negative sentences only, *can*. In each blank, write all the forms that you think express the intended meaning. Use *not* where necessary. Use contractions with *not* where possible.

> Here's some information about me. My name is Nicola Long, MD
>
> In my work, I care for both adults and children
>
> I was born on May 19, 19
>
> In addition to all water sports, I enjoy
>
> You can reach me at home most evenings by calling (604)-447-3914
>
> I'm usually at home after 7 p.m.

It shouldn't (1) be difficult to figure out more about Nicola. There are clues in the message. For example, there's an *MD* after her name. She must/has to/has got to (2) be a doctor. It's the only logical possibility.

But what kind of doctor is she? She ________ (3) be just a children's doctor. There are lots of possibilities, though. ________ (4) she be a surgeon? An eye doctor? Or . . . ?

I wonder how old she is. People don't finish medical school before at least their late 20s. So she ________ (5) be older than 25, but she ________ (6) be older than 30 yet.

Based on the e-mail, it looks like Nicola ________ (7) enjoy swimming and sailing, which are my favorite sports. Apart from that, I'm not very certain that we both enjoy the same things. We ________ (8) have a lot in common—I hope so—or we ________ (9) have a lot in common—that would be too bad.

Her telephone area code is the same as mine. This area code is now used only for my city, so she ________ (10) live in another city. It's 8:30 now. Based on the e-mail, she ________ (11) be at home now. Since she's probably there, I think I'll try calling her.

7 Using Belief Modals About the Present: Singles Seeking Mates

One way to find a mate is to advertise in a newspaper.

1. Work with a partner. Read the following ads and the questions about them. Discuss possible answers, using belief modals.

Example: *Pat's a medical professional. Could Pat be a dentist?* OR
Pat doesn't want to meet anyone who has a pet. Pat mustn't like pets.

2. Write sentences to answer the questions. In each sentence, use one of the following modals: *must*, *have to*, *have got to*, *may*, *might*, *can*, or *could*. For each person include at least two sentences with negative modals.

> **Medical professional.**
>
> In my free time, I read *Sports Illustrated*, *Car and Driver*, *Gourmet*, and *Fine Cooking*. I'm very tall, and I play a team sport.
>
> I drive a red Japanese car, wear red clothing, often have quiet dinners at home, and avoid going to restaurants.
>
> Please don't respond if you have a pet. My name is Pat.

1. What's Pat's profession?
   a. *Pat may be a dentist.* ____________________
   b. ____________________
2. What sport does Pat play? ____________________
3. What brand of car does Pat drive? ____________________
4. What are some of Pat's likes, dislikes, and interests?
   a. ____________________
   b. ____________________
   c. ____________________
5. What is Pat's personality like? ____________________
6. Is Pat a man or a woman? ____________________

Scientist.

(I've published a book, *Distant Galaxies*, and many articles in *Sky and Telescope*.)

In my free time, I read detective stories, *Travel*, and *Art and Architecture*. I play a racquet sport.

I listen to music by Bach and Mozart and have visited museums in many countries.

I'm interested in meeting a vegetarian who is willing to walk or take public transportation everywhere we go. No rock and roll fans, please! My name is Chris.

1. What's Chris's profession? ______
2. What sport does Chris play? ______
3. Does Chris have a car? ______
4. What are some of Chris's likes, dislikes, and interests?
   a. ______
   b. ______
   c. ______
5. What is Chris's personality like? ______
6. Is Chris a man or a woman? ______

GRAMMAR BRIEFING 4

Belief Modals Used to Talk About the Future

FORM and FUNCTION

A. Overview

Speakers use the following modals to express different degrees of certainty about their predictions:

DEGREE OF CERTAINTY	MODALS IN AFFIRMATIVE SENTENCES	MODALS IN NEGATIVE SENTENCES
very certain	**will, be going to**	**will not (won't), be going to + not**
↓	**should, ought to**	**should not (shouldn't)**
not very certain	**may, might, could**	**may not, might not (mightn't)**

Will and *be going to* are the belief modals most often used in questions about the future. Do not use *may*.

Will he/**Is** he **going to** be here tomorrow?
NOT: ~~May~~ he be here tomorrow?

(continued on next page)

B. Expressing Degrees of Certainty in Affirmative Sentences

1. Use *will* and *be going to* if you are very certain about your prediction.	It'**ll** rain tomorrow.
You can weaken the certainty by using an adverb like *probably*.	It'**ll probably** rain tomorrow.
2. Use *should* and *ought to* if you are somewhat certain about your prediction.	The 10:00 train **ought to** be pretty empty. We **should** be able to get there on time.
3. Use *may*, *might*, and *could* if you are not very certain about your prediction.	The economy **may/might** improve soon. We **could** see economic growth by the end of the year.

C. Expressing Degrees of Certainty in Negative Sentences

Use *will*, *be going to*, *should*, *may*, and *might* as in affirmative sentences. *Ought to* and *could* are not used in negative sentences.	Tina probably **won't/isn't going to** have dinner with us. My courses next semester **shouldn't** be hard. **NOT**: My courses next semester ~~ought not to~~ be hard. They **may not/might not** come tomorrow. **NOT**: They ~~could not~~ come tomorrow.

GRAMMAR HOTSPOT!

Notice! *Must*, *have to*, and *have got to* are not used to express certainty about the future. They are **present** belief modals.	It'**s going to** snow a lot this winter. **NOT**: It ~~must~~ snow a lot this winter.

GRAMMAR PRACTICE 4

Belief Modals Used to Talk About the Future

8 Belief Modals About the Future: Finding Mr. or Ms. Right

A. Complete the sentences in the interview using the information in brackets. Use *will, be going to, should, ought to, may, might,* and *could*. In each blank write all the possible forms. Use *not* where necessary. Use contractions with *not* where possible.

Liz: Helen, you've studied recent courtship trends. What are your predictions? Will we see changes in the methods Americans use to find mates?

Helen: Things have been changing. And they will/are going to (1 [very certainly]) continue to change. These changes mightn't/may not (2 [possibly not]) happen everywhere in the country, though.

Liz: What kinds of changes do you expect to see?

Helen: In the past, many Americans just waited to meet a suitable person. This method ______ (3 [probably not]) be the most common way for people to find mates in the future, though. A lot of them are just too busy to meet suitable mates by chance. This situation ______ (4 [certainly not]) change soon.

Liz: Advertising on the Internet ______ (5 [possibly]) become a more popular way of finding a mate.

Helen: Yes. But advertising ______ (6 [possibly not]) become as popular as another strategy that has been used in many cultures—going to a matchmaker. In the future, we ______ (7 [probably]) see more people using professional matchmakers. With matchmakers, people ______ (8 [very certainly]) have a better chance of finding Mr. or Ms. Right.

B. These are some ways in which people find mates: waiting to meet a suitable person by chance, advertising in the newspaper, advertising on the Internet, using matchmakers, and using family connections.

1. As a class, discuss your predictions about how common it will be for people to use each of these methods in the future. What other methods might become common? Why will each method become more or less common?

2. On your own, write five predictions using modals that express your degree of certainty. Include *not* in at least one sentence. Use *probably* with *will* or *be going to* where appropriate to weaken your prediction. Give a reason for each one.

   Example: Advertising for a mate on the Internet could become much more common. People will probably be too busy to search in other ways.

9 **Belief Modals About the Present and Future:** Matchmakers in Action

Rose and Vera are matchmakers. They are trying to find a suitable mate for Lola. Circle the correct form; if both forms are correct, circle both.

Rose: Lola is talented and intelligent. It ought not to / shouldn't (1) be difficult to find suitable men for her.

Vera: Yes, but Lola is very demanding. It is going to / will (2) take a lot of searching to find just the right man.

Rose: Lola is studying engineering. Eddie's an engineer. They should / must (3) get along well if we introduce them to each other.

Vera: Rose, look at Eddie's picture. He must / has to (4) be at least 60 years old. I think he might / should (5) be too old for her.

Rose: What about Chad? He's a handsome 25-year-old. Oh, but he's a vegetarian, and Lola loves steaks. He mayn't / mightn't (6) be right for her. . . . say—Sky's a young, steak-eating engineer. He could / may (7) have all the qualities that Lola wants. He travels occasionally, so he couldn't / may not (8) be home now, but I'm going to call him.

Vera: And what about Lola? May / Will (9) she check with us soon?

Rose: Let me call her. . . . There's no answer. She mustn't / doesn't have to (10) be home now. And she may not / could not (11) check with us until next week. . . . But when she does and she hears about Sky, she has to / is going to (12) be very happy.

GRAMMAR BRIEFING 5

Social Modals I: Modals for Permission, Requests, and Offers

FORM and FUNCTION

A. Overview

Modals for permission, requests, and/or offers include *can*, *could*, *may*, and *will*. Some modals are considered more formal or polite. So the situation and the relationship between the speaker and listener can influence the choice of modal. However, usually you can use any of the possible modals. You can also use *please* to show politeness.	*Student to teacher*: **Could** you (**please**) explain this example? *Student to student*: **Can** you (**please**) lend me your pen?

(continued on next page)

B. Requesting and Giving Permission

more formal ↓	**may**
	could
less formal	**can**

Requesting Permission

To ask for permission, use *may*, *could*, or *can*.	*Request for permission*: **May/Could/Can** I (please) use your phone? *Possible response*: Sure, you **can**. It's on the table.

Giving Permission

To give (or refuse) permission, use *may* or *can*. *Could* is not used.	You **may/can** leave when you finish. You **may not/cannot** leave until you finish. **NOT**: You ~~could~~ leave when you finish. OR You ~~could not~~ leave until you finish.
May in this use is considered very formal. It is often used in public announcements.	Passengers in rows 1–10 **may** board now.

C. Making Requests

more formal ↓	**would, could**
less formal	**will, can**

To make a request (i.e., ask someone to do something), use *would*, *could*, *will*, or *can*.	*Request*: **Would/Could/Will/Can** you (please) open the door for me?
To respond to a request, use *will* or *can*. *Would* and *could* are not usually used.	*Possible response*: Of course I **will/can**. **NOT USUALLY**: Of course I ~~would/could~~.

(continued on next page)

D. Making Offers

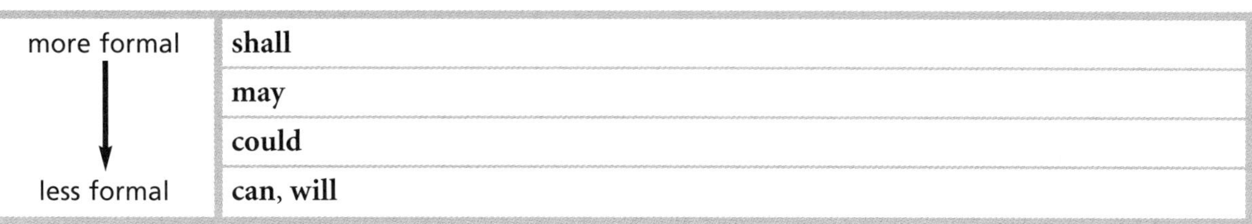

more formal ↓ less formal	
	shall
	may
	could
	can, will

1. To make an offer in a **question**, use *shall, may, could,* or *can.*

   Shall is used only with *I* or *we* and is not very common.

   Offer: **Shall/May/Could/Can** I bring you the menu?
   Possible response: Yes, thank you.

2. To make an offer in a **statement**, use *can* or *will.*

   Offer: I **can/will** help you with those bags.
   Possible response: Thanks.

E. Alternative Responses to Requests for Permission, Requests, and Offers

Responses can take the form of answers to *yes/no* questions. However:

A: Could I (please) borrow a pen?
B: Yes, you can.

- Affirmative responses are often made friendlier with expressions such as *certainly, of course,* and *sure.*

  B: Sure. I have another one.

- Negative responses are often softened with expressions such as *I'm sorry, but . . .* and *I'm afraid . . . .*

  B: I'm sorry, but I don't have one. OR I'm afraid I don't have mine.

GRAMMAR PRACTICE 5

Social Modals I: Modals for Permission, Requests, and Offers

10 Modals for Permission: Situations and Relationships I

Work with a partner. Write dialogues with questions and responses for the following situations. Use each modal in the box in one question, choosing modals appropriate to the situations. Your responses can include an appropriate modal and can be made friendlier or softened.

can	~~could~~	may

1. You're on an airplane that has several empty seats. You want to move to a window seat.

   You: Could I move to a window seat ?

   Flight attendant: Yes, of course you can./I'm sorry, but you can't. .

2. You're sitting with your sister in her kitchen. You want to get a drink of water.

   You: ______________________________ ?

   Your sister: ______________________________ .

3. You're at a formal party at the home of an older woman whom you don't know well. You want to look at her garden.

   You: ______________________________ ?

   The hostess: ______________________________ .

11 Modals for Requests: Situations and Relationships II

Work with a partner. Write dialogues with questions and responses for the following situations. Use each modal in the box in one question, choosing modals appropriate to the situations. Your responses can include an appropriate modal and can be made friendlier or softened.

~~will~~	would

1. You're in class. You ask a friend to lend you his calculator for a few minutes.

   You: Will you lend me your calculator for a few minutes ?

   Your classmate: Sure, I will./I'm afraid I left it at home .

2. You're in class. Your math professor has just explained a problem. You ask her to go over that problem again.

   You: ______________________________ ?

   The professor: ______________________________ .

can	could

3. You're at a party. You ask a good friend to give you a ride home.

   You: ______________________________ ?

   Your friend: ______________________________ .

4. You're at the doctor's office. You ask the doctor to sign your health insurance form.

   You: ______________________________ ?

   The doctor: ______________________________ .

12 Modals for Offers: Situations and Relationships III

Work with a partner. Write dialogues with questions or statements and responses for the following situations. Use each modal in the box in one question or statement, choosing modals appropriate to the situations. Give any appropriate response.

can	~~could~~	may

1. You are in an office at the school where you are a student. The secretary has some letters ready to mail. You offer to mail them for her.

   You: Could I mail those letters for you ____________________?

   The secretary: Yes, thank you./No, thanks. I can do it ____________________.

2. You are walking across the campus of the school where you are a student. You see a professor who is much older than you struggling with the heavy books he's carrying. You offer to carry them for him.

   You: ____________________?

   The professor: ____________________.

3. Your friend just got a new computer program. You offer to show her how to use it.

   You: ____________________?

   Your friend: ____________________.

will	shall	can

4. You're at work. Your boss mentions that the office feels a little warm. You offer to turn on the air conditioner.

   You: ____________________?

   Your boss: ____________________.

5. You've just finished dinner at your brother's house. You offer to help him wash the dishes.

   You: ____________________?

   Your brother: ____________________.

6. Your younger sister's friend calls. Your sister isn't home. You offer to take a message for her.

   You: ____________________?

   Your sister's friend: ____________________.

13 Modals for Permission, Requests, and Offers: Another Matchmaker

Jin has decided to ask a matchmaker to search for a wife for him. Circle the correct form.

Secretary: Good morning, sir. (May) / Will (1) I help you?

Jin: Yes, thank you. I have an appointment with Ms. Mota.

Secretary: Might / Will (2) you have a seat, please? Ms. Mota will be with you in a few minutes. May / Would (3) you fill out this form for her?

Jin: Certainly, I will / would (4). I'm sorry, I don't have a pen. Could / Would (5) I please borrow one?

Secretary: Of course You could / can (6) use this one. Shall / Will (7) I make you a cup of tea to drink while you're waiting?

Jin: Yes, thank you. . . .

Ms. Mota: I may / will (8) help you now.

Jin: Thank you. May / Will (9) I introduce myself? I'm Jin Tanaka.

Ms. Mota: You're a very polite young man. I'm sure we'll find you a bride very soon.

14 Permission, Requests, and Offers: Practicing Politeness

Work with a partner. Think of situations—for example, at school, home, a shop, a restaurant, or a party—in which people need to ask permission, make a request, and make an offer. Make up three dialogues (one asking for permission, one with a request, and one with an offer) similar to those in Exercises 10, 11, and 12. Present your dialogues to the class.

GRAMMAR BRIEFING 6

Social Modals II: Modals for Suggestions, Advice, Expectations, Warnings, and Necessity

FORM and FUNCTION

A. Overview

Modals can be used in telling listeners what to do. Different modals express different strengths; the speaker can be making a suggestion (weak) or stating a necessity or prohibition (strong):

STRENGTH	USE	ONE-WORD MODALS	PHRASAL MODALS; MODAL-LIKE EXPRESSIONS
weak	Suggestion	**could, might, shall**	
↓	Advice/opinion	**should, should not (shouldn't)**	**ought to**
↓	Expectation		**be supposed to, not be supposed to; be to, not be to**
↓	Warning		**had better, had better not**
strong	Necessity/obligation	**must**	**have to, have got to**
strong	Prohibition	**must not (mustn't), cannot (can't)**	**not be allowed to**
	Lack of necessity		**not have to**

(continued on next page)

B. Suggestions

1. *Could* and *might* are the modals generally used to make suggestions.	If Allison is being unfriendly, you **could/might** try talking to her about it.
However, in questions and negative statements, *should* is usually used instead of *could* or *might.*	What **should** I do if she doesn't want to talk? You probably **shouldn't** push her to talk.
2. *Shall* is used mainly in questions with *we.* It is used to make suggestions about possible actions and activities. *Shall* is considered formal and is not very common.	**Shall** we go now?

C. Advice and Opinions

Use *should* and *ought to* to give advice and state opinions.	You **should/ought to** go home if you aren't feeling well. (advice) The city **should/ought to** fix the holes in this road. (opinion)
In negatives and in questions, *should* is usually used.	We **shouldn't** go there. Where **should** we go?

D. Expectations

Be supposed to and *be to* are used to express expectations, for example, about correct behavior. The expectations are sometimes based on rules or instructions.	We**'re supposed to**/**'re to** bring a gift to the party. You**'re supposed to**/**'re to** take two teaspoons of the medicine twice a day. We**'re not supposed to**/**'re not to** be there until nine o'clock.

E. Warnings

Had better is used to give warnings. It implies there will be bad consequences if the warning isn't followed. *Had better* is often contracted (*'d better*). It is not usually used in questions.	You**'d better not** be late for dinner. You **had better** hand that paper in today, or the teacher will lower your grade.

(continued on next page)

F. Necessity and Obligation; Lack of Necessity; Prohibition

Necessity and Obligation

Use *must*, *have to*, and *have got to* to express necessity or obligation. The necessity or obligation is sometimes based on rules or laws.

Although all three can be used:

• *Must* is considered stronger and more formal. It is used more often in written rules and less often in speech.	You **must/have to/have got to** be 18 to vote. (law: in writing, *must* more common; in speech, *have to/have got to* more common) You **must/have to/have got to** send in your transcript in order to apply. (rule: in writing, *must* more common; in speech, *have to/have got to* more common) He **has to/has got to/must** work this weekend. (*have to/have got to* more common)
• In questions, *have to* is used. *Have got to* cannot be used. *Must* in questions is used to make a complaint.	**Do** you **have to** work this weekend? **NOT:** ~~Have you got to~~ work this weekend? **Must** you play your music so loud? (complaint)

Lack of Necessity; Prohibition

1. Use *not have to* to say that something is not necessary.	You **don't have to** eat in the cafeteria, but you can if you want to.
2. Use *must not* to say something is prohibited.	You **must not** eat or drink on the bus.
Prohibition can also be expressed by *cannot* and *not be allowed to.*	You **can't/are not allowed to** eat or drink on the bus.

TALKING THE TALK

Should and *ought* to are usually used by someone who has the authority to give advice.	*Teacher*: For homework, you **should** study for the test. Is there anything I can do to help you prepare for it?
When a person doesn't have this authority, *should* and *ought to* can sound impolite. Instead, *could* and *might* are used to offer suggestions.	*Student*: You **could** give us a study guide.

GRAMMAR PRACTICE 6

Social Modals II: Modals for Suggestions, Advice, Expectations, Warnings, and Necessity

15 Modals for Suggestions, Advice, Expectations, Warning, and Necessity: Wedding Customs

A. Hiro, who is a Japanese visitor to the United States, has been invited to a wedding. He has never been to an American wedding, so he's asking a friend for advice. Complete the sentences with the form that is correct or more appropriate. Use contractions where possible.

Hiro: Laura, I need your advice. What should (1. might / should) I wear to the wedding?

Laura: Well, that depends on the kind of wedding it is. You ______ (2 should not / might not) wear clothes that are too casual. In my opinion, you ______ (3 could / ought to) find out if it's a formal wedding. Men ______ (4 be supposed to / might) wear dark suits to formal weddings. That's expected, so they all do.

Hiro: I need a suggestion for a gift. What ______ (5 ought I to / should I) give the bride and groom?

Laura: There are lots of possibilities. You ______ (6 might / must) give them something special from Japan, but that's just a suggestion.

Hiro: What are my obligations at the wedding reception? ______ (7 have got to / have to) I ______ make a speech?

Laura: No, you don't. After the reception begins, you ______ (8 be to / could) wait in line and give the bride and groom your best wishes, because that's correct behavior. Later, some of the guests may offer toasts, or short speeches, to the newlyweds. If they do, you ______ (9 must / could) offer one, too, but it isn't an obligation. If you want to dance with the bride, you can ask her by saying, "______ (10 Shall / Must) we dance?"

Hiro: I'm worried about being able to do everything properly. You ______ (11 have got to / be supposed to) come to the wedding with me. I'll need you there.

Laura: Oh no, Hiro. You ______________________ take uninvited guests to a
12 (could not / not be allowed to)
wedding. It isn't permitted. But don't worry. You ______________________
13 (must not / not have to)
know much about the customs. It isn't necessary. Oh, there is one thing I need to warn you about. Weddings usually begin on time, so you ______________________
14 (had better not / not have to)
be late.

Hiro: I'll go early, but I'm still going to worry.

Laura: ______________________ you worry so much, Hiro? Just have a good time!
15 (Shall / Must)

B. Work with a partner—if possible, someone who knows about wedding customs in a culture that you're not familiar with. You've been invited to a wedding. Ask your partner for advice and suggestions, and ask about expectations for clothing, gifts, behavior, and customs. In the questions and answers include *should, ought to, could, might,* and *be supposed to,* as appropriate. Then reverse roles.

To learn about wedding customs in the United States and other countries, go to the *Grammar Links* Website.

16 Modals for Opinion, Obligation, Lack of Necessity, and Prohibition: The Roles of Marriage Partners I

A. Kim is leading an international students' discussion on the responsibilities of husbands and wives. Complete the sentences using *should* or *ought to*. If both are possible, write both. Use contractions with *not* where possible.

Kim: What are your opinions? Which tasks should a husband do? Which tasks
1 (a husband)
______________ do?
2 (a wife)

Dana: I think a marriage ______________
3
be a partnership with both people doing everything.

Lesley: Well, there's one thing a husband probably ______________ do—decorate
4 (not)
the house.

Nate: I agree, and I think there's one more thing. A husband ______________ shop
5 (not)
for his wife's clothes!

Tasks

- Earning the money to support the family
- Caring for the children
- Housework
- Cooking
- Repairing and maintaining the house and car
- Managing the money
- Shopping
- Decorating the house

B. Complete the sentences using *have to, have got to,* and *must.* Use contractions with *not* where possible. Write all correct forms.

Kim: What about obligations? Does (1) a wife have to do certain tasks?

Lee: No, I don't think so. These are all things that couples have to/have got to/must (2) talk about and share the responsibility for. The important thing is that if you promise to do something, you ____ (3 (not)) forget to do it. Of course, if people are very rich, they ____ (4 (not)) do the cooking and cleaning themselves, because they can pay someone else. But in general, one person ____ (5 (not)) make a decision without discussing it with the other one.

Kim: Does everyone agree? ____ (6) a couple ____ share in these responsibilities?

Kiko: I think that a wife ____ (7) manage all the money. It's her responsibility. She can tell her husband how she's managing it, but she ____ (8) tell him.

Adel: In my culture, a woman ____ (9 (not)) drive a car—it isn't allowed. So a husband ____ (10) take care of the car and do a lot of the shopping.

Kelly: In my culture, things have changed. In the past, husbands earned the money to support their families. Now a lot of women ____ (11) share that responsibility because one salary isn't enough.

17 Modals for Opinion, Obligation, Lack of Necessity, and Prohibition: The Roles of Marriage Partners II

Work in small groups. Use the list of tasks in Exercise 16 as the basis for a discussion. One student should act as the leader and ask the others to discuss the following questions.

1. In your opinion, are there certain tasks that a husband or a wife should do?
2. Are there certain tasks that a husband or a wife has an obligation to do?
3. Are there tasks that either of them shouldn't or mustn't do?
4. What other responsibilities and obligations do husbands and wives have?
5. Is it necessary for couples to discuss their expectations and opinions about responsibilities and obligations before they marry?

18 Using Ability, Belief, and Social Modals: Points of View

A. As a class, discuss the following statements. Do you agree with either one? Do you have a different point of view?

1.

> *Marriage partners should find each other on their own. They ought to make a decision to marry based on their romantic love for each other. I can't imagine letting my family influence my choice of a partner. They can't understand my situation—or what I need in a partner—as well as I do.*

2.

> *My family should be involved in finding a suitable partner for me. My decision to marry is going to be influenced more by family considerations than by romantic love. My family can understand me better than anyone else. They will suggest possible partners with whom I will be able to get along well. Romantic love may develop later.*

B. Write a paragraph explaining your point of view about finding and deciding on a marriage partner. Use at least two of each of the following types of modals: ability (e.g., *be able to, can*), belief (e.g., *could, will, may, might, must*), and social (e.g., *be supposed to, must, have to, should*).

See the *Grammar Links* Website for a model paragraph for this assignment.

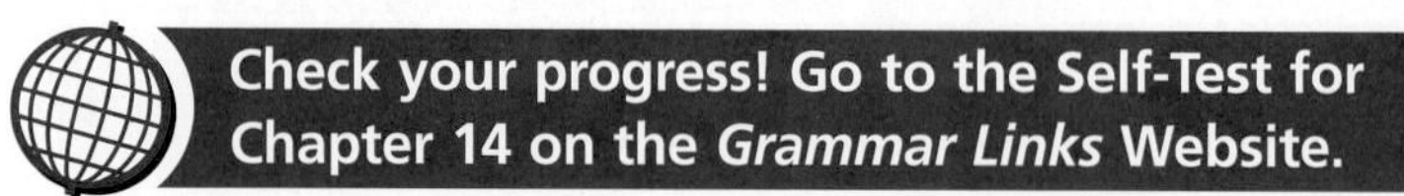

Check your progress! Go to the Self-Test for
Chapter 14 on the Grammar Links Website.

Chapter 15

More About Modals

Introductory Task: Giving Advice

A. You are Addy Viser, the writer of a newspaper advice column. You have received the following letter.

Dear Addy Viser,

I'm 25 years old. A year ago I fell in love with a woman named Irene. Irene and I wanted to get married, but when my parents found out, they didn't approve because they've never gotten along with her family. My friends thought that I should follow my heart and marry Irene. But I listened to my family's advice and decided not to marry her. Irene married another man yesterday. Now I realize that I can never love anyone else as much as I love Irene, and I feel regretful. I **should have listened** to my friends instead of my family. Do you agree?

Regretful

Read the following possible responses to "Regretful." Check the one that you think is best.

_______ Yes, you **should have listened** to your friends. You **shouldn't have let** your parents' opinion influence you. You **ought to have done** what was right for you.

_______ No, you **shouldn't have followed** your friends' advice. Marriages between people whose families don't get along can be very difficult. Besides, you say that Irene married another man. She **couldn't have loved** you as much as you loved her.

_______ You **should have gotten** advice from a professional counselor. With a counselor's help, you **might have worked** things out with your family. Things **could have turned** out more happily for you.

B. As a class, discuss your responses. Does anyone have other ideas about what "Regretful" should have done in this situation? Use *should have* and *shouldn't have* to give your opinion.

Example: "Regretful" should have asked a sympathetic aunt or grandmother to talk to his parents.

GRAMMAR BRIEFING 1

Perfect Modals

FORM

A. Overview

Perfect modals are formed by adding *have* to many of the modals from Chapter 14. They are followed by the past participle of the verb. Perfect modals include:

- *Could have, may have, might have, must have,* and *should have,* formed from one-word modals.

  You **should have known** better.

- *Have to have* and *have got to have,* formed from phrasal modals with *have.*

  He **has to have finished.**

- *Ought to have* and *had better have,* formed from modal-like expressions.

  She **ought to have asked** us.

B. Affirmative Statements

SUBJECT	MODAL + *HAVE*	PAST PARTICIPLE	
They	**might have**	**left.**	
She	**has to have**	**helped**	him.

C. Negative Statements

SUBJECT	MODAL + *NOT* + *HAVE**	PAST PARTICIPLE	
He	**must not have**	**known.**	
You	**should not have**	**done**	that.

The perfect modals formed from phrasal modals and modal-like expressions are not commonly used, except for *had better not have.*

You **had better not have** told him.

*For contractions of modals with *not,* see Chapter 14, Grammar Briefing 1, page 261.

D. Questions

Yes/No *Questions and Short Answers*

QUESTIONS	SHORT ANSWERS
Could they **have gone**?	Yes, they **could have.**
Should we **have helped** him?	No, we **shouldn't have.**

(continued on next page)

D. Questions (continued)

Wh- *Questions*

WH- QUESTIONS ABOUT THE SUBJECT	OTHER *WH-* QUESTIONS
Who could have told him?	**What should** I **have done**?

Questions generally use only perfect modals formed from one-word modals.

When **could** he **have** been here?

TALKING THE TALK

Have in the perfect modal is often pronounced "of" or "a."

"We should-of/shoulda tried harder."

"He couldn't-of/couldn'ta gone there."

GRAMMAR PRACTICE 1

Perfect Modals

1 Perfect Modals—Form: The Dangers of Romantic Love

Use the words in parentheses to complete the sentences. Use contractions with *not* where possible.

Stella: The story of Romeo and Juliet was such a tragedy, but I think that things might have turned out (1 might / turn out) differently for Juliet. A happier ending ________ (2 have to / be) possible.

Maria: But how? Their families were enemies, and Juliet's father had arranged for her to marry another man, Count Paris. ________ (3 Juliet / should / obey) her father?

Stella: No, but Romeo and Juliet ________ (4 should / be) smarter. First of all, Romeo ________ (5 should / not / kill) himself.

Maria: But he thought that Juliet had died.

Stella: Well, she ______________ (6 may / not / seem) to be alive, but she was. Romeo ______________ (7 might / try) to find out for sure. He ______________ (8 ought to / rescue) her.

Maria: What ______________ (9 Juliet / should / do) when she discovered that Romeo was dead? Without him, she ______________ (10 could / not / go on) living.

Stella: She ______________ (11 must / love) him very much. But Juliet was only 13. She ______________ (12 might / meet) someone else.

Maria: How ______________ (13 that / could / happen)? Remember, she had to marry Count Paris.

Stella: Poor Juliet! Romantic love really can lead to tragedy, can't it?

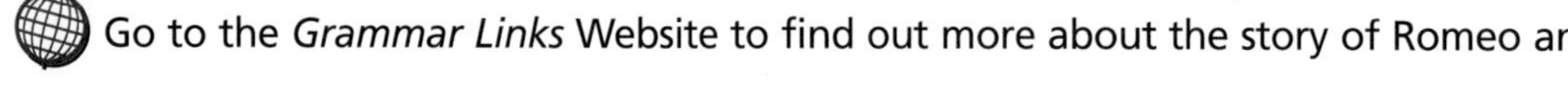

Go to the *Grammar Links* Website to find out more about the story of Romeo and Juliet.

2 Perfect Modals—Contracted and Full Forms: A Communication Problem?

Frank is the host of a radio program, *Speaking Frankly.* People call him for advice about relationships. Listen to the dialogue once for the main ideas. Then listen again and fill in the blanks with the words that you hear. You will hear contracted forms, but you should write full forms.

Frank: Hello! You're on the air. What's your relationship problem?

Elise: Hi, Frank. This is Elise from California. I had a problem with my boyfriend the other night, and I want to know what I should have (1) done about it. We were driving to our friends' new house, and we got lost. We finally found the house, but it should not have (2) taken us two hours to do it.

Frank: Let me guess. Your boyfriend ______________ (3) been driving. He ______________ (4) asked someone for directions, but he didn't do it.

Frank: Let me guess. Your boyfriend ______________ (3) been driving. He ______________ (4) asked someone for directions, but he didn't do it.

Elise: Right! How did you know? There were several times when he ______________ (5) stopped to ask someone, but he didn't.

Frank: Elise, try to think of the situation from your boyfriend's point of view. Imagine that he had stopped to ask someone. You ______________ (6) thought that he wasn't fully in control of the situation.

Elise: He wasn't fully in control of the situation. He ______________ (7) asked someone.

Frank: You ______________ (8) found the house any faster that way. That person ______________ (9) known where it was but ______________ (10) tried to be helpful and given wrong directions.

Elise: When we finally found the house, our friends had gone out without us. They ______________ (11) wanted to keep waiting. I guess I ______________ (12) complained, but I did.

Frank: You ______________ (13) been upset. But your boyfriend probably ______________ (14) done anything differently. A lot of men just have a very hard time asking for directions.

Elise: I understand that now. Thanks, Frank.

GRAMMAR BRIEFING 2

Belief Modals Used to Talk About the Past

FUNCTION

A. Overview

Speakers use perfect modals to express different degrees of certainty about events and situations in the past:

DEGREE OF CERTAINTY	MODALS IN AFFIRMATIVE SENTENCES	MODALS IN NEGATIVE SENTENCES
very certain ↓	**must have, have to have, have got to have**	**could not have (couldn't have), cannot have (can't have), must not have (musn't have)**
	should have, ought to have	**should not have**
not very certain	**may have, might have, could have**	**may not have, might not have (mightn't have)**

(continued on next page)

A. Overview (continued)

1. The belief modals in the past express the same degrees of certainty they do in the present.

Past: Ted **could have** been at the party (weak certainty), but Megan **must not have** been (strong certainty).

Present: Ted could be at the party (weak certainty), but Megan must not be (strong certainty).

2. *Could have* is the modal most often used in questions. *Might have* can also be used.

Could he **have** been at the party?

B. Expressing Degrees of Certainty in Affirmative Sentences

1. *Must have, have to have,* and *have got to have* express very strong certainty about the past.

He **must have/has to have/has got to have** been at the party on Friday. Kim saw him there.

2. *Should have* and *ought to have* express somewhat strong certainty about the past.

He **should have/ought to have** been at the party on Friday. He told me he was going.

3. *May have, might have,* and *could have* express weak certainty about the past.

He **may have/might have/could have** been at the party on Friday. I know he was invited.

C. Expressing Degrees of Certainty in Negative Sentences

In negative sentences, use *must have, should have, may have,* and *might have* the same way as in affirmative sentences.

He **must not have** been at the party. No one saw him.

He **shouldn't have** been at the party. He said he wasn't going to go.

He **may not have/might not have** been at the the party. But he might have been.

However:

- Use *could have* and *can have* when you are very certain.

He **couldn't have/can't have** been at the party. No one saw him.

- *Have to have, have got to have,* and *ought to have* are not used.

He **shouldn't have** been at the party.
NOT: He ~~ought not to have~~ been at the party.

GRAMMAR PRACTICE 2

Belief Modals Used to Talk About the Past

3 Belief Modals About the Past—Form and Meaning: Your Parents' Wedding

Complete the conversation with the appropriate form of the choice that is correct or better expresses the meaning. Use contractions where possible.

Mira: Your parents' wedding must have been in St. Anne's Church. (1 (must have / might have))

If you look closely at one of the photos, you can see a sign that says "St. Anne's."

Who performed their wedding ceremony?

Tony: It ________ been Father Ruiz. He didn't work at St. Anne's then. (2 (must have + not / have to have + not))

It ________ been Father Malley. That's possible. (3 (must have / could have))

Mira: Was the church full of people?

Tony: The church ________ been full. It's very big, so it probably wasn't. (4 (should have + not / ought to have + not))

Mira: Was the ceremony long?

Tony: It ________ been long. I'm not sure. (5 (may have + not / could have + not))

Mira: Your mother's wedding dress was beautiful. Did she sew it herself?

Tony: She ________ sewed it. She doesn't know how to sew. (6 (can have + not / may have + not))

Mira: Where did she get the pearl necklace she wore for the wedding?

Tony: She ________ borrowed it from someone. I'm certain that she's never owned a pearl necklace. (7 (have to have / should have))

Mira: There aren't any pictures of the reception. Do you think they had a white cake?

Tony: They ________ had a white cake. That was the tradition, and everyone had one. (8 (have got to have / might have))

Mira: Your mom's sister ________ been happy about saying goodbye to her. She's crying in this picture. Did anyone take a video of your parents' wedding? (9 (must have + not / should have + not))

Tony: They ________ taken a video! Videos didn't exist yet. (10 (could have + not / might have + not))

4 Belief Modals About the Past: The Mystery of a Long-Term Marriage I

Don's elderly parents live in a small town far from Don. On June 8, he called the captain of the town's police department. Complete the sentences with *must have*, *have to have*, *have got to have*, *should have*, *ought to have*, *may have*, *might have*, *could have*, and, in negative sentences only, *can have*. In each blank, write all the modals that work best in the context. Use *not* where necessary. Use contractions with *not* where possible.

Don: I'm very worried about my parents, Captain. Something strange must have/has to have/has got to have (1) happened to them. There isn't any other explanation for the situation. I tried calling them at noon. They shouldn't have (2) been out then. They almost always have lunch together at home at noon. But no one answered.

Captain: I wouldn't worry. There are lots of possibilities. They ______________ (3) gone for a drive.

Don: I called the neighbors. They said that my parents' car is in the driveway.

Captain: In that case, they ______________ (4) have gone for a drive in their car. Did the neighbors go inside the house to look around?

Don: No. The door was locked. And they couldn't see inside—my parents ______________ (5) left the curtains closed.

Captain: Did the neighbors see anything in the mailbox?

Don: They didn't say, but there probably wasn't any mail. At least, there ______________ (6) been mail, because it usually isn't delivered until later. Also, the neighbors told me that my mother missed the meeting at the Senior Center this morning.

Captain: There are possible explanations for that. She ______________ (7) remembered about the meeting.

Don: My mother writes notes to remind herself of things. My parents have disappeared.

Captain: That's unlikely, but since you're so worried, I'll go over and take a look.

Don: Thank you. They ______________ (8) left a key under the doormat. I know that they usually do.

5 **Belief Modals About the Past:** The Mystery of a Long-Term Marriage II

The police captain didn't find Don's parents, but he did find evidence. He thought about possibilities and drew conclusions. Write sentences using *must have*, *have to have*, *have got to have*, *could have*, *may have*, *might have*, and, for negative sentences only, *can have*. You can write any sentence that fits with the information. Use *not* where necessary.

1. Everything was very orderly in the house.

   He thought: They must not have left in a hurry.
2. Then he found a note that said, "Call travel agency again."

   He thought: They may have gone on a trip.
3. He saw a brochure from a travel agency, "Antarctic Adventures for Seniors."

   He thought: __________
4. All their warm clothes were still in the closets, and it's winter in Antarctica in June.

   He thought: __________
5. He found a box labeled "Beach Umbrellas." It was empty.

   He thought: __________
6. He found a receipt in the desk for two tickets to Honolulu on June 8 at 5 a.m.

   He thought: __________
7. He found a note that said, "Don't forget to tell Don about our 50th wedding anniversary trip."

   He thought: __________

   The captain called Don. What did he tell him?

6 **Using Belief Modals About the Past:** Married Couples

1. 

2. 

3. 

Work with a partner. Look at the couples in the photographs. What are your impressions of their marriages and lives? Use belief modals in the past to describe their life together before the photo was taken.

Example: They must have been married for a long time. They might not have had an easy life. They may have had to work very hard.

GRAMMAR BRIEFING 3

Social Modals Used to Talk About the Past

FORM and FUNCTION

A. Overview

Modals used to talk about the past express degrees of strength similar to those used to talk about the present:

STRENGTH	USE	ONE-WORD MODALS	PHRASAL MODALS; MODAL-LIKE EXPRESSIONS
weak	Suggestion	**could have, might have**	
↓	Advice/opinion	**should have, should not have** (**shouldn't have**)	**ought to have**
	Expectation		**be supposed to, not be supposed to; be to, not be to**
	Warning		**had better have, had better not have**
strong {	Necessity/obligation		**have to**
	Prohibition	**could not** (**couldn't**)	**not be allowed to**
	Lack of necessity		**not have to**

B. Perfect Forms and Other Forms

1. One-word modals occur as perfect modals (*could have, might have, should* [*not*] *have*).

   You **could have** given them a ride.

   The only exception is *could not.*

   He **couldn't** get his driver's license until he was 18.

2. Modal-like expressions occur as perfect modals (*ought to have, had better* [*not*] *have*).

   You**'d better have** done well on the test.

3. Phrasal modals occur with *be* and *have* in their past form (*was/were* [*not*] *supposed, was/were* [*not*] *to, had better* [*not*] *have, was/were not allowed to, had to/didn't have to*).

   You **were supposed to** mail this last week.

   We **weren't allowed to** go in early.

   We **didn't have to** write a paper.

(continued on next page)

FUNCTION

A. Suggestions

Could have and *might have* suggest possibilities that did not occur:	
• *Could have*, which is used more, often implies that an opportunity was lost.	We **could have** gotten free tickets, but we didn't know about it.
• Both modals often imply a criticism.	You're late. You **could have/might have** called.

B. Advice

Should have and *ought to have* are often used to say that:	
• Something was a good idea but didn't happen.	You **should have/ought to have** gone home as soon as you felt sick. (a good idea but you didn't do it; implied criticism)
• Something that was a bad idea happened (in negative sentences with *should*).	I **shouldn't have** stayed up so late last night. (a bad idea and I did it; implied regret).
Both modals imply criticism or regret.	

C. Expectations

Be supposed to and *be to* are used to say that:	
• Something was expected or planned but didn't happen.	You're late. You **were supposed to/were to** get here at nine o'clock.
• Something wasn't expected or planned but happened (in negative sentences).	Mom's going to be mad at us. We **weren't supposed to/weren't to** leave without telling her.

D. Warnings

Had better have is used, in affirmative and negative sentences, to give warnings about past actions.	He**'d better have** told me the truth. You**'d better not have** left all the lights on.

(continued on next page)

E. Necessity: Lack of Necessity; Prohibition

1. Use *have to* to express past necessity.	He **had to** work last weekend.
2. Use *not have to* to express lack of necessity.	We **didn't have to** go to class while we were studying for exams.
3. Use *couldn't* or *not be allowed to* to express prohibition in the past.	As a child, I **couldn't/wasn't allowed to** watch TV until I finished my homework.

GRAMMAR HOTSPOT!

Do not use *must* (*not*) *have* to express necessity and prohibition. Unlike *must*, it is only a belief modal.	Yesterday I **had to** take my brother to the airport. **NOT**: Yesterday I ~~must have taken~~ my brother to the airport. He **couldn't** take more than two bags. **NOT**: He ~~must not have taken~~ more than two bags.

GRAMMAR PRACTICE 3

Social Modals Used to Talk About the Past

7 Social Modals About the Past: An Odd but Happy Couple

Use the expressions given to complete the sentences. Use each expression once. Use contractions where possible.

~~be supposed to~~	not be allowed to	have to	ought to have	should not have

Roxie was supposed to (1) marry an older man. When she broke her engagement to him, a friend said, "What a mistake! You ______ (2) broken your engagement. You ______ (3) married him." Roxie replied, "I ______ (4) end it. It became necessary because he was always telling me what to do. I ______ (5) make my own decisions—he never let me." Then Roxie found Jim, who's five years younger than she is. Jim admired her and gave her confidence.

could have	could not	had better have	have to	not have to

After a few months, Jim and Roxie were sure of their love, but they weren't sure of their families' approval, so they decided to have a secret wedding. They wanted to get married as soon as possible, but they ______ (6) get married without a marriage license. So they ______ (7) wait for a few days. After their wedding, Jim told his family what had happened. Jim's sister complained, "You ______ (8) told me. Roxie may be older, but she's perfect for you. You ______ (9) keep your love a secret." Then she warned him, "You ______ (10) given her a beautiful wedding ring." Jim assured her that Roxie was very happy with the wedding ring and with him.

8 Social Modals About the Past: Nana's Rules

Rachel is talking to her grandmother, Nana. The sentences in brackets tell you what they are thinking. Complete each sentence with all the modals appropriate to expressing their thoughts. Use *could have, might have, should have, ought to have, be supposed to, be to, had better have, have to, could,* and *be allowed to*. Use *not* where necessary. Use contractions where possible.

This was a good idea, but you haven't done it.
You should have found Mr. Right by now.

Nana: Rachel, you're 35 years old, and you're not married yet. You should have/ought to have (1) found Mr. Right by now. [This was a good idea, but you haven't done it.]

Rachel: I've tried, Nana. For example, I met a man named Owen at a party. I went up to him and introduced myself.

Nana: You shouldn't have (2) talked to him first. [It was a bad idea, but you did it.] You ________________ (3) waited for him to introduce himself. [This was a good idea, but you didn't do it.]

Rachel: Owen ________________ (4) call me the next day. [This was what we planned and what I expected.] But he didn't, so I called him and invited him out.

Nana: You ________________ (5) called him. [This was a bad idea, but you did it.] You ________________ (6) waited longer. [This is one suggestion.] Or you ________________ (7) just forgotten about him. [This is another suggestion.] There are plenty of other nice men.

Rachel: Anyway, it turned out that Owen already had a girlfriend. He ________________ (8) told me that at the party. [This was a possibility but it didn't occur, and I'm complaining.] But then I met Eric.

Nana: Rachel, you ________________ (9) invited him out, too. [This is a warning.]

Rachel: I did. He was shy, so I ______________________ (10) do it. [It was a necessity.] But things didn't work out with him, either.

Nana: Rachel, you ______________________ (11) found Mr. Right by now, but you didn't follow the rules. [You lost the opportunity.] When I was young, women ______________________ (12) speak to men first or invite them out. [It was prohibited.] But this was good. We ______________________ (13) worry about getting involved with men who weren't interested. [It wasn't a necessity.] Also, men like to take the lead. If you follow the old rules, Mr. Right will come to you.

9 Using Social Modals About the Past: Communication Problems?

You're Addy Viser. Work with a partner. Read and discuss the following two letters, which people have written to your newspaper advice column. In your opinion, did they do the right thing or should they have done things differently? Write a short paragraph in response to each letter. Use *could have*, *might have*, *ought to have*, and *should have* in your sentences. Include some sentences with *not*.

1.

Dear Addy Viser,

My wife and I recently celebrated our fifth anniversary. As a surprise for my wife, I got tickets to a Dar Williams concert, because I thought that was her favorite singer. I kept our destination a secret until we got to the concert. After we sat down, she told me that the singer she likes is Lucinda Williams. The evening wasn't perfect, because my wife was disappointed. I didn't feel so good, either.

Peter

2.

Dear Addy Viser,

My boyfriend asked me to look after his houseplants for a month while he was gone. I agreed to do it, although I wasn't really sure what to do. I drove ten miles to his house every day to water them, and I put lots of fertilizer on them. I don't know why, but the plants are nearly dead now. My boyfriend came back yesterday. He didn't thank me for looking after the plants, and he hasn't been as cheerful as he usually is.

Barbara

Example:

Dear Peter, Your wife ought to have appreciated the special effort you made to surprise her. . . . OR *You shouldn't have bought tickets before you made sure of the name of your wife's favorite singer. . . .*

See the *Grammar Links* Website for complete model letters for this assignment.

10 Belief and Social Modals About the Past: Which Words Should Addy Viser Have Used?

Circle the correct choice. If both are correct, circle both.

Dear Addy Viser,

I met a woman named Rachel last month and called her the next Saturday afternoon for a date that night. She said that she couldn't go out with me because she (had to help) / must have helped (1) her grandmother. The next week I called her office and left a message for her to call me. I know that she had to get / must have gotten (2) the message because her secretary told me she put it on her desk. I didn't have to work / mustn't have worked (3) that weekend, so I waited at home for her to call, but she never did. I was disappointed. Should I have called her again?

Wondering

Dear Wondering,

Yes, you ought to have called / should have called (4) Rachel again. You know she has to have gotten / must have gotten (5) the message, but you don't know why she didn't respond. Maybe she's decided to follow the old social rules. In the past, women had to let / must have let (6) men take the lead. They couldn't telephone / couldn't have telephoned (7) a man to tell him they wanted to go out. They have to have waited / had to wait (8) for men to call them. And there's another possibility: Rachel might not have wanted / could not have wanted (9) to seem too eager. It was a way to keep you interested in her, and it seems to have worked.

P.S. Why did you wait until Saturday afternoon to call for a date on Saturday night? You might have asked / could have asked (10) her for a date for the following Saturday instead. Next time, don't call later than Wednesday!

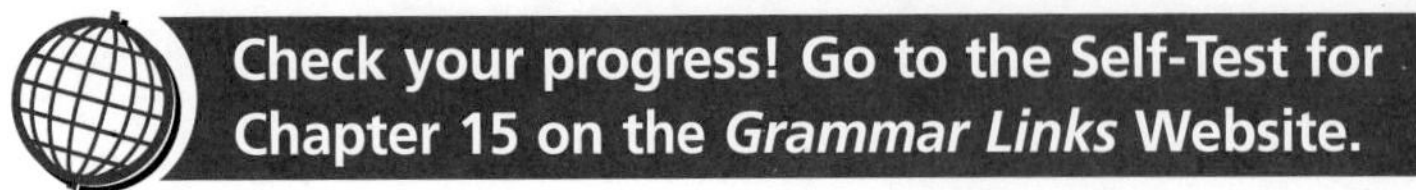

Check your progress! Go to the Self-Test for
Chapter 15 on the Grammar Links Website.

Wrap-up Activities

1 Should Ms. Monish Give Advice? EDITING

Correct the 11 errors in the passage. There are errors in modals and phrasal modals. Some errors can be corrected in more than one way. The first error is corrected for you.

must have heard

By now, you ~~must hear~~ of Ms. Monish, the marriage counselor whose advice column appears in hundreds of newspapers. Every day thousands of people write to Ms. Monish. They ask her, "May you give me some advice?" or "I was confused. What should I have done?" When people tell her they are considering divorce, she responds, "You shouldn't get a divorce. You are able to work out your marriage problems in the future." Recently, she criticized a divorced woman by telling her, "You mustn't have divorced your husband. You should have try harder." Sometimes she writes, "A man's way of communicating can be different from a woman's. You ought to try to understand your husband better."

Because so many people read Ms. Monish's column and follow her advice, I wanted to know more about her background and qualifications. I finally could interview her one day. But when I talked to her, I mustn't find out much because she refused to answer my questions about her past. In order to learn more, I must ask other people. One of her friends told me that Ms. Monish has been married and divorced twice. When I heard this, I thought, "Ms. Monish has to have had marriage problems of her own in the past. She mustn't have worked those problems out very well." Her friend told me, "Ms. Monish's first marriage mustn't break up. And her second marriage hadn't got to break up, either. She couldn't communicate well with her husbands, and now she regrets it. But she must of learned a lot from those experiences."

2 Describing Yourself and Your Ideal Mate: WRITING

Imagine that you have gone to a matchmaker to find your ideal husband or wife. The matchmaker needs some information from you. Write a paragraph responding to the questions in 1 and a paragraph responding to the questions in 2.

1. What abilities do you or don't you have now? What abilities do you expect to have in the future? (Use *can* and *be able to*.)

   Example: I can't cook very well, but I can wash dishes. . . . Two years from now, I'll be able to program computers.

2. What abilities does your ideal mate have? (Use *can* and *be able to*.) What qualities are possible, necessary, or not necessary in your ideal mate? (Use *can, might, could, should, ought to, must, have to,* and *have got to*.)

   Example: My ideal husband is someone who can cook very well. . . . He doesn't have to be handsome, but he must have a sense of humor. . . .

See the *Grammar Links* Website for complete model paragraphs for this assignment.

3 Join the Politeness Patrol: WRITING/SPEAKING

Step 1 Work with a partner. As members of the "Politeness Patrol," your task is to change impolite (i.e., abrupt or inappropriate) requests, offers, and responses into polite ones, using modals and other polite expressions.

	Impolite	Polite
1.	Young student: *Hey, there. I need change for a dollar. Give me some.*	Young student: Excuse me. Could you please give me change for a dollar?
	Older stranger: *Here.*	Older stranger: Certainly I can.
2.	Man, asking for a date: *Want to go to a movie with me?*	Man, asking for a date: ____________
	Woman: *No way. I'm busy.*	Woman: ____________
3.	Student: *I'm going to carry your books for you.*	Student: ____________
	Teacher: *Do it.*	Teacher: ____________
4.	Guest: *Those apples look good. You're going to let me have one.*	Guest: ____________
	Host: *Take it.*	Host: ____________

Step 2 Now think of typical situations where people ask permission, make requests, or make offers. Write two "impolite" dialogues like those in Part A. Then write the same dialogues in a polite version, using modals and polite expressions. Present both versions to the class. Use the tone of your voice to make the impolite dialogues sound very impolite and the polite dialogues sound very polite.

4 Love-Life Dilemmas: SPEAKING/WRITING

Step 1 Work in groups of three. Discuss the following difficult situations. Use belief and social modals in the past—for example, *may* (*not*) *have* and *should* (*not*) *have*. Use belief modals to make predictions about the future—for example, *might* (*not*) and *will* (*not*). Then decide what actions are possible, advisable or not advisable, and necessary or not necessary for Pauline and Carol to take. Use social modals—for example, *could*, *should* (*not*), *must* (*not*), and (*not*) *have to*.

1.

Pauline: I have a good friend named Marcia, who has been married for a year to a man named Bruce. Last Friday night, I went to a movie alone. While I was in the theater, I noticed that Bruce was sitting in the row ahead of me. (I'm sure that Bruce didn't see me.) I was very surprised to see that he was at the movie with a woman that I didn't recognize. I haven't told Marcia about this. I've been worrying about it, and I'm not sure what to do.

2.

Carol: Six months ago, Michael asked me to marry him, and I accepted his proposal because he is a very kind and responsible man. Everyone in my family likes Michael very much. We have invited 300 people to our wedding, which is scheduled to take place in two weeks. Last week I ran into Austin. I had fallen in love with Austin in high school, but we hadn't seen each other for a long time, because we went to colleges in different cities. He was disappointed to hear about my marriage plans. Now all of my old feelings for Austin are coming back.

Step 2 On your own, choose one of the two situations. Write a paragraph about it, discussing the actions you think were and are possible, advisable, or necessary for Pauline or Carol to take. Use any appropriate modals, including at least five of the following: *could* (*have*), *may* (*have*), *might* (*have*), *have to* (*have*), *must* (*have*), *should* (*have*), *and ought to* (*have*).

See the *Grammar Links* Website for a model paragraph for this assignment.

Unit **Eight**

Passives

TOPIC FOCUS

World of Sports

UNIT OBJECTIVES

- **passive sentences in simple present and simple past**
  (Medals ***are awarded*** in every Olympics. A Canadian ***was awarded*** the first Olympic medal for snowboarding.)
- **passive sentences versus active sentences**
  (The ball was caught by the center fielder. The center fielder caught the ball.)
- **passive sentences with and without agents**
  (Sports are played ***by professional and amateur athletes.*** Sports are played in many different places.)
- **passive sentences in progressive and perfect tenses**
  (A new stadium ***is being built.*** The old one ***has*** already ***been torn down.***)
- **passive sentences with modals**
  (The stadium ***must be completed*** before the next football season.)
- ***get*** **passives**
  (Professional athletes ***get paid*** large salaries.)
- **passive causatives**
  (The team ***had*** new seats ***installed*** in the stadium.)

Grammar in Action

Reading and Listening: The World of Sports

Read and listen to this article.

The World of Sports

Sports **are played** by increasing numbers of professional athletes. Moreover, many new records **have been set** in recent years. Nowadays records **are being broken** at a faster pace by stronger and better athletes. Some old records **haven't been broken** yet but likely **will be broken** in the not-too-distant future.

Sports have become a huge entertainment industry. Sports events **are attended** by millions of fans. Many more fans **can be found** in front of their televisions on the days that their teams play.

Sports **are** often **played** in large, modern facilities. Arenas and stadiums that **were built** many years ago **are being replaced**, and more new facilities **will be built** in the future.

Millions of dollars **are spent** on sports every year. Modern stadiums are expensive, and large salaries **are paid** to top professional athletes. Many people believe that too much money **is being spent** on new stadiums and that such large salaries **shouldn't be paid** to professional athletes. **Can** fans **be expected** to share the costs through paying higher ticket prices? Tickets for some sports events have become so expensive that many fans can't afford them. **Will** these fans **be forgotten** by the sports industry as it goes after larger profits elsewhere?

What is the future of sports? Some experts predict that the costs of salaries and stadiums will become greater than the money a team can raise. This may cause problems for one of the world's top entertainment industries.

Think About Grammar

A. Look at the following active and passive sentences. Underline the subject of each sentence, and circle the object of the active sentence. Then complete the statements below.

Active sentence: The goalie threw the ball.

Passive sentence: The ball was thrown by the goalie.

1. The object of the active sentence becomes the ______________ of the passive sentence.

   The subject of the active sentence appears in the passive sentence following the word

   ______________.

2. In the passive sentence, the main verb, ______________, is in its past participle form, and a form of the verb ______________ comes before it.

3. In an active sentence, the subject *performs* the action of the verb and the object *receives* (is affected or changed by) the action of the verb. In a passive sentence, in contrast, the ______________ *receives* the action of the verb.

B. In the passage, the sentences with boldfaced verbs are passive. Find an example of each of the following. Write the boldfaced verb.

1. a passive in the simple present are played
2. a passive in the simple past ______________
3. a negative passive ______________
4. a passive in the present progressive ______________
5. a passive in the present perfect ______________
6. a passive in the future ______________
7. a passive with a modal ______________

Chapter 16

Introduction to the Passive

Introductory Task: Sports Trivia

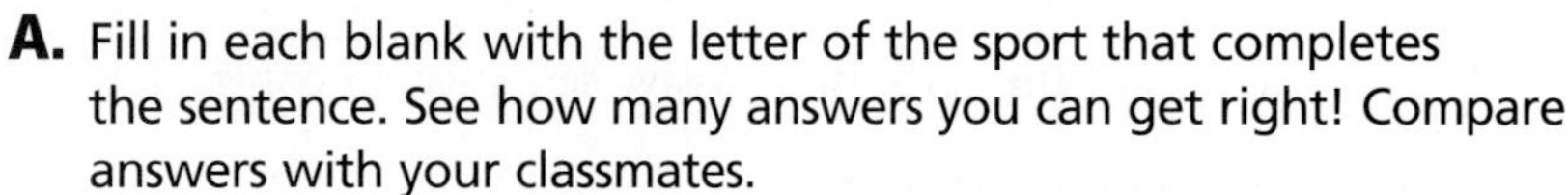

A. Fill in each blank with the letter of the sport that completes the sentence. See how many answers you can get right! Compare answers with your classmates.

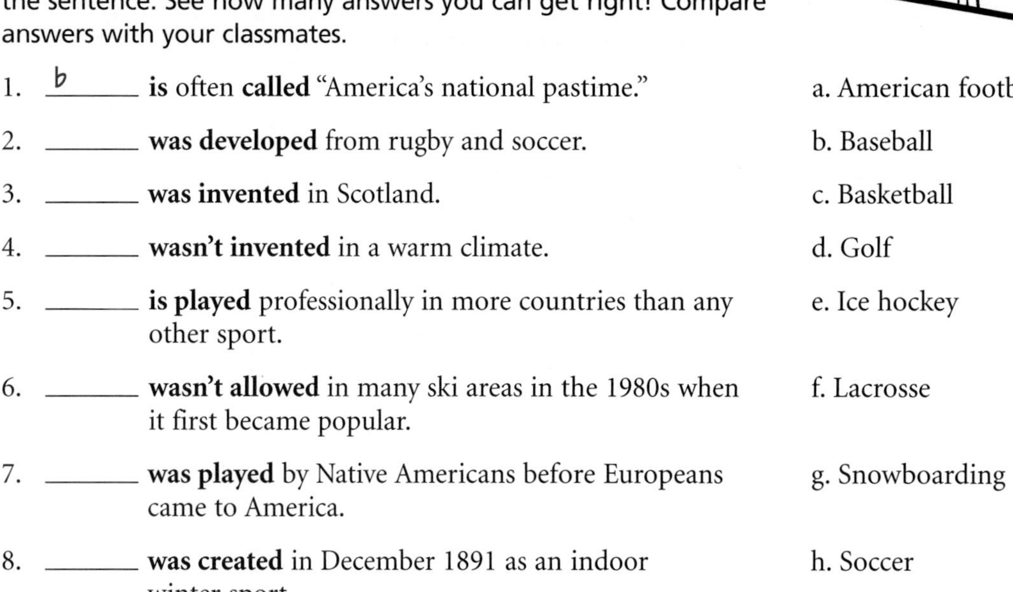

1. ___b___ **is** often **called** "America's national pastime." — a. American football
2. _______ **was developed** from rugby and soccer. — b. Baseball
3. _______ **was invented** in Scotland. — c. Basketball
4. _______ **wasn't invented** in a warm climate. — d. Golf
5. _______ **is played** professionally in more countries than any other sport. — e. Ice hockey
6. _______ **wasn't allowed** in many ski areas in the 1980s when it first became popular. — f. Lacrosse
7. _______ **was played** by Native Americans before Europeans came to America. — g. Snowboarding
8. _______ **was created** in December 1891 as an indoor winter sport. — h. Soccer

Check your answers on page A-4.

B. Work with a partner. Take turns asking and answering the following questions. In your answers, include the sports in Part A and other sports you know about.

1. Which sports **are played** at this time of the year?
2. Which sports **are played** by teams?
3. Which sports **are** usually **considered** individual sports?
4. Which sports **are watched** by many people?
5. Which sports **are televised**?
6. Which sports **were invented** fairly recently?

GRAMMAR BRIEFING 1

The Passive I

Passives in the Simple Present and Simple Past

FORM

A. Affirmative Statements

SUBJECT	*BE*	PAST PARTICIPLE OF MAIN VERB*	(PREPOSITIONAL PHRASE [*BY* . . .])	
Graduation	**is**	**held**	(by the school)	each May.
The graduation ceremony	**was**	**planned**	(by the students themselves)	months ago.

B. Negative Statements

SUBJECT	*BE + NOT/N'T*	PAST PARTICIPLE OF MAIN VERB*	(PREPOSITIONAL PHRASE [*BY* . . .])	
The payments	**aren't**	**recorded**	(by our office)	right away.
The bills	**weren't**	**sent out**	(by the assistant)	on time.

C. *Yes/No* Questions

BE	SUBJECT	PAST PARTICIPLE OF MAIN VERB*	(PREPOSITIONAL PHRASE [*BY* . . .])	
Is	day care	**provided**	(by the company)	for employees?
Was	the doctor's visit	**covered**	(by your insurance)?	

D. *Wh-* Questions

WH- WORD	*BE*	SUBJECT	PAST PARTICIPLE OF MAIN VERB*	(PREPOSITIONAL PHRASE [*BY* . . .])	
Who	**was**		**suspended**	(by the principal)	yesterday?
When	**are**	new students	**admitted**	(by the school)?	

*See Appendix 7 for the past participles of irregular verbs.

(continued on next page)

Passive Sentences Versus Active Sentences

FORM

ACTIVE SENTENCES			
SUBJECT	VERB	OBJECT	
The committee	**wrote**	new rules	last week.

PASSIVE SENTENCES				
SUBJECT	*BE*	PAST PARTICIPLE OF MAIN VERB	(PREPOSITIONAL PHRASE [*BY* . . .])	
New rules	**were**	**written**	(by the committee)	last week.

1. A passive sentence differs from an active sentence in these ways:

Active: Professor Smith (subject) teaches (verb) Psychology 101 (object) every semester.

Passive: Psychology 101 (subject) is taught (verb) (by Professor Smith) (prepositional phrase) every semester.

   - The passive sentence adds *be* and has the main verb in its past participle form.

Active: **teaches**

Passive: **is taught**

   - The object of the active sentence is the subject of the passive sentence.

Active: **Psychology 101** = object

Passive: **Psychology 101** = subject

   - The subject of the active sentence, if included in the passive sentence, is in a prepositional phrase with *by*. It can be omitted.

Active: **Professor Smith** = subject

Passive: **Professor Smith** is in prepositional phrase with *by*

2. Active sentences can have any verb. Passive sentences can have only **transitive verbs**—verbs that, in active sentences, take an object. (Remember, an active sentence object is the passive sentence subject.)

   Passive sentences are not possible with **intransitive verbs**—verbs that don't take an object. Common intransitive verbs include *appear, be, belong, come, die, go, happen, look, occur, seem, sleep, stay,* and *walk.*

Active: A truck **hit** my car. (*hit* is a transitive verb; *my car* = object)

Active: The two vehicles **collided**. (*collide* is an intransitive verb; no object)

Passive: My car **was hit** by a truck.
BUT NOT: My car ~~was collided~~.

GRAMMAR **HOT**SPOT!

Remember! Verbs like *happen* and *seem* are not transitive and are not used in passive sentences.

An accident **happened**.
NOT: An accident ~~was happened~~.

They **seemed** happy.
NOT: They ~~were seemed happy~~.

GRAMMAR PRACTICE 1

The Passive I

1 Passive Sentences in the Simple Present: Baseball Uniforms I

Complete this discussion from a sports history class. Use the words in parentheses to complete passive sentences in the simple present. Use contractions where possible.

Professor: Let's talk for a moment about why a baseball team might adopt a different uniform. After all, uniforms aren't worn (1 (not, wear)) forever. New styles are adopted (2 (adopt)) for some fairly specific reasons. For example, often a change ________ (3 (make)) when a team moves to another city.

Lauren: If a team is losing, ________ (4 (something, do)) to change the uniforms?

Professor: Yes, often different caps ________ (5 (use)), or the style of the shirt ________ (6 (modify)). Not surprisingly, this kind of design change usually ________ (7 (not, consider)) when a team is winning.

Sammy: What happens when new owners buy a team? ________ (8 (the old uniforms, keep))?

Professor: Not usually, and new uniforms ________ (9 (often, design)) when a new stadium ________ (10 (build)).

Mark: What ________ (11 (do)) with the old uniforms?

Professor: Some ________ (12 (put)) in museums, some ________ (13 (keep)) by the players, and some ________ (14 (sell)) to fans or collectors.

Mark: Cool! Maybe I can find some for sale on the Internet.

2 Passive Sentences in the Simple Past: Baseball Uniforms II

Complete the class discussion. Use the words in parentheses to complete passive sentences in the simple past. Use contractions where possible.

Professor: Another interesting fact is that players <u>weren't always identified</u> (1 (not, always, identify)) by names or numbers on their uniforms. Players __________ (2 (give)) identical uniforms, and a fan __________ (3 (expect)) to recognize the players by their faces and positions. In the early 1900s, some teams experimented with using numbers on uniforms, but numbers __________ (4 (not, wear)) by any team for a whole season until 1929.

Ruth: Did all the teams wear numbers that season?

Professor: No, and teams __________ (5 (not, require)) to use them until 1933. The New York Yankees wore numbered uniforms in the 1929 season, and the numbers __________ (6 (assign)) on the basis of the batting order.

Sammy: But, wait a minute. __________ (7 (one player, ever, send in)) to play for another player? What happened then?

Professor: Good point. That was a problem since two players couldn't have the same number. So then the numbers didn't match the batting order. That numbering system was also a problem when a player __________ (8 (trade)) to another team or when a player __________ (9 (drop)) from a team. In these cases, the batting order __________ (10 (often, change)), so players couldn't keep their numbers from one season to the next. Because of all these problems, this system __________ (11 (not, use)) for very long. Okay, let's move on from numbers to names. When __________ (12 (players' names, add)) to the uniforms?

Sammy: I know! Names ______________ on uniforms in 1960 by the Chicago
13 (first, put)

White Sox.

Professor: You're right. The decision to use names ______________ by the fact
14 (probably, influence)

that more and more games ______________ on TV. However, the use of
15 (show)

names ______________ by a number of teams because they wanted fans to
16 (oppose)

buy programs to find out who the players were.

> *batting order* = the order that baseball players take a turn at hitting the ball. *send in for* = replace or substitute one player for another. *program* = a list of players and other information for a sports event.

To find out more about sports uniforms, go to the *Grammar Links* Website.

3 Forming Passive Sentences: Names for Sports Facilities

Underline the objects in the active sentences. Remember to underline the entire noun phrase. Complete the passive sentences. Do not include a *by* phrase.

1. Today sports teams earn a lot of money from the places where sports are played.

   Today <u>a lot of money is earned</u> from the places where sports are played.
2. In many cases, teams name sports facilities for sponsors such as airlines or soft drink companies.

   In many cases, ______________ for sponsors such as airlines or soft drink companies.
3. In the past, teams didn't name sports facilities for sponsors.

   In the past, ______________ for sponsors.
4. They named sports facilities for famous players and coaches.

   ______________ for famous players and coaches.
5. Why do teams give sponsors' names to sports facilities?

   Why ______________ to sports facilities?
6. Sponsors pay large fees to teams to advertise sponsors' names on sports facilities.

   ______________ to teams to advertise sponsors' names on sports facilities.
7. When sponsors support teams, the large fees cover some of the teams' expenses.

   When sponsors support teams, ______________.

> *sponsors* = companies that pay some of the costs of an event, a facility, etc., in return for advertising.

4 Passive Sentences—Questions and Answers: Stadiums

Work with a partner. Student A asks questions with simple present and simple past passives to complete the chart about Invesco Field at Mile High. Use the words given. When no *wh-* word is given, ask a *yes/no* question. Student B uses the information on page A-4 to answer with passive sentences. Then Student B asks questions to complete the chart about the Skydome and Student A answers with the information on page A-4.

Example: Student A: *When was Invesco Field at Mile High first opened to the public?*
Student B: *Invesco Field at Mile High was first opened to the public in 2001.*

Invesco Field at Mile High Denver, Colorado	The Skydome Toronto, Canada
First year: 2001	First year: ______
Uses: ______	Uses: ______
Playing surface: ______	Playing surface: ______
Other fact: ______	Other fact: ______
Other fact: ______	Other fact: ______

Invesco Field at Mile High

1. when/open/to the public
2. what/use/for
3. games/play/on grass
4. why/computerized system/put/under the grass
5. how/money/raise/for art work at the stadium

The Skydome

1. when/open/to the public
2. what/use/for
3. games/play/on grass
4. how/roof/design/to open
5. what/use/to fasten the artificial turf

artificial turf = a substitute surface to grass, as on a playing field.

To find out more about these stadiums, go to the *Grammar Links* Website.

5 Transitive and Intransitive Verbs; Writing Passive Sentences: Player Salaries

A. Label the boldfaced verbs with a *T* for transitive or an *I* for intransitive. All of the sentences are active. There are six transitive verbs and six intransitive verbs.

Sports teams **pay** (T) some of the highest salaries in the world to their top athletes. These athletes **work** (1) hard, but are they worth the money they receive?

Players' salaries **reflect** (2) the popularity of a sport. For example, in the past hockey players didn't earn as much money as football players. Recently, hockey **seems** (3) to have become a more popular sport. Now, nearly all sports fans **recognize** (4) the names of the top hockey players. As a consequence, these players **earn** (5) higher salaries. But basketball players still **appear** (6) to be the top earners in sports year after year. The average salary of a professional basketball player **was** (7) \$3.5 million in 2001 compared to \$1.1 million for a hockey player.

According to one financial expert, paying high salaries **hurts** (8) sports teams. Top players **attract** (9) fans. However, what **happens** (10) when ticket prices are so high that fans can't afford to buy them? When fans **don't come** (11) to watch the teams, will athletes' salaries **change** (12)?

B. Six of the sentences in the passage can be rewritten as passive sentences. Rewrite these sentences. In each, include a prepositional phrase with *by*.

Example: *Some of the highest salaries in the world are paid by sports teams to their top athletes.*

GRAMMAR BRIEFING 2

The Passive II

FUNCTION

A. Active Sentences Versus Passive Sentences

ACTIVE SENTENCES			
AGENT	VERB	RECEIVER OF ACTION	
The janitors	cleaned	**the school**	from top to bottom.

PASSIVE SENTENCES			
RECEIVER OF ACTION	VERB	AGENT	
The school	was cleaned	**by the janitors**	from top to bottom.

1. An **agent** is the noun that performs the action of the verb.

   In active sentences, the subject is usually an agent.

   The cat scratched the child.

   In passive sentences, the agent, if included, is usually in a *by* phrase.

   The child was scratched by **the cat**.

2. A **receiver** is the noun that the action of the verb affects.

   In active sentences, the receiver is usually the object of the verb.

   The cat scratched **the child**.

   In passive sentences, the receiver is usually the subject.

   The child was scratched by the cat.

B. Using Passives Without *By* to Omit the Agent

1. Sometimes, we don't want to mention the agent. In passives, the agent is an optional *by* phrase. So we can omit the agent by using a passive without a *by* phrase.

   The school was cleaned from top to bottom. (*The school* is the receiver; there is no agent.)

2. Speakers may want to omit the agent because:

   - The agent is unknown, unimportant, or unnecessary.

   The Olympics were started in Greece. (The agent is unknown.)

   When it started getting dark, the stadium lights were turned on. (The agent is unimportant.)

   The students were taught fractions this year. (It is unnecessary to mention the agent—obviously, teachers did the teaching.)

(continued on next page)

B. Using Passives Without *By* to Omit the Agent (continued)

• The agent is a general subject (*people, anyone, everyone,* etc.).	Customs are developed over the years. (i.e., by people) The origins of some customs aren't understood. (i.e., by anyone)

C. Using Passives in Writing

Passives are used more in writing than in speech. They are common in news reports and, especially, in scientific and other academic writing, where agents are often less important than processes and results.	Samples of the flies' eggs **are taken**, and the larvae that emerge from the eggs **are grown** in bottles. The fully grown larvae **are** then **examined.** (The scientists who perform these processes are not important; the processes and their results are important.)

GRAMMAR PRACTICE 2

The Passive II

6 Meaning of Passive Sentences: Can the Cougars Win?

Listen to the radio broadcast of a basketball game. Then listen again and put a check next to the sentence that gives the information that is in the broadcast.

1. _______ a. Carson expects to lead his team.
   ___✓___ b. People expect Carson to lead his team.
2. _______ a. Other players passed the ball to Carson.
   _______ b. Carson passed the ball to other players.
3. _______ a. Peterson is playing in the second half.
   _______ b. Young is playing in the second half.
4. _______ a. Thomas hit the ball.
   _______ b. Sanchez hit the ball.
5. _______ a. Phillips tripped Sanchez.
   _______ b. Sanchez tripped Phillips.
6. _______ a. Phillips hurt someone in the last play.
   _______ b. Someone hurt Phillips in the last play.
7. _______ a. The players encourage the fans.
   _______ b. The fans encourage the players.
8. _______ a. Stanley Brown is the coach.
   _______ b. Stanley Brown is a player.

7 Receivers in Active and Passive Sentences: Babe Didrikson Zaharias

Underline the receiver of the action of the verbs in boldface. Circle the performer of the action, if it is given.

1. Most athletes **outshine** their competitors in only one sport.
2. In contrast, many sports **were played** well by the great Mildred "Babe" Didrikson Zaharias.
3. Babe **hit** balls hard like Babe Ruth, the famous baseball player. (This explains her nickname.)
4. In high school, she **achieved** recognition as an All-American basketball player.
5. In the 1932 U.S. track and field championship, more points **were scored** by Didrikson alone than by any team.
6. Two track and field records **were set** by Didrikson in the 1932 Summer Olympics.
7. She **won** two gold medals and a silver medal in the 1932 Olympics.
8. Didrikson **earned** 35 victories in her 21-year golf career.
9. From April 1946 to August 1947, she **defeated** all her opponents, winning 17 consecutive golf tournaments.
10. Many competitions in tennis and bowling **were won** by Didrikson, too.
11. The title "Greatest Female Athlete of the First Half of the Twentieth Century" **was awarded** to Babe Didrikson Zaharias in 1950.

8 Omitting the *By* Phrase: Catch a Wave

Circle the verbs in the following passive sentences. (Some sentences have more than one verb.) Cross out *by* phrases if the agent isn't important or necessary.

1. Some sports, like surfing, are done by individuals, not teams.
2. Surfing is done with or without a surfboard ~~by surfers~~.
3. The sport was popularized by Duke Kahanamoku in the early twentieth century.
4. Kahanamoku, an Olympic swimmer, was recognized by people as an accomplished surfer.
5. This happened when surfing exhibitions were included in swimming competitions by some competition organizers.
6. Today, many people surf, partly because formal training isn't needed by surfers.
7. More and more women are seen on surfboards by other surfers.
8. Women, especially, are inspired by champion surfer Lisa Andersen.
9. They are motivated by her surfboarding skill and her accomplishments.

exhibition = a special, noncompetitive part of a sports event.

9 Writing Passives; the *By* Phrase: Individual Sports

Write passive sentences with the information given. Include the agent in a *by* phrase only if the agent is important or necessary information. Use appropriate tenses.

I. *Snowboarding*

	Agent	Action	Receiver	Other Information
1.	people	often describe	snowboarding	as surfing on snow
2.	Jake Burton and Tom Sims	start	the first snowboard companies	in the late 1970s
3.	organizers	first include	snowboarding	in Olympic competition in 1998

1. Snowboarding is often described as surfing on snow.
2. The first snowboard companies were started by Jake Burton and Tom Sims in the late 1970s.

II. *Cycling*

	Agent	Action	Receiver	Other Information
4.	the French	hold	the first road race	in 1869
5.	millions of people	watch	the Tour de France	every year
6.	Henri Desgranges	organize	the first Tour de France	in 1903

III. *Marathon Running*

	Agent	Action	Receiver	Other Information
7.	officials	define	the length of a marathon	as 42 km, 195 m
8.	athletes	originally run	this distance	in the 1908 Olympic Games
9.	African runners	dominate	the sport	in the 1990s

10 Passives in Academic Writing: Arthroscopic Surgery for Sports Injuries

A. Read the passage on arthroscopic surgery. Find the sentences that have one or more passives and underline the verbs in passive form. Then go back and work with a partner to answer the following questions.

1. How many sentences in the passage have one or more passives? 7
2. How many times is the passive used?
3. In how many of the passives is an agent included in a *by* phrase?
4. Why is the *by* phrase omitted in so many of the passive sentences?
5. Why is the passive used so often in the passage?

Arthroscopic Surgery

Injuries occur in all sports, and injuries to joints, especially the knee, are common. Surgery for these injuries has become simpler because of the advances in arthroscopic surgery, one of the most common procedures in sports medicine today. Arthroscopic surgery was first performed in the mid-1950s by a Japanese doctor, Masaaki Watanabe, who also designed one of the first widely used arthroscopes. The procedure was brought to North America in 1965 by a Canadian doctor, Robert W. Jackson.

Using an arthroscope, a surgeon can examine and treat joint problems that used to require extensive surgery and long recovery periods. An arthroscope is a thin tool containing a fiber-optic light, a magnifying lens, and a video camera. In arthroscopic surgery, a small incision, or cut, is made and the arthroscope is inserted into the incision. Sterile fluid is injected into the joint space to enlarge the space, and the tissues are examined. Repairs are made to the injury through another small incision. Usually, because the incisions are so small, stitches are not required, and surgical tape is used to close them instead. When injuries are treated with arthroscopic surgery, they heal faster, so little time is needed for recovery, and normal activity is resumed by the patient within a short time.

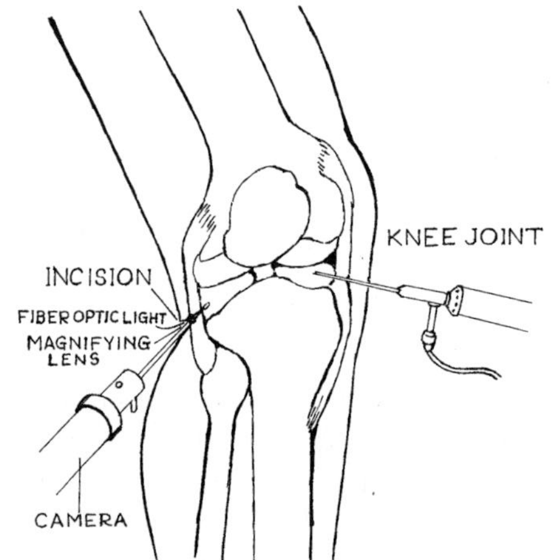

joint = a place where two or more body parts are joined. *fiber-optic* = using glass or plastic fibers that are capable of transmitting light around curves. *magnify* = make something appear larger than it really is. *sterile fluid* = a liquid that is free from living microorganisms, especially those that cause disease. *tissue* = the substance that plants and animals are made of. *stitch* = a piece of thread used to close an incision in surgery.

B. Write a paragraph that explains a process or procedure like the one in Part A. Possibilities include biological, chemical, mechanical, mental, physical, and social processes, or any other process you know or can find out about. Use at least five passive sentences in your paragraph. Use the simple present and simple past tense and at least one negative. Make sure to use the passive appropriately.

See the *Grammar Links* Website for a model paragraph for this assignment.

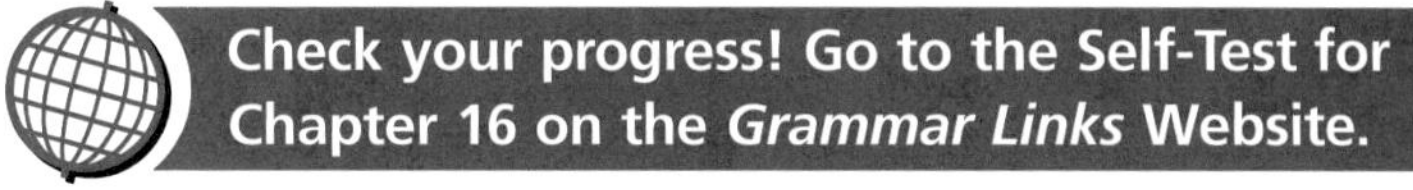

Check your progress! Go to the Self-Test for
Chapter 16 on the *Grammar Links* Website.

Chapter 17

More About Passives

Introductory Task: The Things Fans Do

A. Sports fans do some strange things to support their teams and bring them good luck. Put a check next to each statement that you think is true.

___✓___ 1. Fans **got** their faces **painted** red, white, and blue to support the U.S. soccer team.

______ 2. A barrel (and very little else) **was being worn** by one football fan to every game, even when the weather was cold.

______ 3. A couple with World Cup tickets **got married** in the stadium an hour before the game started.

______ 4. A fan **got** his hair **cut** and **colored** to look like a soccer ball.

______ 5. A fan **had** a soccer-ball dress **made** for the World Cup.

______ 6. Stuffed animals, even very big ones, **get taken** to games for good luck.

______ 7. Rubber rats **were being thrown** on the ice at hockey games until officials stopped this for safety reasons.

______ 8. A fan **won't have** his lucky shirt **washed** and wears it to all his team's games.

Then turn to page A-4 for the answers.

B. Read the three items, and then complete them.

1. Two of the sentences in Part A are passives with *be* + past participle. That is, they are like the passives in Chapter 16, although they are not in the simple present or simple past. The passive forms are: was being worn and ______________.

2. Two of the sentences in Part A are passives that are not formed with *be.* Instead, they include the verb ______________ + past participle. These passive forms are ______________ and ______________.

3. Four of the sentences in Part A are passive causatives. Passive causatives include an object. They are formed with the verb ______________ or ______________ + object + past participle. The examples here (verb + object + past participle) are ______________, ______________, ______________, and ______________.

GRAMMAR BRIEFING 1

Passives in Progressive and Perfect Tenses

Passives in the Present and Past Progressive Tenses

FORM

A. Affirmative Statements

SUBJECT	*BE*	PRESENT PARTICIPLE OF *BE*	PAST PARTICIPLE OF MAIN VERB*	
The package	**is** / **was**	**being**	**sent**	by our office.

B. Negative Statements

SUBJECT	*BE*	*NOT*	PRESENT PARTICIPLE OF *BE*	PAST PARTICIPLE OF MAIN VERB*	
The notices	**are** / **were**	**not**	**being**	**delivered**	on time.

C. *Yes/No* Questions

BE	SUBJECT	PRESENT PARTICIPLE OF *BE*	PAST PARTICIPLE OF MAIN VERB*	
Is / **Was**	that sofa	**being**	**thrown out**?	

D. *Wh-* Questions

WH- WORD	*BE*	(SUBJECT)	PRESENT PARTICIPLE OF *BE*	PAST PARTICIPLE OF MAIN VERB*	
Why	**is** / **was**	the problem	**being**	**ignored**?	
What	**is** / **was**		**being**	**done**	about the problem?

*See Appendix 7 for past participles of irregular verbs.

Passives in the Present and Past Perfect Tenses

FORM

A. Affirmative Statements

SUBJECT	*HAVE*	PAST PARTICIPLE OF *BE*	PAST PARTICIPLE OF MAIN VERB*	
The bills	**have** / **had**	**been**	**paid.**	

(continued on next page)

B. Negative Statements

SUBJECT	*HAVE*	NOT	PAST PARTICIPLE OF *BE*	PAST PARTICIPLE OF MAIN VERB*	
The grass	**has** / **had**	**not**	**been**	**watered**	for days.

C. *Yes/No* Questions

HAVE	SUBJECT	PAST PARTICIPLE OF *BE*	PAST PARTICIPLE OF MAIN VERB*	
Have / **Had**	new plans	**been**	**made**	yet?

D. *Wh-* Questions

WH- WORD	*HAVE*	(SUBJECT)	PAST PARTICIPLE OF *BE*	PAST PARTICIPLE OF MAIN VERB*	
When	**have** / **had**	those issues	**been**	**discussed**	before?
What	**has** / **had**		**been**	**discussed**?	

*See Appendix 7 for past participles of irregular verbs.

GRAMMAR PRACTICE 1

Passives in Progressive and Perfect Tenses

1 Passive Sentences in Progressive Tenses: A Baseball Stadium Is Being Built

Complete the passive sentences in the sports radio interview from 2003. Use the words in parentheses and the present progressive and past progressive tenses.

Eric: Bob, what's the latest news on Petco Ballpark here in San Diego?

Bob: Eric, I'm happy to report that lots of work is being done (1 do) on the ballpark right now. As everyone knows, work on the stadium stopped in late 2000. The money that was needed to pay for the work ______ (2 not, raise), as a result of legal problems. Although significant progress ______ (3 make) before work stopped, nothing was done for more than a year, so the ballpark won't be ready when originally scheduled.

Eric: Yes, the delay was unfortunate, but we were thrilled to learn that last week the construction crews ________________ (4 give) the go-ahead, so now work has started again. Tell us about some of the features of the new ballpark. The plans ________________ (5 describe) by the experts as exciting and different.

Bob: It will be great, Eric. When it ________________ (6 plan) back in 1998, the architects wanted to give all fans the best possible view. They felt that this just ________________ (7 not, do) in many ballparks of the 1980s and 1990s.

Eric: How does their plan solve the problem?

Bob: It solves it partly by a special design involving "neighborhoods." These neighborhoods ________________ (8 create) because seats ________________ (9 install) in sections that are clearly separated from each other. Also, all of the seats ________________ (10 put in) at an angle so they'll all face the pitcher's mound.

Eric: What other features ________________ (11 include) in the design of the stadium?

Bob: In early 2000, as the plans for the seating ________________ (12 finalize), the designers turned their attention to fans who might not be able to afford the best seats. As a result, now several areas ________________ (13 place) around the ballpark where fans who pay a small admission fee can stand and watch the game. In addition, a unique "Park at the Park" area ________________ (14 design) where people can sit on the grass instead of in a seat.

Eric: It sounds like a fun experience ________________ (15 plan) for every fan in every price range. We're going to have a great new ballpark. Thanks for talking to us today.

raise money = collect money. *pitcher's mound* = the place on a baseball field where the pitcher stands to throw the ball.

To find out more about stadiums and arenas, go to the *Grammar Links* Website.

2 Passive Sentences in Perfect Tenses: Sports Records Have Been Broken

Complete the passive sentences about sports records. Use the words in parentheses and the present perfect and past perfect tenses.

1. The Masters golf tournament has been won (win) six times by Jack Nicklaus.
2. A mile hadn't been run (not, run) in under four minutes until Roger Bannister ran a 3-minute-59-second mile in England on May 6, 1954.

3. A 63-yard field goal ______________ (kick) by New Orleans Saints kicker Tom Dempsey in 1970 before Denver Broncos kicker Jason Elam tied the record in 1998.

4. A perfect ten ______________ (not, achieve) by a gymnast until Nadia Comaneci of Romania did it in the 1976 Olympic games.

5. Twenty-six touchdowns ______________ (make) in a season by running back Marshall Faulk of the St. Louis Rams.

6. Seventy home runs ______________ (hit) by Mark McGwire, of the St. Louis Cardinals in 1998 before Barry Bonds of the San Francisco Giants hit 73 in 2001.

Tiger Woods

7. A 12-stroke lead ______________ (not, reach) by the winner of the Masters golf tournament until Tiger Woods did it in 1997.

8. Two gold medals ______________ (earn) in the heptathlon by Jackie Joyner-Kersey, one of the top women athletes of the twentieth century.

9. Ninety-two goals ______________ (score) in a hockey season by Wayne Gretzky of the Edmonton Oilers.

10. More than 100 points ______________ (not, score) by a basketball player in a single game, but Philadelphia basketball center Wilt Chamberlain scored 100 points in a game against the New York Knicks on March 2, 1962.

11. The record of 2,130 consecutive baseball games played ______________ (set) by Lou Gehrig of the New York Yankees but was broken by Cal Ripken of the Baltimore Orioles, who played 2,632 consecutive games.

Nolan Ryan

12. Three hundred eighty-three batters ______________ (struck out) in a single season by Nolan Ryan of the California Angels.

13. The record for the most losses to the same opponent in Grand Slam tennis tournament finals ______________ (set) by Venus Williams. Interestingly, her opponent was her sister Serena Williams.

Venus and Serena Williams

GRAMMAR BRIEFING 2

Passives with Modals

FORM

A. Overview

Passive sentences can include modals, phrasal modals, and modal-like expressions.

It **might be discussed**.

It **has to be discussed**.

It **ought to be discussed**.

B. Affirmative Statements

SUBJECT	MODAL	BASE FORM OF *BE*	PAST PARTICIPLE OF MAIN VERB*	
The new plan	**might**	**be**	**discussed**	at the meeting.
The packages	**had better**	**be**	**mailed**	today.

C. Negative Statements

SUBJECT	MODAL + *NOT*	BASE FORM OF *BE*	PAST PARTICIPLE OF MAIN VERB*	
The package	**will not**	**be**	**delivered**	today.
The lawn	**isn't supposed to**	**be**	**watered**	again yet.

D. *Yes/No* Questions

MODAL + SUBJECT	BASE FORM OF *BE*	PAST PARTICIPLE OF MAIN VERB*	
Should the files	**be**	**reorganized**?	
Are the awards **going to**	**be**	**announced**	tonight?

E. *Wh-* Questions

WH- WORD	MODAL (+ SUBJECT)	BASE FORM OF *BE*	PAST PARTICIPLE OF MAIN VERB*	
Who	**should**	**be**	**invited**	to the ceremony?
When	**do** the applications **have to**	**be**	**submitted**?	

*See Appendix 7 for past participles of irregular verbs.

GRAMMAR PRACTICE 2

Passives with Modals

3 Passives with Modals: Should a New Stadium Be Built?

Complete the passive sentences in the sports article. Use the words in parentheses.

Many sports teams want new stadiums. For a stadium to be built, it must be funded (1 must, fund). Sports teams believe that to be successful, a stadium project ________ (2 can, not, pay for) by the teams alone and that it ________ (3 ought to, finance) by the public—that is, by a city and its taxpayers—as well as by the teams that will play there. For this to happen, stadium funding usually ________ (4 has to, approve) by voters. Teams therefore try to convince voters that a new stadium will be good for the city because, for example, new jobs ________ (5 are going to be, create) as a result.

Recently, financial experts have begun to question whether stadiums are good investments for cities. Many believe that the benefits that teams promise ________ (6 will, not, bring about) by constructing a new stadium. These experts argue that the money for a stadium ________ (7 should, pay) mainly or entirely by the teams that will profit from playing there. They don't believe that the money a city spends ________ (8 will, pay back) by the teams. For example, the money ________ (9 might, not, pay back) if the teams don't sell enough tickets. Teams argue back by saying that the pleasure that stadiums bring to fans ________ (10 can, not, measure).

________ (11 should, a stadium, build)? As long as teams want new stadiums and ask cities for funds, the question ________ (12 will, debate). ________ (13 can, something, do) to make a stadium project work for both the teams and the cities? For one thing, a limit ________ (14 can, place) on the city's contribution. Additional costs ________ (15 could, absorb) by the teams. Other uses for the stadium ________ (16 might, consider) by both the teams and the cities. When sports teams and cities work together, a profitable stadium project can be a reality.

4 Using Passives with Modals: Can This Problem Be Solved?

Think of a problem at your school or in your community. In small groups discuss this problem. Use modals with passives to express an opinion about what could be done, should be done, is supposed to be done, and must be done to correct the problem. Report your problem and solutions to the class.

Example: *Our school doesn't have a place for students to eat lunch together, and there isn't enough time to go out. Students need a place to eat together. A place of some kind should be provided. An office might be converted. If space can't be found, more time for lunch ought to be given so students can go out to eat.*

5 Passives in Different Verb Tenses: What a Place!

Find information on a public place you are interested in. It can be a sports stadium or arena or any other building or monument anywhere in the world. Write a paragraph telling about the place—when and where it was built, who it was designed by, what it is being used for, who it is visited by, and other interesting facts. Use at least three passive sentences in different tenses and two passive sentences with modals.

Example: *The Roman Coliseum was the world's largest early sports arena for 18 centuries after it was constructed. It was built over a 10-year period starting in AD 72. It had eighty entrances and could hold 50,000 spectators. Public events such as gladiator fights and wild animal hunts were held at the Coliseum. At times in its history, stones were removed to build other buildings. It is visited every year by many tourists from all over the world. . . .*

To find information on famous world monuments, go to the *Grammar Links* Website. See the *Grammar Links* Website for a complete model paragraph for this assignment.

GRAMMAR BRIEFING 3

Get Passives

FORM and FUNCTION

A. Passive Sentences with *Get*

Passive sentences can be formed with *get* instead of *be*, including:	
• Affirmative sentences.	She **gets teased** by the other kids. That player **got sent** to another team.
• Negative sentences.*	The soup **didn't get eaten**. Those notices **haven't gotten sent out** yet.
• *Yes/no* questions.*	**Does** the mail **get picked up** on Sundays? **Have** those bills **gotten paid** yet?
• *Wh-* questions.*	When **did** your bike **get stolen**? Who **got fired**?
• Sentences in any tense.	We **are getting cheated**. My car **has gotten broken into** several times.
• Sentences with modals.	You **could get arrested** for doing that. All the students **are going to get promoted**.

**Do* is used in negatives and questions in the simple present and simple past.

B. *Get* Passives Versus *Be* Passives

1. *Get* passives are used mainly in conversation and informal writing. They are not usually used in formal writing. *Be* passives can be used in informal or formal contexts.	The mayor **got reelected**. (informal—e.g., conversation, informal letter) *Compare*: The mayor **was reelected**. (more formal—e.g., TV or newspaper story, as well as conversation, informal letter)
2. *Get* passives are used just with certain verbs—mainly verbs that emphasize some change, especially bad change. *Be* passives can be used with any verbs that allow the passive.	The cake **got eaten** before we arrived. (emphasis on change) OR The cake **was eaten** before we arrived. My bike **got stolen**. (bad change) OR My bike **was stolen**. *But*: Protective clothing **must be worn** here. **NOT**: Protective clothing ~~must get worn~~ here. We **haven't been told** the truth. **NOT**: We ~~have gotten~~ told the truth.

GRAMMAR HOTSPOT!

Be or *get* followed by an *-ed* adjective can look like a passive. (In fact, this structure is sometimes called "stative passive.") Here is how to tell the difference:

- With ***be/get* + *-ed* adjective**, the *-ed* word is an adjective, so:

The sentence is about a feeling or quality (e.g., the feeling of worry).	We were/got worried.
The intensifier *very* can be put before it.	We were/got very worried.

- With **passive with *be/get***, the *-ed* word is a verb, so:

The sentence is about an action (e.g., the action of robbing).	We were/got robbed.
The intensifier *very* cannot be put before it.	**NOT**: We were/got ~~very~~ robbed.

GRAMMAR PRACTICE 3

Get Passives

6 *Get* Passives: Bad Things Can Happen to Good Players!

Use the words in parentheses to complete the *get* passive sentences. Use appropriate tenses.

Playing professional sports is the ambition of many young athletes. These youngsters dream of one day being as famous as Shaquille O'Neal, and they hope that they will get paid (1 (pay)) a salary like his. But playing professional sports isn't easy, and it can be dangerous.

Professional athletes often get hurt. Over the years, many baseball players ____________ (2 (hit)) by pitched balls. Few quarterbacks ____________ (3 (not, injure)) by much bigger football players at various points in their careers. Basketball players ____________ (4 (probably, will, knock down)) while playing, too. Hockey players often ____________ (5 (cut)) by other players' sticks and soccer players ____________ (6 (can, kick)).

Behavior on and off the field can also lead to problems and to lost playing time. Players ____________ (7 (may, suspend)) for bad behavior during games and as a result may have to sit out for several games. Hockey players are notorious for fighting. They often ______________________ (8 kick out) of the game. Unfortunately, these days more and more professional athletes ______________________ (9 arrest) for their behavior off the field.

Finally, a professional athlete's career is often short. When their performance begins to decline, players ______________________ (10 trade) to other teams. Sometimes they simply ______________________ (11 not, hire) for the next season.

None of this stops young athletes from hoping they ______________________ (12 choose) to play professionally.

> *ambition* = a strong desire to achieve something. *pitched* = thrown toward a batter in baseball. *notorious* = known widely and regarded unfavorably. *kick out* = make someone leave. *decline* = become less good.

7 *Get* Passives: Lucky Larry and Poor Pete

Work with a partner. Look at the chart about Lucky Larry and Poor Pete. Student A reads sentence 1 about Lucky Larry to Student B. Student A asks Student B a *yes/no* question about Poor Pete based on this sentence and using the same tense. Student B should use the information about Poor Pete to answer. After sentence 4, Student B reads about Poor Pete and asks Student A questions about Lucky Larry. Student A answers with the information given.

Example: Student A: Lucky Larry got hired by the top team in his league. Did Poor Pete get hired by the top team in his league?
Student B: No, he didn't. He got hired by the worst team in the league.

Lucky Larry	Poor Pete
1. Lucky Larry got hired by the top team in his league.	1. (hire) by the worst team in his league
2. Lucky Larry is getting promoted to head coach.	2. (demote) to assistant coach
3. Lucky Larry gets recognized by the fans.	3. (confuse with) the equipment manager
4. Lucky Larry is going to get paid to write a book.	4. (charge) for his parking space
5. (praise) for his team's success	5. Poor Pete has gotten blamed for his team's failure.
6. (invite) to many social events	6. Poor Pete gets ignored by his friends.
7. (elect) to the Sports Hall of Fame	7. Poor Pete may get ejected from the game for bad behavior.
8. (choose) to be coach of the year	8. Poor Pete will get fired at the end of the year.

> *demote* = reduce somebody in rank or status. *confuse with* = be unable to tell the difference between two people. *eject* = make someone leave; throw out.

8 Using Passive Sentences: The Games We Play

A. Read the paragraph. Underline the *be* and *get* passives.

Baseball <u>is played</u> on a field by two teams. A point (or "run") is scored when a batter-runner safely touches all four bases. Sometimes a runner can run only to the next base, but when the ball gets hit out of the ballpark, the player who hit it is allowed to run to all the bases and score.

B. Write a paragraph like the one in Part A about a game that you know how to play (a sport, a card game, a board game, etc.). Focus on the actions or the receivers of the actions, not on the agents. Use at least two passive sentences with *be* and one *get* passive.

9 True Passives Versus Stative Passives: Fan Superstitions

Read the passages. Label the boldfaced verbs with a *P* if they are true passives or an *S* if they are stative passives. (Remember, stative passives can take the intensifier *very*.)

I. *The Sock Monkey*

Brett Morris lost his sock monkey when he was 10, but he never forgot it. So when Brett, who is now an adult, **was given** (1) [P] another sock monkey by a friend, he **was delighted** (2) [S]. While watching a football game involving his favorite team, Brett put the sock monkey in front of the TV. Brett **is devoted** (3) to his team, and when his team won, he and his friends decided the sock monkey was responsible. Now, they make sure that the sock monkey **gets put** (4) in front of the TV before every game!

II. *Pulled-up Socks*

Cleveland Indian baseball fans believed pulled-up socks made their team win. This practice **got started** (5) because player Jim Thome wore his socks that way in games. On Thome's birthday, the other players on the team wore their socks pulled up in his honor, and the Indians won the game. Fans **were excited** (6). They believed that pulling up their socks would help the team win, so at Indians games many fans **could be seen** (7) wearing pulled-up socks.

devoted = showing strong affection for; loving.

To find out more about funny fan behavior, go to the *Grammar Links* Website.

GRAMMAR BRIEFING 4

Passive Causatives

FORM

A. Overview

Passive causatives can occur in any tense and with modals. *Get* or *have* is followed by an object + a past participle. The form of *get* or *have* depends on the tense.

I **got/had** the washing machine **fixed.**

I **haven't gotten/had** the washing machine **fixed** yet.

When **are** you **going to get/have** the washing machine **fixed**?

B. Affirmative Statements

SUBJECT	(AUXILIARY)	*GET/HAVE*	OBJECT	PAST PARTICIPLE OF MAIN VERB*	(*BY* PHRASE)	
Emily		**gets/has**	her hair	**done**		every week.
I	**am**	**getting/having**	my hair	**done**	by a professional	next time.

C. Negative Statements

SUBJECT	AUXILIARY + *NOT*	*GET/HAVE*	OBJECT	PAST PARTICIPLE OF MAIN VERB*	(*BY* PHRASE)	
We	**didn't**	**get/have**	our house	**painted**	by the company that usually does it.	
We	**haven't**	**gotten/had**	our house	**painted**		since 2000.

D. *Yes/No* Statements

AUXILIARY	SUBJECT	*GET/HAVE*	OBJECT	PAST PARTICIPLE OF MAIN VERB*	(*BY* PHRASE)	
Did	you	**get/have**	your car	**repaired**	by the new mechanic?	
Are	**you**	**getting/having**	your car	**repaired**		this week?

E. *Wh-* Questions

WH- WORD	AUXILIARY	(SUBJECT)	*GET/HAVE*	OBJECT	PAST PARTICIPLE OF MAIN VERB*	(*BY* PHRASE)
Why	**did**	you	**get/have**	your cabinets	**built**	by that carpenter?
Who	**is**		**getting/having**	a cabinet	**built**?	

F. Passive Causatives with Modals

SUBJECT	MODAL	*GET/HAVE*	OBJECT	PAST PARTICIPLE OF MAIN VERB*	(*BY* PHRASE)
You	**should**	**get/have**	your groceries	**delivered**	by the store.
We	**are going to**	**get/have**	these groceries	**delivered.**	

*See Appendix 7 for past participles of irregular verbs.

FUNCTION

Meaning and Use

1. Passive causatives express the idea that someone "causes" someone else to perform a service.	I **got/had** the food for the party **prepared** by a restaurant. (I "caused" the restaurant to prepare the food.)
A *by* phrase can be included to tell who performs the service.	I got/had my car repaired **by a new mechanic.** (*by a new mechanic* included because information is not obvious)
Often, however, a *by* phrase is not included, if this information is obvious or unimportant.	I got/had my car repaired (by a mechanic). (*by a mechanic* often not included because information is obvious)
2. With passive causatives, the sentence is about the person receiving the service, not the person performing the service or the service itself.	**I'm getting** a new phone **put in.** (sentence is about the person getting the phone) *Compare:* The phone company is putting in a new phone. (active sentence; sentence is about the phone company—the performer of the action) A new phone is being put in (for me). (passive; sentence is about the new phone)

GRAMMAR PRACTICE 4

Passive Causatives

10 Passive Causatives: Supporting the Team

A. The Cougars basketball team is very good, but the players are very lazy. As a result, people do things to support the team. Match the agents in List A with their actions in List B. Then write five sentences with passive causatives, using *get* or *have*, telling how the agents support the team. Use *the players* as the subject of each sentence.

List A		List B
1. an athletic trainer	______	a. make their travel arrangements
2. a gourmet chef	______	b. wash their uniforms
3. the coach	______	c. cut their hair
4. a travel agent	______	d. choose their positions
5. a laundry service	______	e. cook their meals
6. a hairstylist	1	f. tape their ankles

Example: The players get/have their ankles taped by an athletic trainer.

B. Change the sentences in Part A by adding one of the following time expressions: *last year, next year, since they won the championship, right now, before they became famous, by the time the game starts*. Use an appropriate verb tense.

Example: The players had a travel agent make their travel arrangements last year.

C. Mismatch the agents in List A with the actions in List B. Then write **three** sentences with a passive causative that tell how the agents don't support the team. Use *the players* as the subject of each sentence.

Example: The players don't get their ankles taped by a gourmet chef.

11 Using Passive Causatives: Getting Things Done

Work with a partner. Student A asks Student B *wh-* and *yes/no* questions about things he/she has done by someone else. Each question should include a passive causative with *get* or *have*. Student B answers Student A's question and adds more information. Use a variety of tenses in both the questions and answers. Use items in the box and your own ideas.

hair/cut; shoes/shine; clothes/dryclean; apartment, room, house/paint; car/repair; pet/feed; TV, watch, etc./repair; dinner, groceries, etc./deliver; gift/wrap

Example: Do you get your hair cut by a hairdresser? Yes, I do. How often do you have your hair cut? I have my hair cut every two months. I had it cut last week, but I'm not very happy with it.

Have you ever gotten your shoes shined? No, I haven't, but I'd like to get them shined sometime. Maybe when I visit New York I can get them shined.

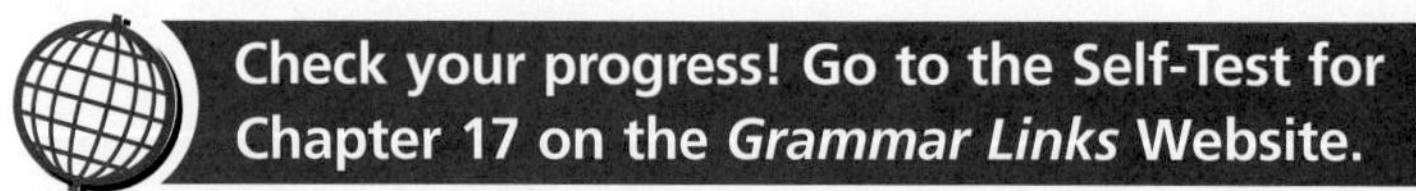

Check your progress! Go to the Self-Test for
Chapter 17 on the *Grammar Links* Website.

Wrap-up Activities

1 Sports Nicknames: EDITING

Correct the 10 errors in these true stories. There are errors with passives. Some errors can be corrected in more than one way. The first error is corrected for you.

are given/have been given

There are many nicknames in sports. Some athletes ~~given~~ interesting nicknames as a result of their actions in games. One such athlete was "Wrong-Way" Riegels, who played in the 1929 Rose Bowl. The Rose Bowl is an important college football game that is play on January 1st every year. In the 1929 game, the football was dropped by a player from Georgia Tech, and Roy Riegels, from the University of California, picked it up and began to run. It was seemed that Riegels would score easily. But, for some reason, he got confused and ran 65 yards the wrong way. By the time he got turn around by a teammate, the other team had also run down the field, and Riegels got tackled on the one-yard line on the wrong end of the field. Because of Riegels' run down the field, his team was lost the game 8–7, and he was nicknamed "Wrong-Way" Riegels.

Sometimes the play, not the player, gets the nickname. A famous soccer goal knows by its nickname, the "Hand of God" goal. This goal was scored by Argentinean superstar Diego Maradona against the English in the 1986 World Cup. When the ball kicked over the heads of the English defense by another Argentinean player, both Maradona and the English goalkeeper, Peter Shilton, jumped for it. Maradona was appeared to have hit the ball into the goal with his head, but Shilton protested that Maradona had been hit it with his hand. The goal was permitted to stand, and the game was won by Argentina, 2–1. When the television replays proved that Shilton was correct, Maradona was declared that the goal had been "a little bit Maradona, a little bit the hand of God."

2 Guess That Sport: SPEAKING

Student A thinks of a game or a sport. The other students in the class ask *yes/no* questions about the game or sport, using the passive when possible. The first person who guesses the game or sport gets to think of the next game or sport.

Example: Is this game played professionally in the United States? Is a ball used in this game?

3 "Get" the Answer: SPEAKING

Step 1 Work with a partner. Write eight interview questions to find out interesting things about your classmates. Include a *get* passive in four of the questions and a passive causative (with *get* or *have*) in the other four. You can use the phrases in the box or your own ideas.

> *Get* passives: get hired for an unusual job, get invited somewhere special, get charged for something you didn't buy, get offered something for free, get chosen for an award, get fired from a job, get elected to an office or position
>
> Passive causatives: get/have special clothing made for you, get/have your hair cut in a style you hated, get/have your picture taken with someone famous, get/have something special done for you, get/have something valuable stolen

Example: Have you ever gotten hired for an unusual job?

Step 2 On your own, interview someone other than your partner, using the questions you wrote. When the person answers *yes* to a question, ask for details. Report the most interesting answers to the class.

4 All About . . . : WRITING

Step 1 Find out about a sport on the Internet or from encyclopedias, books, or magazines. Find out about when, where, and by whom it was invented; who it is played by; when and where it is played; what records have been set; and what is predicted for the future of the sport. You might also look for interesting stories about the sport and successes and failures.

Step 2 Write two paragraphs of at least six sentences each about the sport. Use at least five passives in several tenses, including one negative passive and one passive with a modal.

Example: The inventor of golf isn't known, but the game was probably developed in Scotland. However, in 1457, the Scots were forbidden to play golf by the King of Scotland because he thought that young men were wasting time on the golf courses instead of practicing with bows and arrows. . . .

Golf is played on specially designed courses. . . .

See the *Grammar Links* Website for complete model paragraphs for this assignment.

Unit **Nine**

Conditionals

TOPIC FOCUS
Natural Disasters

UNIT OBJECTIVES

- **factual conditionals**
  (***If*** the temperature ***falls*** below 32°F, water ***freezes. If*** she ***saw*** the weather report, she ***knew*** about the storm.)
- **future conditionals**
  (***If*** it ***continues*** to rain, there ***will be*** a flood.)
- **present unreal conditionals**
  (***If*** I ***were*** you, I ***would watch*** the weather forecast.)
- **past unreal conditionals**
  (***If*** an earthquake ***hadn't occurred***, the building ***wouldn't have collapsed***.
- **sentences with *hope* or *wish***
  (I ***hope*** the storm ***will stop*** soon. I ***wish*** the storm ***would stop*** soon.)

Grammar in Action

Reading and Listening: The Two Faces of Nature

Read and listen to this passage from a book.

If you were looking at the earth from a satellite now, you would see a beautiful and peaceful-looking planet. But the peaceful appearance of the earth from space is misleading. Within the earth's atmosphere and beneath its surface, there are powerful, and often violent, forces at work. **If it's a late afternoon in the early summer, a tornado is probably forming somewhere in North America. If it's late summer, a hurricane is probably moving across an ocean toward land.** And, regardless of time of year, an earthquake may occur and a volcano may erupt.

A Tornado

These events—severe weather, earthquakes, and volcanoes—are part of the cycles of nature and the forces that shaped the earth. **The earth would be a very different place if these events didn't occur.** For example, **the Hawaiian islands wouldn't have formed if volcanoes hadn't erupted in the middle of the Pacific Ocean.** Severe natural events continue to have beneficial effects for life on the earth. For example, both volcanoes and floods make the soil more fertile, which is good for farming. However, **these natural events can become natural disasters if they negatively affect people and their property.**

A Volcano Erupting

A Hurricane Coming Ashore

More and more people are being affected by violent natural events because the population is increasing in areas where these events are most likely to occur. More and more, then, natural events are causing disasters. Our ability to predict some natural events—hurricanes and blizzards, for example—is relatively good, so we have time to escape from them or to prepare for them. But others—earthquakes, for example—occur without warning. **If earthquakes could be predicted, many lives could be saved.** In short, even though our scientific knowledge has increased, at this point humans still can't defend themselves against some of the most powerful forces of nature. **If we can learn more about prediction of natural events, then perhaps someday we'll be able to keep more of these events from becoming natural disasters.**

After an Earthquake

Adapted from Kendrick Frazier, *The Violent Face of Nature: Severe Phenomena and Natural Disasters.* New York: Morrow, 1979.

satellite = a mechanical device going around earth in space. *misleading* = giving a false idea. *erupt* = release melted rock, steam, etc. *severe* = extreme. *beneficial* = good, helpful. *fertile* = favorable to the growth of plants and crops.

Think About Grammar

The boldfaced sentences in the passage are conditional sentences. These sentences contain a condition clause, sometimes called an *if* clause, which expresses a condition, and a result clause, which expresses the result of the condition.

A. Look again at the conditional sentences in the passage. For each one, underline the condition (*if*) clause once and the result clause twice. The first one has been underlined for you.

B. Mark these statements *T* for true or *F* for false.

1. F______ The author of the passage believes that you are looking at the earth from a satellite now.
2. ______ It's possible for tornadoes to form in North America in the early summer.
3. ______ The Hawaiian islands formed because volcanoes erupted in the middle of the Pacific Ocean.
4. ______ It's possible for people to predict earthquakes now.
5. ______ The author of the passage believes that it might be possible for us to learn more about prediction of natural events.

Chapter 18

Factual Conditionals; Future Conditionals

Introductory Task: Hazardous Conditions and Results

A. Work with a partner. Fill in each blank in the conditions column with the letter of the result that best completes the sentence.

Conditions

1. If we have a *thunderstorm*, g______
2. If it rains heavily for several days, ______
3. If you see a funnel-shaped column of rapidly spinning wind, ______
4. If the winds of a tropical storm reach 74 miles (120 km) per hour, ______
5. If a severe snowstorm with high winds is expected, ______
6. If there is a long period with no rainfall, ______
7. If the ground is moving violently, ______
8. If a *volcano* erupts, ______

Results

a. a *blizzard* warning will be issued.
b. a *flood* might occur.
c. the result is a *drought*.
d. a major *earthquake* is probably occurring.
e. the storm is officially classified as a *hurricane*.
f. it's probably a *tornado*.
~~g.~~ we will experience hard rain with noise and flashes of lightning.
h. lava, ash, and steam come out of the ground.

B. The sentences in Part A describe various natural events. Discuss them as a class. Which ones have you experienced? Where do or might they occur? Then use a sentence with an *if* clause to tell your classmates about a natural event they might experience in a particular place. Use the simple present in the *if* clause and use *will* or *might* in the result clause.

Example: Thunderstorms are frequent in the summer here. If you stay here in the summer, you will experience a thunderstorm. OR Major earthquakes have occurred in California. If you go to California, you might experience an earthquake.

hazardous = full of danger. *funnel-shaped* = with a wide top and long, narrow bottom. *tropical storm* = a storm that begins in a warm-weather region. *lava* = melted rock.

GRAMMAR BRIEFING 1

Overview of Conditionals*

FORM and FUNCTION

A. Conditional Sentences

1. A conditional sentence has two clauses: an *if* clause and a result clause. The clauses can come in either order. When the *if* clause is first, use a comma between clauses.

   if clause: If the sun shines, / result clause: water evaporates more quickly.

   result clause: Water evaporates more quickly / *if* clause: if the sun shines.

2. A conditional sentence expresses a condition and a result: Something might happen (the condition). That will make something else happen (the result).

   condition: If the sun shines, / result: water evaporates more quickly.

B. Statements

AFFIRMATIVE STATEMENTS

IF CLAUSE	RESULT CLAUSE
If it snows,	(then) we'll go skiing this weekend.

NEGATIVE STATEMENTS

IF CLAUSE	RESULT CLAUSE
If it doesn't snow,	(then) we won't go skiing.

1. The result clause can begin with *then*. There is no difference in meaning. Use *then* only if the result clause comes second.

   If the air is cold enough, **then** rain turns to snow.
   NOT: ~~Then~~ rain turns to snow if the air is cold enough.

2. The negative can be:
   - In the *if* clause. — If it **doesn't** rain, I'll water the lawn.
   - In the result clause. — If it rains, I **won't** water the lawn.
   - In both clauses. — If it **doesn't** rain, the lawn **won't** get enough water.

*The example sentences are factual conditionals and future conditionals. For factual conditionals, see Grammar Briefing 2, page 350. For future conditionals, see Grammar Briefing 3, page 355. This overview also applies to unreal conditionals (Chapter 19, Grammar Briefings 1 and 2, pages 361 and 369).

(continued on next page)

C. Questions

YES/NO QUESTIONS		SHORT ANSWERS
IF CLAUSE	RESULT CLAUSE	
If it snows,	will the schools be closed?	No, they won't. OR Yes, they will.

WH- QUESTIONS	
IF CLAUSE	RESULT CLAUSE
If it rains tomorrow,	when will we have the picnic?

Use question word order only in the result clause.	**Will you go** if I go?

GRAMMAR PRACTICE 1

Overview of Conditionals

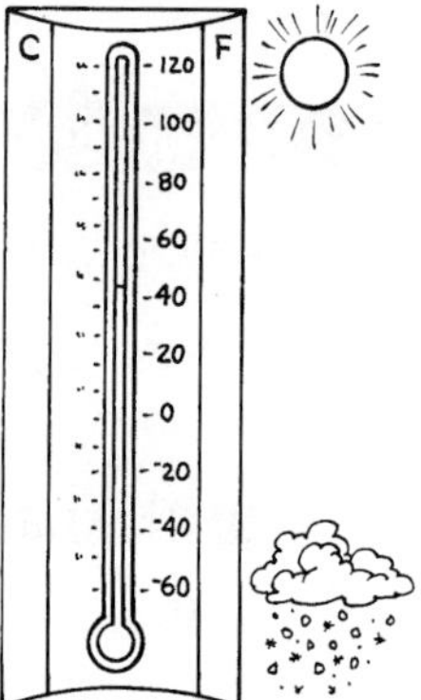

1 Conditional Questions and Statements—Form: Temperature Facts and Figures

A. Use the words given in parentheses to write *yes/no* questions, short answers, and statements in the simple present tense. Write the *if* and result clauses in the order given, in the questions and answers. Use *then* in the answers where possible. Use commas where necessary.

1. (if/you/heat/water/to 100°C) (it/boil)

   Q: If you heat water to 100°C, does it boil?

   A: Yes, it does. If you heat water to 100°C, then it boils.

2. (water/boil) (if/you/heat/it/to 100°F)

   Q: ______________________________?

   A: No, ____________. ______________________________.

3. (if/water/be heated/to 212°F) (it/boil)

   Q: ______________________________?

   A: Yes, ____________. ______________________________.

4. (water/freeze) (if/its temperature/be/32°C)

   Q: ______________________________?

   A: No, ____________. ______________________________.

B. Use the words given in parentheses to write *wh-* questions and answers in the simple present tense. In each item, write the *if* and result clauses in the order given, and use the same order in the answer. Use *then* in the answers where possible. Use commas where necessary.

1. Q: What happens to water if its temperature is 32°F ?
   (what / happen / to water) (if / its temperature / be / 32°F)

   A: Water begins to freeze if its temperature is 32°F .
   (begin / to freeze)

2. Q: ______________________________?
   (if / the temperature / be / 20°C in their classroom) (how / students / feel)

   A: ______________________________.
   (feel / comfortable)

3. Q: ______________________________?
   (how / students / feel) (if / the temperature / be / 20°F in their classroom)

   A: ______________________________.
   (not / feel / at all comfortable)

4. Q: ______________________________?
   (if / you / want / to convert temperatures from Celsius to Fahrenheit) (what / you / do)

   A: ______________________________.
   (use / this formula: $F = 9C/5 + 32$)

C = Celsius. *F* = Fahrenheit.

GRAMMAR BRIEFING 2

Factual Conditionals

FORM

A. Factual Conditional Sentences*

IF CLAUSE	RESULT CLAUSE
If you **mix** blue and yellow,	you **get** green.
If you **are** hungry,	we **should get** lunch now.
If the Indian restaurant **was** closed,	they probably **went** to the Chinese restaurant.

*For general information on the form of conditional sentences, see Grammar Briefing 1, page 347.

B. Factual Conditionals with Present Tense Verbs

Factual conditionals often have present tense verbs. The verbs may be simple and/or progressive.

If I **have** money, I **spend** it.

If they**'re skiing**, they**'re having** a good time.

If the children **are getting** tired, it**'s** time to leave.

C. Factual Conditionals with Past Tense Verbs

Factual conditionals often have past tense verbs. These may be simple and/or progressive.

The teachers always **helped** us if we **needed** help.

If he **was missing** class a lot, he **wasn't learning** much.

If I **was having** trouble with my homework, I **asked** for help.

D. Modals in Factual Conditionals

Modals can be used in:

- The *if* clause.

  We often take the five o'clock train if we **can get** to the station on time.

- The result clause.

  If you're leaving now, **can** I **go** with you?

- Both clauses.

  You **should make** a lot of money if you **can work** a lot this month.

(continued on next page)

E. Imperatives in Factual Conditionals

The imperative can be used in the result clause.	If you need $20, **take** it from my wallet. **Turn off** the TV if you have homework to do.

FUNCTION

A. General Truths and Habits

1. Factual conditionals can express general truths. These conditionals usually use the simple present.	If it**'s** five o'clock in New York, it**'s** two o'clock in California. If clouds **cover** the sun, then the temperature **goes** down.
2. Factual conditionals can express habits. These can be present or past habits. The simple tenses are most often used.	If I **get** up early, I **take** the eight o'clock bus to work. If I **cooked**, my roommate **washed** the dishes.
3. In factual conditionals that express general truths or habits, you can use *when* or *whenever* instead of *if*. There is little or no difference in meaning.	**When**(**ever**) it's five o'clock in New York, it's two o'clock in California. **When**(**ever**) I cooked, my roommate washed the dishes.

B. Possibility, Certainty, Ability, and Other Modal Meanings

Factual conditionals can express possibility, certainty, ability, advice, and other meanings connected with modals. These conditionals often use modals.	If he's not in his office, he **might be** at the gym. (present possibility) If he was talking on the phone all day, then he wasn't doing much work. (certainty about the past) If he **can't do** the work, you **should talk** to the teacher. (ability, advice)

C. Commands

Factual conditionals with imperatives can be used for commands.	If you're not feeling well, **stay** in bed.

Factual Conditionals

2 Factual Conditionals with Present Tense Verbs and Modals: The Nature of a Tornado

A. Combine the sentences in parentheses to form one sentence with an *if* clause and a result clause. Use the sentences in the order they are given. Decide which sentence should become which clause. Use *then* where possible. Use commas where needed.

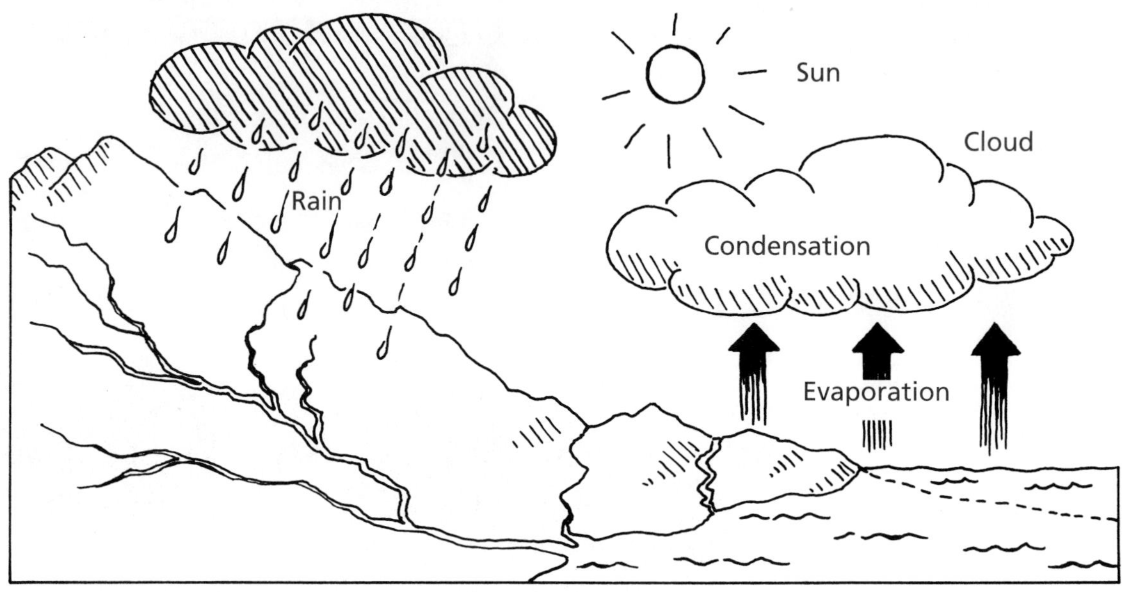

Storms occur as a result of natural processes involving the sun, air, water, and gravity. The sun heats the earth and the air around it. Air rises if it is heated.
1 (Air rises. It is heated.)
The sun heats the water on earth, too. If the sun shines on water, then the water evaporates.
2 (The sun shines on water. The water evaporates.)
This means that the water goes into the air as vapor. As warm air and the water vapor in it rise, the warm air becomes cooler. ______
3 (The air cools. The water vapor in it condenses.)
That is, the vapor becomes tiny drops of water and forms clouds. The drops may join other drops.
______
4 (The drops become too heavy for the air to hold. They fall to earth.)
The temperature determines the form in which the drops fall to earth.
______
5 (The drops fall as rain. The temperature isn't below the freezing point.)
Thunderstorms occur under certain conditions.
______
6 (A mass of warm, moist air is rising very rapidly. A thunderstorm can occur.)

Tornadoes are funnel-shaped windstorms that occur only under one condition.

____
7 (A tornado can't occur. There is no thunderstorm.)

An area that includes Texas, Oklahoma, and Kansas is known as "Tornado Alley" because tornadoes are most frequent there.

____
8 (Thunderstorms are moving across Tornado Alley at this moment. A tornado is probably forming.)

Tornadoes can be extremely destructive.

____
9 (A house is hit by a tornado. The house might explode.)

> *gravity* = the natural force that causes objects to move toward earth. *vapor* = water in the form of a gas. *destructive* = causing great damage; able to destroy.

B. Look at the sentences you wrote in Part A. In which sentence is it **not possible** to use *when* in place of *if*? ____________

To learn more about thunderstorms and tornadoes, click on the *Grammar Links* Website.

3 Factual Conditionals with Past Tense Verbs: The Making of a Television Meteorologist

A. In his book *Weathering the Storm*, Gary England describes his experiences growing up in Oklahoma. Use the words given to write factual conditionals with past tense verbs. Write the words in the order in which they are given. Decide which group of words should become the *if* clause and which should become the result clause. Use commas where needed.

1. Before the 1950s, people often had no warning of approaching tornadoes.

   If people didn't have warning, disasters occurred.
   (people / not / have / warning) (disasters / occur)

2. England's parents and grandparents often told stories about life in the old days.

   ____
   (he / listen / with fascination) (they / tell / stories about terrible tornadoes)

3. As a child, England learned to be cautious about severe weather. Sometimes he would see a thunderstorm approaching.

   ____
   (he / play / outside) (he / race / into the house)

4. In those days, weather radar and television didn't exist yet.

   ____
   (people / see / threatening clouds or tornadoes) (they / report / them to the sheriff)

5. The sheriff would then sound a warning siren.

   ____
   (everyone in England's family / run / into the cellar) (they / hear / the siren)

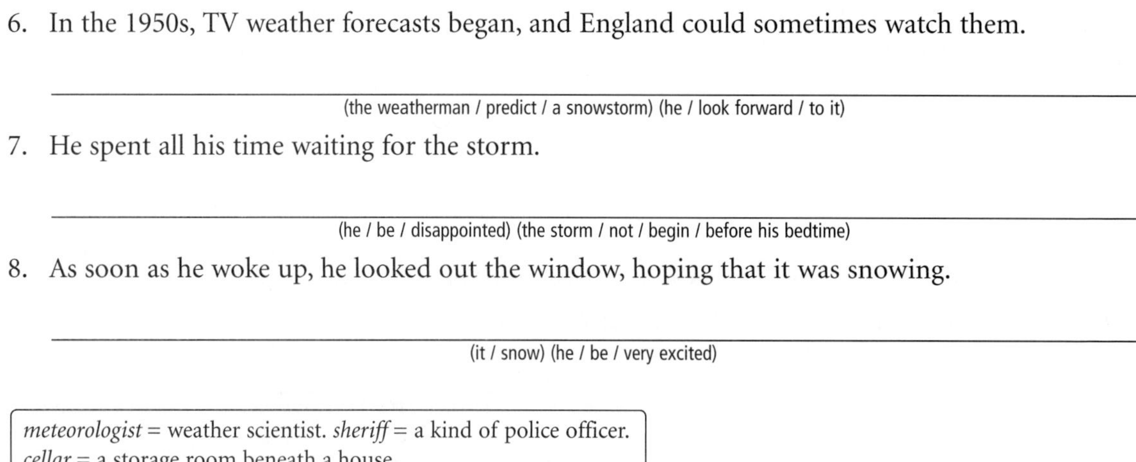

6. In the 1950s, TV weather forecasts began, and England could sometimes watch them.

   ____
   (the weatherman / predict / a snowstorm) (he / look forward / to it)

7. He spent all his time waiting for the storm.

   ____
   (he / be / disappointed) (the storm / not / begin / before his bedtime)

8. As soon as he woke up, he looked out the window, hoping that it was snowing.

   ____
   (it / snow) (he / be / very excited)

meteorologist = weather scientist. *sheriff* = a kind of police officer.
cellar = a storage room beneath a house.

B. Write five sentences about what you often did in storms or other weather situations when you were a child. Use a progressive in at least one sentence.

Example: If it was snowing, I built a snowman. OR I stayed inside if it was very hot.

4 Using Factual Conditionals with Modals and Imperatives: The Weather Helpline

A. Work with a partner. Your task is to respond to calls to the Weather Helpline. Read the situations and think of at least two factual conditionals to say in response to each one. Use the caller's last sentence to form the *if* clause and use a modal or imperative in the result clause. You can give advice or suggestions with *must, should, ought to, may, might, could,* or *can*. You can give commands with imperatives.

1. I'm outside. I can see dark clouds and lightning nearby.
   If you can see dark clouds and lightning nearby, it could be dangerous for you to be outside.
   If you can see dark clouds and lightning nearby, go inside as soon as possible.
   You shouldn't stay outside if you can see dark clouds and lightning nearby.
2. My English class starts in a few minutes. I'm in another building, so I have to walk across the campus to get to it. It's raining hard and lightning.
3. I've been on the beach in my swimming suit for a couple of hours. My skin is beginning to turn red.
4. I'm in my car on the highway, driving through a terrible rainstorm. I can't see where I'm going.
5. The weather is very cold and wet. I have a sore throat and a headache.
6. My plane is supposed to leave in two hours, so I need to drive to the airport soon. It's snowing hard.
7. The weather has been extremely hot and dry recently, and I'm worried about my garden. The flowers are turning brown.

B. For each situation in Part A, write at least one factual conditional with a modal or imperative in the result clause.

GRAMMAR BRIEFING 3

Future Conditionals

FORM

A. Future Conditional Sentences*

IF CLAUSE	RESULT CLAUSE
If I'**m** in the neighborhood,	I'**ll stop** by to see you.
If I **have** time this weekend,	I'**m going to clean** the house.
If you **can wait** until next week,	the doctor **can see** you in the evening.

*For general information on the form of conditional sentences, see Grammar Briefing 1, page 347.

B. *If* Clause

1. In future conditionals, the *if* clause generally has a present tense verb—simple present or present progressive.

   If it **rains/is raining** tomorrow, we'll reschedule the picnic.

   If we **reschedule** the picnic, the students will be disappointed.

2. The ability modal *can* is sometimes used.

   We'll reschedule for Sunday if everyone **can come** then.

C. Result Clause

1. The result clause usually has *will* or *be going to.* (*Will* is more common than *be going to.*)

   If it rains tomorrow, we'**ll reschedule**/'**re going to reschedule** the picnic.

2. Instead of *will* or *be going to*, you can use:

   • Another modal.

   If I go to the picnic, **can** you **give** me a ride home?

   • An imperative.

   If you're coming to the picnic, **bring** a main dish or a dessert.

(continued on next page)

FUNCTION

A. Predictions

Future conditionals express what will happen in the future if certain conditions occur. They are therefore often used to make predictions.	If you study for the test, you'll do well.

B. Other Common Uses

Other common uses include:

• Plans.	If you come when the weather is warm, we'll go to the beach.
• Offers.	We can take you to the airport tomorrow if you need a ride.
• Suggestions and advice.	If your boss doesn't give you a raise soon, you should talk to him.
• Requests.	If you finish your work early today, can you help me with mine?
• Threats.	If you don't obey the baby sitter, then you're not going to go to the party tomorrow.
• Commands.	Lock the door if you're the last one to leave.

GRAMMAR PRACTICE 3

Future Conditionals

5 Future Conditionals—Form: The Hurricanes of the Future

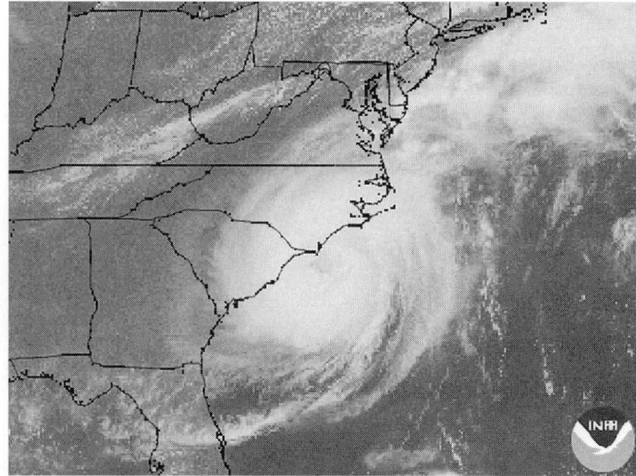

Use the words in parentheses to complete the future conditionals. You can use *will* or *be going to*.

1. The weather everywhere on Earth will/is going to change (change) if global temperatures continue (continue) to rise.

2. If the climate __________ (become) warmer, the water in the Atlantic Ocean __________ (get) warmer.

3. If the water in the Atlantic ______________ (become) warmer, hurricanes ______________ (increase) in number and severity.

4. Also, hurricanes ______________ (affect) more people if the population along the coastlines ______________ (continue) to grow.

5. But people ______________ (not / be) injured by hurricanes if they ______________ (take) precautions.

6. People who live where hurricanes are common should have a weather radio which they can tune in at any time. They ______________ (hear) warnings and instructions on the radio if a hurricane ______________ (come) toward land at the time they tune in.

7. If meteorologists' forecasts ______________ (be) accurate, during the next hurricane season seven hurricanes ______________ (form) over the Atlantic.

8. To find out how the National Hurricane Center follows hurricanes, visit its website. If a hurricane ______________ (form) at that time, you ______________ (be able to see) satellite images of it on your computer screen.

coastlines = land areas next to the ocean. *precaution* = an action taken to guard against danger.

Visit the *Grammar Links* Website for links to information about and images of hurricanes.

6 Future Conditionals—Uses: If You Come Visit Me . . .

A friend or relative who lives in another place has written that she or he might be able to come visit you. The following sentences are part of your response. Complete the sentences. In each sentence, use *will* or another modal or an imperative. The content should be appropriate for the function in brackets.

1. *If you come visit me,* we'll have a great time [prediction].
2. *If you can come when the weather is warm,* ______________ [plan].
3. *If you want to spend a lot of time outdoors here,* ______________ [command].
4. *If you would like to do some shopping here,* ______________ [suggestion].

5. *If I can't be with you all the time,* ______________________________ [prediction].

6. *If you need a ride from the airport,* ______________________________ [offer].

7. *If you have any questions about what to expect,* ______________________________ [command].

8. *If you have time,* ______________________________ [request]?

9. *I'm really looking forward to seeing you. If you don't come visit me,*

______________________________ [threat].

7 Using Factual and Future Conditionals: If You Like Cold/Warm Weather . . .

International Falls, Minnesota

Average high temperature in January: 14°F
Outdoor activities:

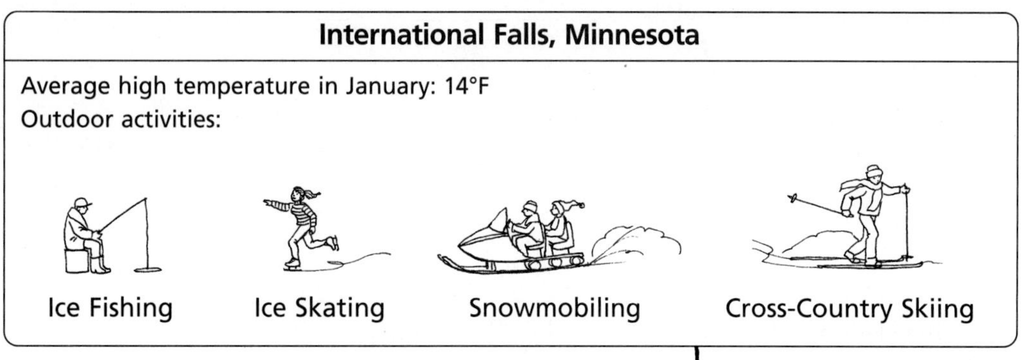

Ice Fishing | Ice Skating | Snowmobiling | Cross-Country Skiing

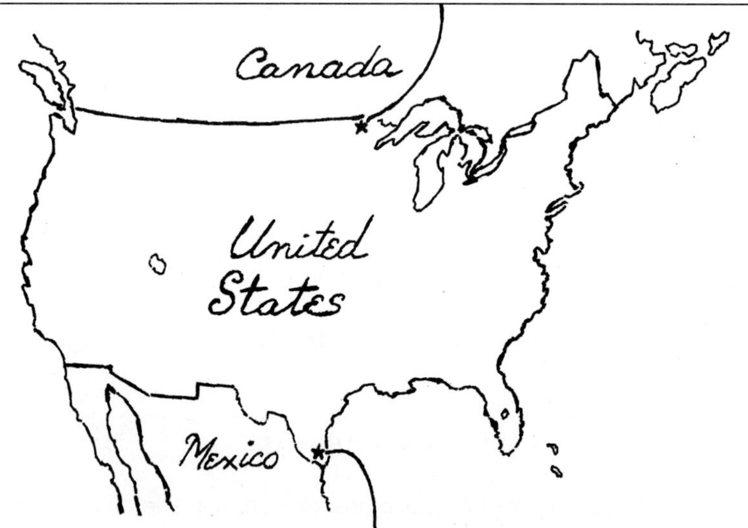

Brownsville, Texas

Average high temperature in January: 70°F
Outdoor activities:

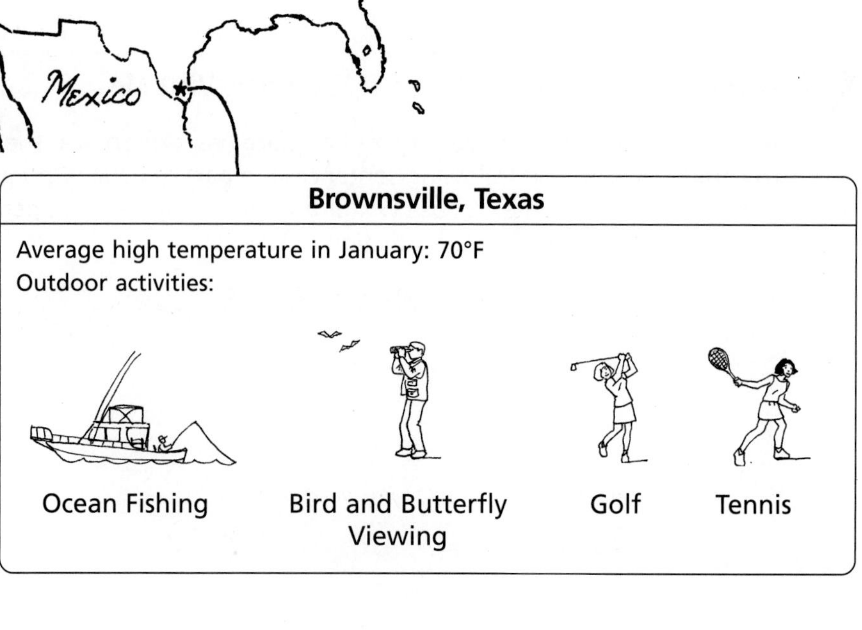

Ocean Fishing | Bird and Butterfly Viewing | Golf | Tennis

You are a writer for IfYouGo.net, a travel and weather website. Your assignment is to write a one-paragraph article about January vacations in International Falls and Brownsville. Use the information given on page 358 and your imagination to write about the places, the weather, and what visitors can do there. Use at least five conditionals, including conditionals with modals and imperatives.

Example: *If you want to take a vacation in January, then you might want to visit International Falls or Brownsville. If you like cold weather, you'll have a great time in International Falls. . . . When you're in International Falls, it's easy to visit Canada.*

See the *Grammar Links* Website for a complete model paragraph for this assignment.

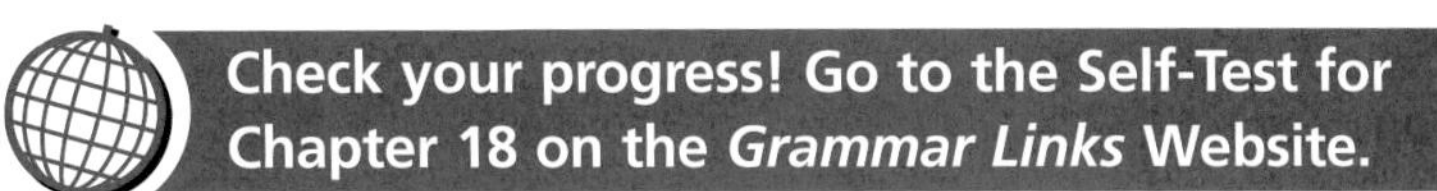

Check your progress! Go to the Self-Test for Chapter 18 on the *Grammar Links* Website.

Chapter 19

Present and Past Unreal Conditionals; *Hope* and *Wish*

Introductory Task: At Home in the Storm

A. The pairs of pictures show different situations. In the space before each sentence, write the letter of the more logical choice.

1.

2.

a. We don't have any bread.
b. It's possible that we have some bread.

3.

4.

a. It's possible that the storm is over.
b. The storm isn't over yet.

B. The sentences given in pictures 1 and 3 are factual conditionals. The sentences given in 2 and 4 are present unreal conditionals.

1. Complete the sentences with *factual* and *unreal.*

   a. In ____________________ conditionals, the *if* clause expresses a condition that is possible.

   b. In ____________________ conditionals, the *if* clause expresses a condition that is impossible, untrue, or very unlikely.

2. Complete the sentences with *present* or *past.*

   The sentences in 2 and 4 are different from those in 1 and 3 because the sentences in 2 and 4 use ____________________ tense forms instead of ____________________ tense forms. But all four sentences take place in the ____________________ time.

GRAMMAR BRIEFING 1

Present Unreal Conditionals

FORM

A. Present Unreal Conditional Sentences*

IF CLAUSE	RESULT CLAUSE
If we **had** a car,	we **would drive** to the mall.
If I **were working** more hours at my job,	I **couldn't do** all my school work.
If I **could live** anywhere,	I **might live** near the ocean.

* For general information on the form of conditional sentences, see Chapter 18, Grammar Briefing 1, page 347.

B. *If* Clause

1. In present unreal conditionals, the *if* clause has a **past tense** verb—simple or progressive.	If I **knew** the answer, I would tell you. If I **were leaving** now, I would give you a ride.
2. *Were* is used with all persons of *be*, including first and third person singular.	If **I were working** on a computer, I could finish more quickly. If **he were** here, we could finish more quickly.
3. *Could* to express ability is sometimes used.	If she **could sing**, she would take voice lessons.

C. Result Clause

In the result clause, use *would*, *could*, or *might*.	If you studied more, you **would/could/might get** better grades.

(continued on next page)

FUNCTION

A. Talking About What Is Impossible or Unlikely in the Present

1. The *if* clause of a present unreal conditional expresses a condition that is unreal at the present time.

   The result clause tells what would happen if this condition were real.

   The sentence expresses an unreal condition and an unreal result.

   The unreal condition may be:

   - Impossible or definitely untrue.

     unreal condition / unreal result
     If your grandparents were alive, they would be very proud of you.

     unreal condition / unreal result
     If I were the teacher, I'd give a lot less homework.

   - Very unlikely but still possible.

     unreal result / unreal condition
     Ray would call us if he were in town.

2. Instead of *would* in the result clause, you can:

   - Use *could* or *might* to say that, if the unreal condition were true, the unreal result would be only possible, not certain.

     If I had money, I **might/could travel** around the world. (a possibility if I had money)
     Compare: If I had money, I **would travel** around the world. (a definite plan if I had money)

   - Use *could* to express ability.

     If you were here, we **could talk** more.

B. Talking About What Is Impossible or Unlikely in the Future

Present unreal conditionals can be used to talk about the future. In this use, they express an unreal condition and unreal result in the future.

The unreal condition may be impossible or very unlikely.

Could and *might* have the same meanings as when these conditionals are used to talk about the present.

These sentences differ from future conditionals (Chapter 18, Grammar Briefing 3, page 355) because they are about what is impossible or unlikely in the future.

unreal condition / unreal result
If wars were never fought again, the world would be a much better place.

unreal condition / unreal result
If they were coming tonight, we could go to a movie. (They probably or definitely aren't coming.)

Compare: If they're coming tonight, we can go to a movie. (It's quite possible that they are coming.)

C. Giving Advice

Present unreal conditionals with *if I were you* are used to give advice.	**If I were you**, I would be more careful. (= You should be more careful.)

GRAMMAR **HOT**SPOT!

Remember! In present unreal conditionals, past forms do not express past time. They express the idea that something in the present or future is not real.	If I **asked** him for help now, he would help me. (present unreal conditional: I'm not asking him for help) *Compare*: If I **asked** him for help when we worked together, he always helped me. (factual conditional: in the past I asked him for help)

TALKING THE TALK

1. In spoken English and informal writing, *would* is often contracted as *'d.*	I**'d** have a talk with him if I were you.
2. In informal spoken English, *was* is sometimes used with first and third person singular subjects. This use is **not** considered acceptable in formal English.	If he **was** a real friend, he'd be here helping you. (informal speech only) If he **were** a real friend, he would be here helping you.

GRAMMAR PRACTICE 1

Present Unreal Conditionals

Mount St. Helens and Mount Rainier

1 Present Unreal Conditionals—Form: Natural Hazards in the U.S. Pacific Region

Complete the present unreal conditionals, using the words in parentheses. Use *might* in the result clause where given. Use progressives where appropriate.

1. Mount Ranier is a volcano near Seattle, Washington. If it erupted (erupt) without warning, many people would be (be) in danger.
2. Mount Ranier isn't expected to erupt soon. I ______ (not, feel) worried if I ______ (be) near it.
3. Mount St. Helens is another volcano in Washington. It could erupt again, so scientists are monitoring it continuously. People who live around it ______ (be) concerned about their safety if scientists ______ (not, monitor) it.
4. Mount St. Helens isn't erupting now. If it ______ (erupt) at this moment, lava and mud ______ (flow) down its sides, and gases and ash ______ (shoot) into the air.
5. The top of Mount St. Helens is steep and icy, so climbing it is difficult. If it ______ (be) easy to climb to the top, I ______ (might, do) it next summer.
6. More and stronger earthquakes occur in Alaska than in any other state, but Alaska isn't densely populated. If it ______ (become) more densely populated, future Alaskan earthquakes ______ (might, be) very destructive.
7. Tectonic plates are the thick pieces of solid rock that rest on the melted rock of earth's mantle. Two tectonic plates meet along the San Andreas Fault in California. If two tectonic plates ______ (not, meet) there, earthquakes ______ (not, be) so common in that region.

8. My home is not close to the San Andreas Fault. But I ______________________ (take) precautions against earthquakes if my home ______________________ (be) close to it.

9. Tsunami are waves caused by volcanoes or earthquakes near or under the sea. If a giant tsunami ______________________ (come) ashore in Hawaii, it ______________________ (cause) a great deal of damage.

10. Tsunami, earthquakes, and volcanoes are hazards in Hawaii. If you ______________________ (vacation) in Hawaii now, ______________________ you ______________________ (think about) the hazards?

> *densely populated* = having many people living close together.
> *mantle* = a layer beneath the earth's surface.

2 Present Unreal Conditionals—Meaning: Visiting Hawaii's Volcanoes

Work with a partner. Read each sentence and mark the sentences that follow it *T* (true) or *F* (false).

1. If Mount Kilauea in Hawaii Volcanoes National Park weren't erupting, I wouldn't be so interested in visiting the park.

   F_______ Mount Kilauea isn't erupting.

   T_______ I'm interested in visiting the park.

2. If it were dangerous to observe the lava flows, the park rangers wouldn't let visitors do it.

   _______ It isn't dangerous to observe the lava flows.

   _______ The park rangers let visitors do it.

3. If flowing lava weren't so hot, you could touch it.

   _______ Flowing lava isn't very hot.

   _______ You can touch it.

4. The flowing lava would appear to be red if it were night.

   _______ The flowing lava doesn't appear to be red.

   _______ It's night.

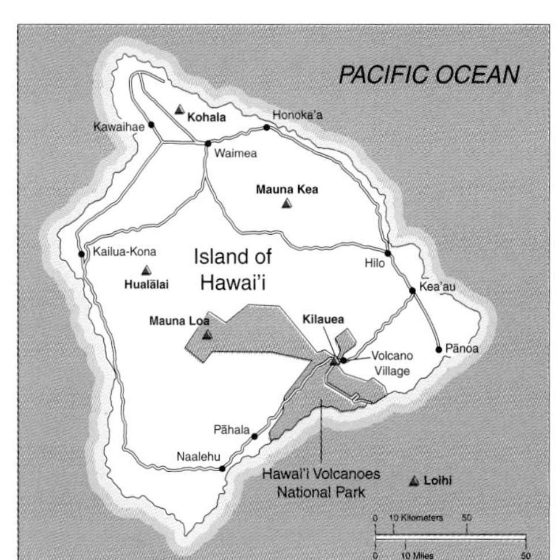

5. I might drive around the island if I had time.

   _______ I definitely want to drive around the island.

   _______ I don't have time to drive around the island.

6. If there weren't a "hot spot" in the earth's crust underneath Hawaii, volcanoes couldn't form new islands there.

   _______ There is a "hot spot" in the earth's crust underneath Hawaii.

   _______ It's possible for volcanoes to form new islands there.

crust = outer layer.

3 Present Unreal Conditionals with *Would* and *Could*: Waiting to Be Rescued

Suppose that all the statements below are true. Use each pair of statements to write present unreal conditionals. Use *would* or *could* in the result clause, as appropriate. Use *could* in the *if* clause where appropriate.

1. We're trapped inside our house. We need to use our disaster supplies.

   If we weren't trapped inside our house, we wouldn't need to use our disaster supplies.

2. We don't have electricity. We can't cook.
3. We have plenty of canned food. We're not hungry.
4. We don't have hot water. I can't take a bath.
5. I have a flashlight. I can find my way in the dark.
6. Our battery-powered radio is working. We can listen to news reports.
7. We can play card games. We're not bored.
8. Our sleeping bags are keeping us warm at night. We're sleeping very well.
9. I'm prepared for disasters. I'm not worried.

4 Factual Versus Unreal Conditionals: Earthquakes

Complete the factual conditionals and unreal conditionals with the correct form of the verbs in parentheses. Use *would* in the result clause of the unreal conditionals.

A Seismologist and a Seismograph

1. The earth's crust moves. As a result, earthquakes occur. If the earth's crust didn't move (not, move), earthquakes wouldn't occur (not, occur).
2. Seismographs are instruments used to record the movements of the earth's crust. If an earthquake occurs (occur), a seismograph records (record) its strength.
3. Seismologists study the movements of the earth's crust. I'm not a seismologist. But I ________ (know) a lot about earthquakes if I ________ (be) a seismologist.
4. Seismologists use the Richter Scale (0–9.0) to measure the intensity of earthquakes. Earthquakes ________ (be) classified as "moderate" if they ________ (measure) 5–5.9 on the Richter Scale.
5. Many very minor earthquakes occur every day. If someone ________ (pay) you a dollar for every earthquake, you ________ (earn) about $9,000 per day.
6. People build earthquake-resistant structures in areas where earthquakes are frequent. Earthquakes ________ (cause) less damage if people ________ (build) these structures.
7. Earthquakes are a hazard in California, so people build earthquake-resistant structures there. If they ________ (not, build) these structures, earthquakes ________ (cause) more damage.

> *earthquake-resistant* = able to withstand an earthquake without much damage.

Check out the *Grammar Links* Website for more information about volcanoes, earthquakes, and seismology.

5 Using Present Unreal Conditionals to Give Advice: Avoiding Risk

Work with a partner. For 1–5, read each situation to your partner and get your partner's advice. The advice should be phrased as *If I were you, ...* For 6–9, reverse roles.

1. A big storm just blew a power line down next to my house.

   If I were you, I wouldn't touch the power line. OR *If I were you, I'd call the power company.*

2. I'm outside playing soccer. Dark clouds are moving in, and I can see lightning.
3. I recently moved from Florida to Vermont, where the winters are very cold and snowy. It's October, and I don't have any warm clothes.
4. I'm driving to school through a heavy rainstorm. The underpass ahead of me is flooded.
5. I'm in Hawaii. I want to hike to the top of a volcano, but I'm not sure whether it's safe or not.
6. Because of a storm, the power has been off since yesterday. The food in my refrigerator is getting warm.
7. When I drove to school this morning, the weather was fine, but it's been snowing hard all day. Now it's time to go home. I've never driven in snow before.
8. I'm on vacation in California. I don't know what to do in case of an earthquake.
9. I want to move to a place where natural disasters are rare.

6 Using Unreal Present Conditionals: Things Would Be Different If . . .

A. Use the following statements and your own ideas to write unreal present conditionals. Include at least two conditionals with *could* or *might* in the result clauses.

1. There are thunderstorms.

   If there were no thunderstorms, parts of the earth might be very dry. OR *I could spend more time playing soccer if there were no thunderstorms.*

2. The weather isn't the same everywhere.
3. There are weather forecasts on the radio and television.
4. The weather isn't nice every day.
5. People talk about the weather a lot.
6. Earthquakes can't be predicted.
7. We can't control nature.

B. As a class, compare sentences.

GRAMMAR BRIEFING 2

Past Unreal Conditionals

FORM

A. Past Unreal Conditional Sentences*

IF CLAUSE	RESULT CLAUSE
If I **had known** about the concert,	I **would have gone** to it.
If he **hadn't failed** the final,	he **could have gotten** a B for the course.
If he **had been telling** the truth,	he **wouldn't have gotten** in trouble.

* For general information on the form of conditional sentences, see Chapter 18, Grammar Briefing 1, page 347.

B. *If* Clause

1. In past unreal conditionals, the *if* clause has a past perfect verb—simple or progressive.

   We would have had a better vacation if it **hadn't rained** every day.

   He wouldn't have had that accident if he **had been paying** attention.

2. *Could* to express ability is sometimes used.

   We would have been happy if they **could have come**.

C. Result Clause

In the result clause, use *would*, *could*, or *might* + *have* + a past participle.

If there hadn't been so much traffic, we **would have gotten/might have gotten** there on time.

If you had told me you needed help, I **could have helped** you.

(continued on next page)

FUNCTION

A. Talking About What Was Not Real in the Past

1. The *if* clause of a past unreal conditional expresses a condition that was not real in the past. The result clause tells what would have happened if the condition had been real. The sentence expresses an unreal condition in the past and its unreal result.	unreal condition / unreal result If Lou had come earlier, you would have met him. (Lou didn't come earlier, so you didn't meet him.) unreal condition / unreal result If you hadn't spoken up, the situation wouldn't have changed. (You spoke up, so the situation changed.)
2. Instead of *would* in the result clause, you can:	
• Use *could* or *might* to express that the result would have been possible, instead of certain.	If you had explained things to your boss, she **could/might have changed** her mind.
• Use *could* to express ability.	If I had studied algebra, I **could have solved** those problems.

B. Expressing Regret

Because they are about what could have happened but didn't happen, past unreal conditionals often express regret.	If I had studied, I could have done a lot better in school. If the car hadn't been in the repair shop, we could have helped you with your move.

GRAMMAR **HOT**SPOT!

Although some native speakers use *would* in the *if* clause, this is considered incorrect.	If you **had told** me, I would have done something. **NOT**: If you ~~would have~~ told me, I would have done something.

GRAMMAR PRACTICE 2

Past Unreal Conditionals

7 Past Unreal Conditionals—Form: The Dust Bowl

Use the words in parentheses to complete the past unreal conditionals. Use *could* or *might* where given.

In the 1930s, an environmental disaster occurred in the southwestern Great Plains. This area became known as the Dust Bowl. In the 1920s, the price of wheat was very high. If the price for wheat __hadn't been__ (1 (not, be)) so high, thousands of people __wouldn't have moved__ (not, move) to the Great Plains to start farms. In the 1920s, a great deal of rain fell in the region. If the rainfall __hadn't been__ (2 (not, be)) unusually good, people __might have known__ (might / know) not to start farms there.

A terrible drought began in 1931. This drought ______________ (3 (not, have)) such serious consequences if the farmers ______________ (manage) the land more carefully. If the farmers ______________ (4 (not, plow up)) the natural grass to grow wheat, the soil ______________ (not, get) so dry. If the farmers ______________ (5 (plant)) trees around their farms, they ______________ (could / protect) the soil from the wind.

Terrible windstorms began in 1932. These storms blew the soil away and were dangerous to people's health. You ______________ (6 (might / get)) "dust pneumonia" if you ______________ (live) in the Dust Bowl. The dust blew all the way across the country. If you ______________ (7 (be)) in New York City on May 21, 1934, you ______________ (could / see) huge clouds of dust in the air.

The farms in the Dust Bowl were ruined. In the 1930s, the United States experienced economic depression. If the economy ______________ (8 (be)) better, the situation in the Dust Bowl ______________ (not, be) so tragic. Thousands of farmers moved to California. If the government ______________ (9 (not, give)) jobs to many who stayed, they ______________ (might / starve). Finally, in the late 1930s, rain began to fall again.

economic depression = a period of severe decline in the economy, with many people unemployed.

Visit the *Grammar Links* Website to learn more about the Dust Bowl.

8 Present Versus Past Unreal Conditionals: The Weather Here and There, Then and Now

Use the information given to complete the present and past unreal conditionals.

1. We had a heat wave last summer. The heat was unbearable, so I bought a new air conditioner. If the heat hadn't been unbearable, I wouldn't have bought a new air conditioner.
2. It's extremely dry here. We're having a drought, so the grass isn't green. If we ______________ a drought, the grass ______________ green.
3. An ice storm broke all the power lines last winter. Some people didn't have electricity, so they had to go to emergency shelters to keep warm. If they ______________ electricity, they ______________ go to the shelters.
4. It's been raining for days, and houses near the river are being flooded. My house isn't near the river, so it isn't full of water. If my house ______________ near the river, it ______________ full of water.
5. This thunderstorm is violent and dangerous. The storm isn't over, so it isn't safe to go outside. If the storm ______________ over, it ______________ safe to go outside.
6. After the blizzard last month, we couldn't leave our house for three days. We didn't run out of food because I went to the store before the storm started. We ______________ food if I ______________ to the store before the storm started.
7. A hurricane was moving in this direction last summer. It didn't come ashore, so it didn't cause a lot of damage. If it ______________ ashore, it ______________ a lot of damage.

9 Past Unreal Conditionals: Weather Pleasures

Suppose that all the statements below are true. Use each pair of statements to write past unreal conditionals. Use *would* in the result clause except where *could* is given.

1. We swam across the lake so often because the weather was unusually hot.
   We wouldn't have swum across the lake so often if the weather hadn't been unusually hot.
2. You could skate on the pond all winter because the ice didn't melt.
3. The vegetables in our garden grew so fast because it rained every afternoon last summer.
4. People could go skiing in the park because the snow was so deep.
5. We could fly kites because the wind was blowing so hard.
6. I sat by the fire drinking cocoa and reading because I couldn't get to my office.
7. I got to know my neighbors because they needed help after the storm.

10 Past Unreal Conditionals—Meaning: Johnstown, Pennsylvania, 1889

Listen to the description of a disaster. You will hear each item twice. Decide whether the written statement given for an item is similar in meaning to what you heard. If it is similar, mark it with an *S*; if it is different, mark it with a *D*.

In 1852, a dam was built across the Little Conemaugh River, 15 miles above Johnstown, Pennsylvania. Thirty years later, the dam and the lake created by it were sold to new owners. These owners wanted to develop the lake into a fishing resort for people on vacation.

1. S______ The fish didn't escape because wire screens were installed in front of the lake's natural outlets.
2. ______ The screens didn't become filled with dirt and plants, so the water could go through them.
3. ______ The water wasn't able to go through the screens, so it created a lot of pressure on the dam.
4. ______ The dam was strong because they repaired it properly.
5. ______ It didn't rain very hard in the spring of 1889, so the lake didn't overfill.
6. ______ People in Johnstown had been warned about the danger of flood often, so they didn't pay attention to the warning they got on May 31, 1889.
7. ______ People jumped onto the pile in front of the bridge, so they had a chance to survive.
8. ______ The pile didn't burst into flames, so hundreds of lives were saved.
9. ______ The deadliest flood in American history wasn't avoided because people didn't pay attention to the warnings.

dam = wall built across a river to create a lake.

11 Expressing Regret with Past Unreal Conditionals: If I Had Known . . .

Use your own ideas to complete the past unreal conditionals. Use *would*, *could*, and *might* at least once each in the result clauses. Use commas where needed.

1. If I had known about your problem , I would have tried to help you. OR I might have been able to think of a solution. OR I could have helped you solve it.
2. If I had had more time yesterday ______
3. I might have gotten a better grade ______
4. If I had been more careful ______
5. I could have gone to the party ______
6. If I hadn't made a mistake ______
7. I would have felt better ______
8. I might not have had a problem ______
9. Would things have turned out differently for me ______

12 Using Past Unreal Conditionals: My Life Might Have Been Different If . . .

A. Write four true statements about important events or situations in your life in the past. Then write a past unreal conditional sentence about each of the events or situations.

Example: *When I was six years old, my family got a piano. If my family hadn't gotten a piano, I wouldn't have been able to take music lessons.*

B. Write four true statements about things that you didn't do or that didn't happen to you. Then write a past unreal conditional sentence about each thing.

Example: *I didn't study enough for the entrance examination. If I had studied enough, I wouldn't have had to take it again.*

GRAMMAR BRIEFING 3

Sentences with *Hope* or *Wish*

Overview; Sentences with *Hope*

FORM and FUNCTION

A. Overview

1. Sentences with *hope* and sentences with *wish* express desires. The difference is:
   - Sentences with *hope*, like real conditionals, are about what is possible.

     I **hope** Mary is here. (Mary might be here.)
   - Sentences with *wish*, like unreal conditionals, are about what is impossible or highly unlikely.

     I **wish** Mary were here. (Mary isn't here.)
2. These sentences have a main clause followed by a noun clause that can begin with *that.* (For noun clauses, see Chapter 20.)

   main clause: I hope — noun clause: (that) I did well on the test.

   main clause: I wish — noun clause: (that) I had done well on the test.

B. Sentences with *Hope*

Sentences with *hope* express desires that something that is possible did happen, is happening, or will happen.

The verb forms used correspond to the time the hope is about.

I hope you **were having** a good time.

I hope he**'s enjoying** his vacation now.

I hope you**'ll be able to get** a lot done tomorrow.

(continued on next page)

Sentences with *Wish*

FORM

A. Sentences About the Present

In wishes about the present, you can use:

• A past tense verb—simple or progressive. (Use *were* with all persons of *be*.)	He wishes (that) he **had** more money. We wish (that) she **were spending** more time with us.
• *Could* to express ability.	I wish (that) I **could be** with you now.

B. Sentences About the Future

In wishes about the future, you can use:

• *Would*.	It never snows here—I wish it **would snow** this winter.
• *Could* to express ability.	I wish I **could study** full time next semester.
• *Were going to*.	They wish he **weren't going to miss** the party.
• The past progressive.	I wish I **were taking** a trip this summer.

C. Sentences About the Past

In wishes about the past, you can use:

• The past perfect.	We wish you **had been** there. I wish I **hadn't said** that.
• *Could have* to express ability.	I wish I **could have helped** you.

FUNCTION

A. Sentences About the Present or Future

1. Sentences about the present or future express a desire for something that is impossible or unlikely.	I wish I could earn more money soon. (The speaker sees this as impossible or unlikely.) *Compare*: I hope I can earn more money soon. (The speaker sees this as possible.)
2. Sometimes they express:	
• A complaint.	I wish my neighbor would stop playing the piano.
• A regret.	I wish I could go on the trip with you.

(continued on next page)

B. Sentences About the Past

Sentences about the past express a desire for a situation that did not occur. They often express regrets.	I wish that I'd traveled a lot when I was young. (I didn't, and I regret it.) I wish I hadn't spent so much money. (I did, and I regret it.)

GRAMMAR PRACTICE 3

Sentences with *Hope* or *Wish*

13 Sentences with *Hope* and *Wish*: Delayed Due to Weather

Use the information given to complete the sentences with *hope* and *wish*.

1. a. Maybe the weather is good there. I hope (that) the weather is good there.

   b. The weather isn't good there. I wish (that) the weather were good there.

2. a. Maybe he's having a good time. I hope ______.

   b. He isn't having a good time. I wish ______.

3. a. Maybe the storm will end soon. I hope ______.

   b. The storm won't end soon. I wish ______.

4. a. Maybe his plane can take off soon. I hope ______.

   b. His plane can't take off soon. I wish ______.

5. a. Maybe he's coming home tomorrow. I hope ______.

   b. He isn't coming home tomorrow. I wish ______.

6. a. Maybe he heard the forecast. I hope ______.

   b. He didn't hear the forecast. I wish ______.

14 *Hope* and *Wish* About the Present and Future: Natural Disasters Make TV News

Complete the sentences by using the information given. Where more than one form is possible, use any appropriate form.

Hurricane on the Coast of Texas

Reporter: The hurricane is approaching your home. How do you feel about this?

Resident: Well, of course, I wish that the hurricane __weren't approaching__ (1) my home. But it's possible that my house won't be badly damaged.

Reporter: I hope that your house __won't be badly damaged__ (2). The emergency officials are going to ask everyone to go to a shelter soon.

Resident: I wish they __weren't going to ask__ (3) everyone to go. I'm not ready.

Reporter: It seems that the eye of the hurricane, with the strongest winds around it, will come ashore here.

Resident: That doesn't sound good. I wish that the eye of the hurricane ______________ (4) ashore here.

Reporter: Unfortunately, we can't control hurricanes.

Resident: Right now I wish that we ______________ (5) them. But maybe I'll be able to come back home soon.

Reporter: I hope that you ______________ (6) back home soon. Good luck!

Flood in Ohio

Reporter: As a result of heavy rain, the river has flowed over its banks, causing serious flooding. Is the water level going down now?

Resident: No, it isn't. I wish that it ______________ (7) now, because the first floor of my house is covered with water.

Reporter: Do you have flood insurance?

Resident: No, I don't. I wish that I ______________ (8) flood insurance. But that's not my only problem. My cat is lost. Maybe she's in a safe place, though.

Reporter: I hope that your cat ______________ (9) in a safe place. . . . It's possible that the president will make disaster aid available.

Resident: That's good news. I hope that the president ______________ (10) disaster aid available soon, so we can clean up and repair the damage.

Reporter: Unfortunately, floods happen often along this river. Of course, we wish that they ______________ (11) so often. But whenever they happen, we'll be here to give you the news.

Blizzard in Baltimore

Reporter: This evening I'm talking to people about the blizzard that's headed toward Baltimore. It's going to snow very hard.

Snowplow Operator: I wish it ______ (12) very hard. Because of this storm, I can't spend the evening with my family.

Reporter: Big storms can really disrupt family life. Notice how crowded this supermarket is.

Shopper: I wish it ______ (13) so crowded.

Reporter: Let's find out how your son feels about the storm.

Child: I'm looking forward to it. But it isn't snowing now. I wish it ______ (14).

Reporter: The storm won't start until later this evening.

Child: I wish the storm ______ (15) soon. If we get a lot of snow, school will be canceled.

Reporter: I see. The blizzard won't be a disaster for the children of Baltimore!

15 *Hope* and *Wish* About the Past: Talking About the News

Complete the sentences by using the correct forms of the words in parentheses to express wishes or hopes about the past.

Vicky: Did you watch television last night?

Joe: No, I didn't, because I had to work. I wish I had had (1 (have)) a chance to watch television last night. I hope I didn't miss (2 (not, miss)) anything important.

Vicky: You missed a news program about natural disasters. I wish I ______ (3 (know)) how they were going to present the stories. If I had known, I wouldn't have watched.

Joe: What do you mean? How did they present the stories?

Vicky: The reporters kept making the situations as dramatic as possible. I wish they ______ (4 (not, keep)) asking people to talk about their feelings. First, they interviewed a man in Texas. I hope that hurricane ______ (5 (not, destroy)) his house. Then they interviewed a woman in Ohio. She was really upset because her house was flooded and she'd lost her cat. She probably wishes she ______ (6 (not, have to talk)) about her problems on national television.

Joe: I hope the poor woman ______ (7 (find)) her cat.

Vicky: Then they talked to people about a blizzard that hadn't even started yet. Of course, I hope the blizzard ______________ (8 (not, cause)) serious problems, but the report was really silly. I wish you ______________ (9 (could, see)) it. Why do you think reporters try to make the weather news so dramatic?

Joe: They know that if the weather news is dramatic, more people watch television.

16 Using *Hope* and *Wish*: Questions and Answers

A. Use the words given to write questions.

1. What is something that you wish/you/experience/in the past?
   What is something that you wish you had experienced in the past?
2. What is something that you/hope/happen/yesterday?
   ____
3. What is something that you/wish/happen/yesterday?
   ____
4. What is something that you hope/not/happen/now?
   ____
5. What do you wish that you/do/now?
   ____
6. What is something that you hope/happen/soon?
   ____
7. What do you wish that you/do/tomorrow?
   ____

B. Work with a partner. Ask your partner the questions you wrote in Part A. Your partner answers, beginning each answer with *I wish* or *I hope*.

Example: Student A: What is something that you wish you had experienced in the past?
Student B: I wish that I had seen Brazil win the World Cup in 2002.

17 Using Unreal Conditionals, *Hope*, and *Wish*: What Are Your Regrets? What Are Your Dreams?

We all have regrets about the past. We also have fantasies about how our lives might be different in the present and future. Write two paragraphs.

1. In the first paragraph, tell about something that you did or didn't do that you now regret. Use *wish* and past unreal conditionals.

Example: When I was in high school, I got a job at a fast-food restaurant in order to earn money to buy a car. I spent every night at work. Now I wish I hadn't spent those nights at work. I wish I had spent that time studying. If I had had more time to study, I might have gotten much better grades. I could have taken advanced chemistry and physics if I hadn't been serving fried chicken until midnight every night.

2. In the second paragraph, tell about your hopes and wishes, including those that seem impossible, for the present and future. Use *hope*, *wish*, and present and future unreal conditionals.

Example: I'm happy with my life, but I sometimes wish that it were different. For example, I often wish that I were rich. If I were rich, my life would be easier. . . . I have dreams about the future, too. I wish that I could become a famous musician. If I could become a famous musician, I would give concerts all over the world. . . . I hope that at least some of my wishes come true.

See the *Grammar Links* Website for complete model paragraphs for this assignment.

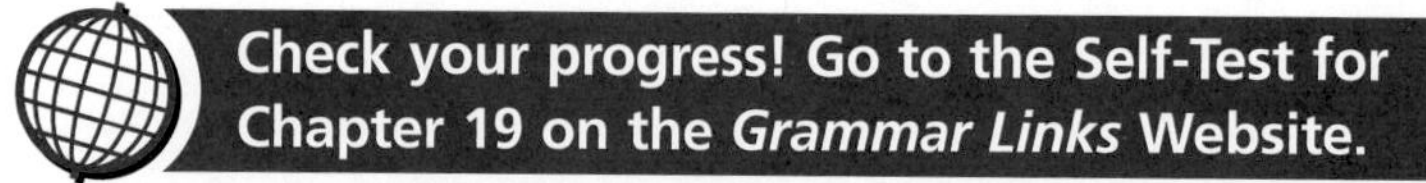

Check your progress! Go to the Self-Test for Chapter 19 on the *Grammar Links* Website.

Wrap-up Activities

1 A Disastrous Prediction: EDITING

Correct the nine errors in the following passage. There are errors in conditional sentences and in sentences with *wish* and *hope*. Some errors can be corrected in more than one way. The first error is corrected for you.

In 1811–1812, the small town of New Madrid, Missouri, was the center of some of the biggest earthquakes ever recorded in the United States. ~~When~~ If the area had been densely populated then, the earthquakes would have caused great devastation. The shock waves from the earthquakes traveled for hundreds of miles. If you had lived in Boston at the time, you could of felt them. The area around New Madrid is still a dangerous earthquake zone. If the area wasn't so dangerous, people who live there might not take earthquake predictions so seriously.

In 1989, Iben Browning, a business consultant, made this announcement: "If my calculations are correct there is a 50 percent chance of a destructive earthquake striking New Madrid on December 3, 1990." Because many people believed that Browning had predicted previous earthquakes, hundreds of news reporters went to New Madrid. One reporter said, "If an earthquake will occur, it will be the best-recorded event in Missouri history. If nothing happens, people's reaction to the prediction will make an interesting news story." New Madrid experienced an "earthquake hysteria." Thousands of people bought disaster supplies, many residents decided to spend the week elsewhere, and the schools closed.

December 3 came and went. No earthquake occurred. Many people blamed the reporters for the hysteria. A physicist said, "Browning had not accurately predicted previous earthquakes. The reporters would have found this out if they would have investigated. Earthquakes cannot be predicted. I wish we can predict them!" Red Cross officials were glad that the prediction raised awareness about earthquakes, but they wished the hysteria wouldn't have happened. A government official said, "I hope an earthquake wouldn't ever come. But now we will be better prepared if one comes."

2 The Chain Reactions Game: SPEAKING

Step 1 Play this game as a class. Use your imagination to describe the possible results of the past unreal conditions given in the box. One student gives a result for the first condition. Then the next student changes that result into a condition and gives a result for it. Continue until everyone has contributed a sentence to the chain of events.

Example: Student A: *If it had snowed yesterday, I wouldn't have come to class.*
Student B: *If I hadn't come to class, I would have spent the day at home.*
Student C: *If I had spent the day at home, I might have baked a cake.*
Student D: *If I had baked a cake, . . .*

1. If it had snowed yesterday, . . .
2. If I had been alive a hundred years ago, . . .
3. If everyone in our class had gone to Hawaii last month, . . .

Step 2 To continue the game, think of your own conditions to start the chain of events.

3 A Guide to Disaster Preparation: WRITING

Step 1 Work in small groups. Each group should choose a natural disaster, for example, hurricanes or earthquakes. Get information from the library or the Internet about preparing for that kind of disaster.

Step 2 Write a one-page guide to inform your classmates about how to prepare for the disaster and advise them about where to go and what to do if it occurs or is about to occur. Use at least five factual conditionals.

Example: *If you live in an area with earthquakes, remove all heavy objects from high shelves. If you leave these objects on shelves, they might fall during an earthquake and injure someone. . . . If an earthquake occurs, do not go outside.*

For links to information on disaster preparation, see the *Grammar Links* Website.
See the *Grammar Links* Website for a complete model guide for this activity.

4 A Disaster Movie: WRITING/SPEAKING

Step 1 Work in groups of three. Write a script for a dramatic scene in a movie about a volcano eruption, a tornado, a blizzard, or any other natural disaster. The scene should include a part for each member of the group. Use each of the following at least once: *hope*, *wish*, future conditionals, present unreal conditionals, and past unreal conditionals.

Example:
Sabrina: *I wish we hadn't climbed to the top of the volcano. I hope it doesn't erupt before we can escape.*
Shinji: *If the helicopter can land here, it might be able to rescue us. . . .*

Step 2 Present your scene to the class.

See the *Grammar Links* Website for a complete model scene for this activity.

Unit **Ten**

Noun Clauses

TOPIC FOCUS
Popular Fiction

UNIT OBJECTIVES

- **noun clauses with *that***
  (I think ***that those stories are by Agatha Christie.***)
- **noun clauses with *wh-* words**
  (She wonders ***when they will fall in love.***)
- **noun clauses with *if/whether***
  (Can you tell me ***if/whether you have the new Catherine Coulter romance***?)
- **quoted speech and reported speech**
  (Brent said, ***"I'm in love with Katie."*** Brent said ***that he was in love with Katie.***)
- **changes in reported speech**
  (I'm leaving and I'll be there tomorrow. → He said that ***he was leaving*** and ***he would*** be ***here today.***)
- **reported questions, commands, and requests**
  (David asked ***if we had homework.*** The teacher told us ***to write a paper.*** Tanya asked us ***to help her.***)

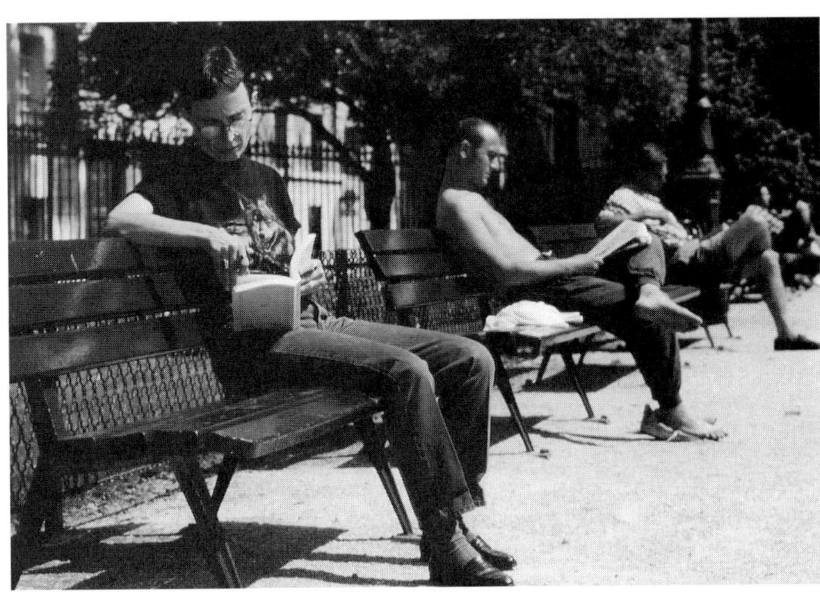

Grammar in Action

Reading and Listening: Explaining Popular Fiction

Read and listen to this lecture about popular fiction.

In almost any bookstore, you'll see a large Fiction/Literature section. You'll probably also see that **many works of fiction are in other sections instead**. These sections have labels such as *Romance*, *Mystery*, *Science Fiction*, *Horror*, and *Westerns*. You might wonder **how these books are different from the books you find under *Fiction/Literature***.

The answer is **that these books belong to genres** (pronounced JAHN-ruhz), types of fiction that follow certain formulas, or rules. If you pick up an unfamiliar novel from the Fiction/Literature section, you won't know **what kind of story it tells**. But if you pick up a novel from the Romance section, you can be pretty sure **that it's about a young woman who falls in love**. The reason is **that books in the romance genre almost always follow a certain formula**.

That genre fiction is popular is something no one would question. Booksellers say **that two-thirds of *all* books sold are genre fiction**. In fact, another name for genre fiction is "popular fiction."

However, experts wonder **why genre fiction is so popular**. Experts also wonder **whether books based on formulas can be considered literature the way, for example, Shakespeare's plays are literature**.

The first question might not be very hard to answer. A careful look at genre fiction shows **that it's like real life but much better**. The hero, man or woman, of a work of genre fiction has an important goal—whether it's to save the world from creatures from outer space, find the murderer before he strikes again, or marry the handsome millionaire. Readers are afraid **that the hero will fail**. When they close the book for the last time, they are relieved and gratified **that the hero has succeeded**. They care about **what happens to the hero** because they can identify with the hero and his or her goal. The second question is probably a harder one. See **if you can come up with an answer**.

work of fiction = a book that tells a story based on the imagination, not fact. *novel* = a book-length work of fiction. *relieved* = not worried anymore. *gratified* = pleased, satisfied. *identify with* = feel sympathy for.

Think About Grammar

A. Look at the pair of sentences from the lecture. Complete the statements that follow with words from the box.

a. In almost any bookstore, you'll see **a large Fiction/Literature section.** (noun phrase)

b. You'll probably also see **that many works of fiction are in other sections instead.** (noun clause)

a clause	a subject and a verb	a word such as *that*	the object of a verb

1. A noun clause functions like a noun or a noun phrase, because it can be, for example, ________________.

2. A noun clause is ____________ because it includes ________________.
   It is linked to the rest of the sentence with ________________.

B. Look at each boldfaced noun clause in the lecture and circle the word that it begins with. List these words. (List each word just once.)

that ________ ________

________ ________ ________

C. There are three types of noun clauses: *that*, *wh-*, and *if/whether.* Write two examples of each from the lecture.

1. *that* noun clauses: that many works of fiction are in other sections instead
   ____

2. *wh-* noun clauses: ____________________________
   ____

3. *if/whether* noun clauses: ____________________________
   ____

Chapter 20

Noun Clauses

Introductory Task: Judging a Book by Its Cover

A. Look at the four book covers. What kinds of stories do these books tell? Each of the sentences with a noun clause on page 387 is about one of the books. Write the number of the book that the sentence is about.

Book 1

Book 2

Book 3

Book 4

1. I think

   a. that this book is a horror story. __4__

   b. that this book is a mystery. ______

   c. that this book is a romance. ______

   d. that this book is science fiction. ______

2. She is telling him

   a. that they must report what they've seen to the commander of the Space Fleet. ______

   b. that she knows that he prefers someone from his own social class. ______

   c. that, if he knows anything about the crime, he'd better talk now. ______

   d. that he can't make her into a monster like him. ______

3. The reader will keep turning the pages to find out

   a. whether the man and woman will discover each other's true feelings. ______

   b. whether the murderer will be caught. ______

   c. whether people will learn the truth before creatures from another planet take over the world. ______

   d. whether the unnatural evil that has lasted for centuries will be destroyed. ______

B. Compare answers in a group. What other ideas do you have about these books from their covers? Which one of these books do you think that you'd like to read? Why? Discuss these questions. Use *I think that . . .* and *I think that I'd read . . . because . . . .*

Example: I think that she becomes a prisoner in his castle. . . . I think that I'd read the horror story because I like to feel scared. . . .

GRAMMAR BRIEFING 1

Overview of Noun Clauses

FORM and FUNCTION

A. Sentence and Clause Structure

MAIN CLAUSE	NOUN CLAUSE			
		SUBJECT	VERB	
He realizes	**that**	**the work**	**isn't**	**easy.**
I wonder	**where**	**they**	**are going.**	
We don't know	**if**	**she**	**arrived**	**yet.**

(continued on next page)

A. Sentence and Clause Structure (continued)

1. A noun clause occurs in a sentence with a main clause.

   main clause / noun clause
   I think **that the movie started.**

2. Like any clause, a noun clause must have a subject and a verb.

   subject / verb
   I think that **the movie started.**

3. Noun clauses begin with:

   - *That* (see Grammar Briefing 2, page 390).

     I think **that** the movie started.

   - A *wh-* word (see Grammar Briefing 3, page 394).

     I don't know **when** the movie started.

   - *If* or *whether* (see Grammar Briefing 4, page 397).

     I wonder **if/whether** the movie started.

B. Uses of Noun Clauses

1. Like nouns, noun clauses can be used as:

   - Subjects.

     What she said isn't true.

   - Subject complements.

     My opinion is **that they won't care.**

   - Objects of verbs.

     I **wonder whether they are coming.**

   - Objects of prepositions.

     I will think **about how you can help us.**

2. Noun clauses can follow certain adjectives.

   I am **sure that they talked to her.**

3. The verbs and adjectives that noun clauses follow usually express mental activities or feelings.* (For lists of these verbs and adjectives, see Grammar Briefing 2, page 390.)

   We **agree/feel/think** that you should come with us.

   I am **afraid/angry/convinced/surprised** that he didn't tell them about our plans.

*Noun clauses also follow verbs that report speech—for example, *say*, *ask*, and *tell* (see Chapter 21).

GRAMMAR HOTSPOT!

Do not confuse *that* noun clauses with adjective clauses with *that*. Noun clauses can occur where nouns occur. Adjective clauses modify, and follow, nouns.

I **know that the restaurant is good.** (noun clause; object of verb *know*)

I'm looking for a **restaurant that is good.** (adjective clause; modifies noun *restaurant*)

GRAMMAR PRACTICE 1

Overview of Noun Clauses

1 Identifying Noun Clauses and Their Uses: Two Views of Popular Fiction

A. Work with a partner. Read the following letters sent to a literary magazine. Underline each noun clause (*that, wh-, if/whether*) and circle the word that introduces it. (Remember: Do not confuse noun clauses with adjective clauses.) Including the examples, there are 11 noun clauses.

Dear Editor:

I am extremely disappointed that you included an article about genre fiction in your magazine last month. That this inclusion is inappropriate is obvious to any serious reader.

A literary magazine is supposed to be about literature—written works of art. Literature is fiction that is original and uses poetic language. With literature, you must read carefully and think about whether you understand the meaning.

It is clear that genre fiction is the opposite of literature. Genre fiction just follows formulas: for example, boy meets girl, and boy and girl fall in love and get married. Reading genre fiction is like watching TV.

My position is that you should stick to literature from now on.

Professor Harold Burton

Dear Editor:

As a writer of genre fiction, I feel that I must respond to Professor Burton.

First, 90 percent of all new fiction published is genre fiction. I don't know why the professor wants us to ignore 90 percent of all new fiction.

Second, I'm not sure if any fiction is fully original. Even Shakespeare got most of his stories from other sources!

Third, genre fiction deals with the same issues that the greatest works of literature deal with. Undoubtedly, the professor admires Dostoyevsky's *Crime and Punishment.* Doesn't he realize that mysteries are about crime and punishment?

Finally, I don't understand why the professor thinks watching TV is so bad. Perhaps he's a snob. That TV and genre fiction can bring people pleasure seems obvious and important.

Lydia Burgess

literary magazine = a magazine with literature and articles about literature. *Crime and Punishment* = a famous novel by nineteenth-century Russian writer Fyodor Dostoyevsky.

B. Look at the noun clauses that you underlined in Part A. Label the function of each noun clause: *S* (= subject); *O* (= object); *O Prep* (= object of preposition); *SC* (= subject complement); *adj + NC* (= noun clause following adjective).

Example: adj + NC
I am extremely disappointed that you included an article about genre fiction in your magazine last month.

GRAMMAR BRIEFING 2

Noun Clauses with *That*

FORM and FUNCTION

A. Structure of Noun Clauses with *That*

MAIN CLAUSE	NOUN CLAUSE	
	(THAT)	
I think	(**that**)	**this book will be interesting.**
I am sure	(**that**)	**class is canceled tomorrow.**

Noun clauses with *that* are introduced with the word *that. That* can usually be omitted.

We hope **that you will come.** = We hope **you will come.**

B. Uses of Noun Clauses with *That*

1. Noun clauses with *that* can be the subject of a sentence.

   That he's late doesn't surprise me.

   However, usually *it* is put in subject position and the *that* clause is put at the end of the sentence.

   It doesn't surprise me (**that**) **he's late.**

   The only time *that* **cannot** be omitted is when the noun clause is in subject position.

   NOT: ~~He's late~~ doesn't surprise me.

2. *That* noun clauses can be subject complements.

   The truth is (**that**) **she's not a very happy person.**

3. *That* noun clauses can be the object of the verb.

   I **hope** (**that**) **you'll like my friends.**

   Verbs that can be followed by *that* clauses include:

agree	doubt	guess	imagine	realize	show	understand
believe	feel	hear	know	remember	suppose	
decide	forget	hope	notice	see	think	

4. *That* noun clauses can follow an adjective.

   I'm **happy** (**that**) **you like my friends.**

   Adjectives that can be followed by *that* clauses include:

afraid	certain	glad	positive	sure
angry	convinced	happy	sad	surprised
aware	disappointed	pleased	sorry	worried

GRAMMAR **HOT**SPOT!

1. Unlike other noun clauses, a *that* clause **cannot** be the object of a preposition. Omit the preposition if possible or use a gerund phrase instead.	I **heard** that they have problems. OR I heard **about** their having problems. **NOT**: I heard about ~~they have problems~~.
2. Be careful! Some verbs are used with gerunds and/or infinitives but not with noun clauses.	I **want** you **to help** me. **NOT**: I want ~~that you help me~~.
3. If the main clause verb is past tense, the noun clause:	
• Has a past tense verb if the action of the main clause and the noun clause occur at the same time.	Around noon, I suddenly **realized** that she **wasn't** with us. **NOT**: Around noon, I suddenly realized that she ~~isn't~~ with us.
• Has *would* or *was/were going to* if the action of the noun clause occurs after that of the main clause.	I **didn't think** that we **would find** her. **NOT**: I didn't think that we ~~will~~ find her.

GRAMMAR PRACTICE 2

Noun Clauses with *That*

2 *That* Noun Clauses—Form: The Rules of the Game

Use the words in parentheses to complete the sentences with *that* clauses. Include *that*. Use appropriate tenses.

It's obvious that each genre has its own formula, or "rules" (1 (each genre / have / its own formula, or "rules")). For mysteries, a main rule is ________ (2 (the crime / must / be / important))—for example, a murder. When readers begin a mystery book, they know ________ (3 (they / find / clues)) but also "red herrings," or false clues.

It's equally obvious, however, ________ (4 (all genres / share / certain rules)). An important shared rule is authenticity: Even minor details must seem vivid and real. One well-known publisher of Westerns often refused to publish books because he felt ________ (5 (they / not / be / authentic enough)). In many cases, he actually thought ________ (6 (the books / be / good)), but he was disappointed ________ (7 (he / not / "smell the gunsmoke")).

authenticity = seeming real. *publish* = print and sell books.

3 Forming Sentences with *That* Clauses: And Then There Are Subgenres—A Tale of Two Detectives

A. Combine the two sentences to form a sentence with a *that* clause. When possible, write the sentence in two ways. Include *that*. Do not omit any words other than *this*.

Every genre can be divided into subgenres.

1. For example, readers of mysteries know **this**. There are "classic" mysteries and "hard-boiled" mysteries.

   For example, readers of mysteries know that there are "classic" mysteries and "hard-boiled" mysteries.

2. **This** is a well-known fact. There are great differences between the two kinds of mysteries.

   It is a well-known fact that there are great differences between the two kinds of mysteries.

   That there are great differences between the two kinds of mysteries is a well-known fact.

3. One of the first things a reader notices is **this**. The tone of the writing is very different.
4. The reader of classic mysteries, like Agatha Christie's, expects **this**. The crime will take place in an upper-class setting, like a mansion in England.
5. The detective in these mysteries, for example, Christie's Hercule Poirot, knows **this**. He'll be able to solve the crime through logical thinking.
6. **This** is usually the case. The classic detective is an amateur with an interest in crime.
7. Experts have shown **this**. The hard-boiled mystery developed in the United States as authors tried to write more authentically about crime.
8. The reader of hard-boiled mysteries expects **this**. The action will occur in the streets of a city and will involve tough "lowlifes" as well as the rich.
9. The detective, like Raymond Chandler's Philip Marlowe, is a professional who knows **this**.
   He may need to use his weapon as well as his brains.
10. **This** doesn't surprise me. Many people read one kind of mystery but not the other.

tone = sound, style. *mansion* = a very large house, usually of a rich person. *amateur* = not a professional. *lowlife* = someone who does not have a good moral character.

B. Work with a partner. Read the following quotes. Two are from a hard-boiled detective novel by Raymond Chandler. Two are from classic detective stories by Agatha Christie. Use the tips in the box to discuss which quotes are from which author and why you think this. Use noun clauses after verbs such as *think*, *believe*, *agree*, *decide*, and *doubt* and after adjectives such as *certain*, *convinced*, and *sure*. When you have decided, compare answers with your classmates.

Example: I (don't) think that the quote in *a* is from a hard-boiled detective book because the woman seems . . . and because . . . I (don't) agree that the quotes in *a* and *b* are by the same writer, because I'm convinced that . . .

a. I [the detective] went on up the street and parked and walked back. In the daylight it seemed an exposed and dangerous thing to do. . . . She stood there straight and silent against the locked front door. One hand went up to her teeth and her teeth bit at her funny thumb. There were purple smears under her eyes.

b. "So you're tough tonight," Eddie Mars' voice said.
"Big, fast, tough, and full of prickles. What can I do for you?" [said the detective.]
"Cops over there—you know where. You keep me out of it?"
"Why should I?"
"I'm nice to be nice to, soldier. I'm not nice not to be nice to."
"Listen hard and you'll hear my teeth chattering."

c. "Mrs. Robinson did not seem to notice anything amiss. Very curious, is it not? Did she impress you as being a truthful woman, Hastings?" [asked the detective.]
"She was a delightful creature!"
"[Evidently,] since she renders you incapable of replying to my question. Describe her to me, then."
"Well, she's tall and fair; her hair's really a beautiful shade of auburn—"

d. . . . The side door in question was a small one in the angle of the wall, not more than a dozen yards from the scene of the tragedy. As we reached it, I [the detective] gave a cry. There. . . lay the glittering necklace, evidently dropped by the thief in the panic of his flight. I swooped joyously down on it. Then I uttered another cry which Lord Yardly echoed. For in the middle of the necklace was a great gap. The Star of the East was missing!

Sources: Agatha Christie, *Poirot Investigates* (Harper Paperbacks, 1992); Raymond Chandler, *The Big Sleep* (Vintage, 1976).

Tips

- Characters: tough lowlifes? upper class?
- Language/characters' language: tough tone? formal tone?
- Setting: in the streets? an upper-class setting?
- Detective: thinking a lot? involved in dangerous action?

Go to the *Grammar Links* Website find out more about Agatha Christie, Raymond Chandler, and their detectives.

4 *That* Clauses—Editing: He Said, She Said

Correct the errors involving *that* clauses. Including the example, there are six errors.

That
^ Conversation adds interest to our daily life is something we all know. And all readers know that dialogue—the conversations of characters in a book—adds interest to fiction. Dialogue brings characters to life for readers. Good writers realize dialogue can also be a way of introducing information without taking up much space. There are limits to this use of dialogue to provide information. One writer decided that he will start a book with the following line: "Oh, Uncle, if you had come into my life years ago, I wouldn't have been alone, then in the orphanage, then with that cruel family, and then . . ." (And this writer was surprised about that nobody publishes his book!)

Dialogue should be like real conversation—but not too much like it. Listen to a real conversation. It is filled with *um*s and pauses is the first thing you will notice. You will probably also notice it is often boring and hard to understand. Readers would wonder about a book that had lines like this: "Um, . . . those canned tomatoes on the shopping list . . . uh, never mind." If writers want that people enjoy their books, they shouldn't have their characters sound exactly the way we do!

GRAMMAR BRIEFING 3

Noun Clauses with *Wh-* Words

FORM and FUNCTION

A. Structure of Noun Clauses with *Wh-* Words

MAIN CLAUSE	NOUN CLAUSE	
	WH- WORD	
I understand	**why**	**they can't come.**
I don't remember	**when**	**the concert starts.**

1. Noun clauses with *wh-* words begin with a *wh-* word (*who, what, why, when, where, how*).

   I wonder **why/when/how** they came.

   I wonder **who/what** he knows.

2. *Wh-* noun clauses have statement word order, even when they are used in questions.

   I don't know what **he is** doing.
   NOT: I don't know what ~~is he~~ doing.

   Can you see where **they are**?
   NOT: Can you see where ~~are they~~?

B. Uses of Noun Clauses with *Wh-* Words

1. Noun clauses with *wh-* words have all the possible uses of noun clauses:
   - Subject.

     Why the meeting was canceled isn't clear to me.
   - Subject complement.

     The question is **how we can finish on time.**
   - Object of a verb.

     I **didn't notice when they left.**

     However, *wh-* noun clauses can follow only some of the verbs that *that* noun clauses can follow. These include:

decide	hear	notice	remember	understand
forget	know	realize	see	wonder

   - Object of a preposition.

     We finally decided **on when to take our trip**.
   - After an adjective.

     However, *wh-* noun clauses can follow only a few of the adjectives that *that* noun clauses can follow. These include *certain* and *sure.*

     I'm not **certain what the teacher told us about that**.

(continued on next page)

B. Uses of Noun Clauses with *Wh-* Words (continued)

2. *Wh-* clauses are often used in statements that express uncertainty.	I **wonder** **how he knows that**.
These statements are often negative.	I **don't remember** **how the teacher explained those sentences**. I'm **not sure** **when the assignment is due**.
3. *Wh-* clauses are often used in indirect requests for information. These requests begin with *Do you know* or *Can/Could you tell me.* They are considered polite.	Do you know **what time it is**? Could you tell me **where the post office is**?

GRAMMAR HOTSPOT!

1. Remember! Use statement word order in *wh-* noun clauses.	I wonder when **Mark will** get here. **NOT:** I wonder when ~~will Mark~~ get here.
2. Remember! If the main clause verb is past tense, in the noun clause use past tense verbs instead of present tense verbs and *would* or *was/were going to* instead of *will* or *am/is/are going to.*	I **wondered** why she **wasn't** with us. **NOT:** I wondered why she ~~isn't~~ with us. I **wondered** when we **would** see her. **NOT:** I wondered when we ~~will~~ see her.

GRAMMAR PRACTICE 3

Noun Clauses with *Wh-* Words

5 Noun Clauses with *Wh-* Words—Form: Page Turners

Complete the noun clauses with the words in parentheses. Use appropriate tenses.

1. Why books like mysteries are called "page turners" isn't much of a puzzle.
   (why / books like mysteries / be called / "page turners")
2. When Evelyn recently read her first Agatha Christie book, she was surprised at ______________________.
   (how / she / not be able to / put the book down)
3. She knew who was murdered, but she didn't know ______________________.
   (who / the murderer / be)
4. As she read, she tried to notice ______________________.
   (what / the clues / be)
5. But it was hard for her to notice the clues because she kept turning the pages to find out ______________________.
   (how / the book / end)

6. If readers are familiar with the genre, they understand ______________________.
(why / characters / behave / the way they do)

7. The heroine in a romance novel is confused about ______________________,
(why / the hero / seem / unfriendly)

but the reader knows it's because he's falling in love!

heroine = female hero.

6 Indirect Requests for Information: Can You Tell Me Why He Is Asking These Questions?

Make each question more polite by including it in an indirect request.

1. Where is the Martha Blikenstrop Library?

   Can you tell me where the Martha Blikenstrop Library is?

2. Who is Martha Blikenstrop? Do you know ______________________?
3. When does the library close today? Can you tell me ______________________?
4. What time is it now? Do you know ______________________?
5. How do I get downstairs? Can you tell me ______________________?
6. Where can I find a good place for lunch?

   Do you know ______________________?

7 Using Noun Clauses with *Wh-* Words: I Wonder Wh- . . .

1. Work with a partner. In a few sentences, tell your partner the basic plot (story) of a book, movie, or TV program he or she isn't familiar with. Don't reveal any details or the ending.

Example: A man and a woman send each other e-mail messages but have never met. They think they have a lot in common and they want to meet. But they live far from each other.

2. Your partner should think of some things he or she would like to know about the book, movie, or program and express these in statements beginning *I wonder* + *wh-* word. Satisfy your partner's curiosity.

Example: I wonder what they look like. . . . I wonder when and how they finally meet.

3. Reverse roles. Your partner tells you the plot of a book, movie, or program. Find out about the things you'd like to know about it, by making statements beginning with *I wonder* + *wh-* word.

GRAMMAR BRIEFING 4

Noun Clauses with *If/Whether*

FORM and FUNCTION

A. Noun Clauses with *If/Whether*

MAIN CLAUSE	NOUN CLAUSE	
	IF/WHETHER	
I don't know	**if/whether**	**my flight will leave on time.**
I wonder	**if/whether**	**Laura is home now.**

Noun clauses with *if/whether* begin with *if* or *whether*. They always have statement word order, even when they are in questions.

I'm not sure **if/whether** he is coming.

Have you heard **if/whether he is coming**?
NOT: Have you heard if/whether ~~is he~~ coming?

B. Uses of Noun Clauses with *If/Whether*

1. Noun clauses with *if/whether* have all the possible uses of noun clauses:
   - Subject.
     Whether he was here isn't obvious.
   - Subject complement.
     The question is **whether the work will be done on time.**
   - Object of verb (the verbs are the same as for clauses with *wh-* words; see Grammar Briefing 2, page 390).
     I **wonder if/whether Sean and Dave know each other**.
   - Object of preposition.
     I often think **about whether I should change my major**.
   - After an adjective (as for clauses with *wh-* words, these include *certain* and *sure*).
     She's not **certain if/whether they left yet**.

   Use *if* **only** in clauses that are objects of verbs or follow an adjective. (*Whether* can always be used.)

   I **don't know if/whether** he's home.
   I'm not **sure if/whether** he's home.
   NOT: ~~If~~ he's home isn't obvious.
   NOT: I'm not sure about ~~if~~ he's home.

(continued on next page)

B. Uses of Noun Clauses with *If/Whether* (continued)

2. Like *wh-* clauses, *if/whether* clauses are often used:	
• In statements that express uncertainty.	I **wonder** **if/whether it's going to rain**. I **don't know** **if/whether my aunt will visit this year**.
• In indirect requests for information, after *Do you know* or *Could/Can you tell me*.	Do you know **if/whether the bus stops here**? Can you tell me **if/whether the financial aid office is in this building**?

GRAMMAR HOTSPOT!

1. Remember! Use statement word order in *if/whether* noun clauses.	Do you know if **they are** planning to come? **NOT**: Do you know if ~~are they~~ planning to come?
2. Remember! If the main clause verb is past tense, in the noun clause use past tense verbs instead of present tense verbs and *would* or *was/were going to* instead of *will* or *am/is/are going to*.	I **wondered** if she **wasn't** here. **NOT**: I wondered if she ~~isn't~~ here. I **wondered** if we **would** see her. **NOT**: I wondered if we ~~will~~ see her.

GRAMMAR PRACTICE 4

Noun Clauses with *If/Whether*

8 Noun Clauses with *If/Whether*—Form: I Wonder If . . . ?

Stuart Forrester is wondering whether he can write a book. Use the questions to complete his sentences with *if/whether* noun clauses. If both *if* and *whether* are possible, use both. Make only necessary changes.

1. Do I have enough talent to write fiction?

   I often think about whether I have enough talent to write fiction.

2. Could I write the story of my own life as a book?

   I wonder if/whether I could write the story of my own life as a book.

3. Would my story fit into the romance genre?

   I can't make up my mind about ____________________.

4. Would I find readers who are interested in my story?

   I'm not sure ____.

5. Can readers accept something a little bit different?

   ____ is the main issue.

   (*983 pages later . . .*) There's a writers' conference coming up. My favorite author, Lydia Burgess, will be there.

6. Should I go?

   I wonder ____.

7. Would Lydia Burgess have time to read the manuscript for my book?

   It's not clear ____. I hope so!

manuscript = papers intended for publication.

9 Indirect Requests and Statements of Uncertainty: Do You Know If . . . ?

Use the questions to complete the indirect requests for information with noun clauses. Use *whether* in the noun clauses. Use the words in parentheses to answer with statements expressing uncertainty.

At the writers' conference:

1. Would you have time to read my manuscript?

   Stuart: Ms. Burgess, it's a privilege to meet you. I've written a book. Do you know

   whether you would have time to read my manuscript ?

   LB: I don't know whether I would have time to read your manuscript.
   (don't know)

2. Does your book belong to the romance genre?

   LB: Well, can you tell me ____?

   Stuart: ____.
   (not certain)

   I think so.

3. Would your story interest readers?

   LB: Well, can you tell me ____?

   Stuart: ____.
   (not sure)

   Maybe it would interest them because it's the story of my life. I went to work for a nice boss. I liked her a lot. But she fired me. . . . Let me give you my manuscript.

Next year, in a bookstore:

4. Do you have that new romance by Stuart Forrester?

   Woman: Do you know ______________________________?

   Owner: ______________________________ (don't know). Everyone's been buying it!

Go to the *Grammar Links* Website find out more about romance novels and writing romance novels.

10 Using Noun Clauses: I Think That . . . I Wonder If . . .

A. Work in a small group. Pick two of the following topics. Discuss what you think about the topics, and discuss something that you would like to know about them. Use *that* clauses, *wh-* clauses, and *if/whether* clauses. Include negatives. Use verbs including *agree*, *believe*, *doubt*, *guess*, *know*, *realize*, *think*, *understand*, and *wonder*. Use adjectives including *certain*, *convinced*, *sure*, and *surprised*.

Topics:

1. Whether popular fiction can be considered literature
2. Why people read popular fiction in general and why they read particular genres (romance fiction, mysteries, horror fiction, science fiction, Westerns)
3. How reading genre fiction is similar to watching romances, mysteries, etc., on TV and how it is different
4. Whether fiction can be educational and what people can learn by reading it
5. Whether writing fiction would be hard or easy

Example: I think it would be hard to write fiction. . . . I wonder how writers get the information that they need for their stories. . . .

B. Write a paragraph on one of the topics that your group discussed. Use each type of noun clause at least once.

Example: I think that people can learn a lot by reading fiction. They can find out about how people live in different parts of the world and how people lived in different times. They can see whether other people would do the same things they would do in difficult situations. . . .

See the *Grammar Links* Website for a complete model paragraph for this assignment.

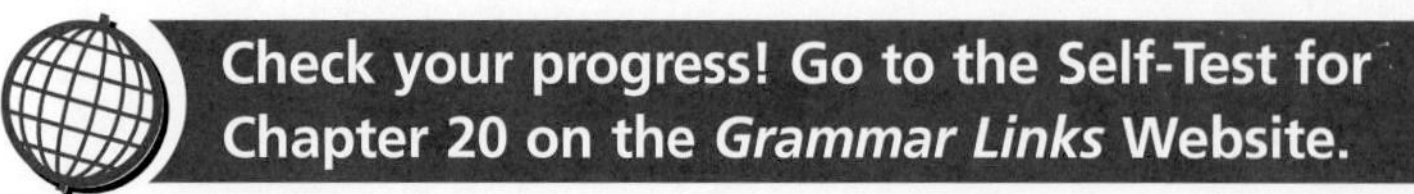

Check your progress! Go to the Self-Test for
Chapter 20 on the Grammar Links Website.

Chapter 21

Quoted Speech; Noun Clauses with Reported Speech

Introductory Task: Passing Along a Message

A. Work with a partner. Read the following lines from two telephone conversations.

Claire to Miriam: I will be in San Francisco Wednesday on my way to Tokyo. Can Carlos and you meet me for dinner? I really am sorry I didn't call sooner.

Miriam to Carlos, the next day: Claire said that she would be here tomorrow on her way to Tokyo. She asked if you and I could meet her for dinner. She said that she really was sorry she hadn't called sooner.

The lines from the second conversation are reported speech: Miriam reports what Claire said. The reported speech adds some words and replaces some words. Underline all the new or different words. Answer these questions.

1. In reported speech, verbs that were present tense in the original speech become ________________ tense verbs. Past tense verbs become ____________________ tense verbs.
2. What are the two modals in Claire's original speech? ________________ ________________
   What modals do they become in the reported speech? ________________ ________________
3. In addition to verbs, modals, and time and place words, what other kind of words can change in reported speech? ________________

B. Read what Carlos told Miriam. Then complete Miriam's message to Claire.

Carlos to Miriam: I'm glad, and I can't wait to see her. I will pick her up at the airport. . . .

Miriam to Claire: Carlos said that ________________________ and that ______________________________. He said that ______________________________ at the airport. . . .

GRAMMAR BRIEFING 1

Quoted Speech and Reported Speech

Overview of Quoted Speech and Reported Speech

FORM and FUNCTION

QUOTED SPEECH	REPORTED SPEECH
Betty said, "You are in love with Mary."	Betty said (that) I was in love with Mary.
Betty asked, "Why do you love Mary?"	Betty asked why I loved Mary.
Betty asked, "Does Mary love you?"	Betty asked if/whether Mary loved me.

1. Quoted and reported speech differ in function:
   - Quoted speech is used to give the **exact words** that someone said, thought, or wrote.

     Betty said, "**You are in love with Mary**." (Betty's exact words)
   - Reported speech is used to tell what someone said, thought, or wrote. It usually does not give the exact words.

     Betty said **I was in love with Mary**. (not Betty's exact words)
2. Quoted and reported speech differ in form:
   - Quoted speech occurs in a sentence between quotation marks.

     sentence
     Betty asked, **"Why do you love Mary?"**
   - Reported speech occurs in a noun clause (*that*, *wh-*, or *if/whether*; see Chapter 20).

     noun clause
     Betty asked **why I loved Mary**.

Quoted Speech

FORM

INTRODUCTORY WORDS	QUOTED SPEECH
The police officer asked,	"Did you see it happen?"

QUOTED SPEECH	INTRODUCTORY WORDS
"Yes, I did,"	she replied.

1. Quoted speech can come before or follow the words introducing it. Even when it follows, quoted speech begins with a capital letter.

   Dad said, "**M**aybe we should stop soon."
   "Are you tired?" Mom asked. "The kids look tired."
2. If the introductory words come first, use a comma before the quoted speech.

   Dad said, "I *am* tired."
3. If the quoted speech comes first, use a comma before the introductory words instead of a period. (Questions end with a question mark; exclamations end with an exclamation point.)

   "Let's stop for the night**,**" Mom said.
   "Does this motel look OK**?**" Dad asked.
   "It looks great**!**" Mom replied.

(continued on next page)

Verbs Introducing Quoted or Reported Speech

FORM

INTRODUCTORY WORDS	SPEECH
She said (to him),	"They have problems."
She said (to him)	that they had problems.

Say, *tell*, and *ask* are the verbs most commonly used to introduce quoted or reported speech.

Verbs introducing speech follow four patterns:

- V (+ *to* + noun phrase): *admit*, *comment*, *complain*, *explain*, *mention*, *reply*, *say*.

  He **said** (**to her**), "Tom is unhappy."
  He **said** (**to her**) (that) Tom was unhappy.

- V + noun phrase: *remind*, *tell*.

  He **told her**, "Tom is unhappy."
  He **told her** (that) Tom was unhappy.

- V (+ noun phrase): *answer*, *ask*, *promise*, *warn*.

  He **asked** (**her**), "Why is Tom unhappy?"
  He **asked** (**her**) why Tom was unhappy.

- V only: *think*.

  He **thought**, "Tom is unhappy."
  He **thought** (that) Tom was unhappy.

GRAMMAR PRACTICE 1

Quoted Speech and Reported Speech

1 Punctuating Quoted Speech; Identifying Reported Speech: A Woman from His Past

A. Add the missing punctuation to the following quoted speech.

Brent grabbed his coat and, glancing at his watch, said, "I'm leaving, Tom. I've told my clients that they can reach me tomorrow."

Are you off to another night on the town, Brent Tom asked You told me that you'd reformed. Who are you going out with this time

Live your life the way you want Brent replied Let me do what I want with mine

Sure, you're the boss Tom said Hey, do you know who's back in town? That secretary of yours who left so suddenly. When she left, I thought that was too bad. But you said you were glad she was gone. . . . What was her name

In a strange voice, Brent replied Katie

night on the town = a night out having a good time. *reform* = improve one's behavior.

B. Underline the sentences in Part A that include reported speech.

2 Verbs Introducing Speech: Brent and Katie

A. Work with a partner. Complete the sentences with the verbs in the box. Use each verb once. Include a noun or pronoun after the verb only if necessary.

admit	ask	promise	say	think
answer	~~explain~~	remind	~~tell~~	

1. "Katie, you look as beautiful as ever—but somehow more mature and sophisticated," Brent told Katie/her.
2. "I've traveled," Katie explained. "I've gone to school."
3. "Would you have dinner with me tonight, Katie?" Brent ________.
4. "No. I can't. I'm sorry," Katie ________.
5. "Come on, Katie," Brent ________. "You've got to. I won't take no for an answer."
6. "Remember what I told you the last time we spoke," Katie ________. "I said that I never wanted to have anything to do with you again."
7. "I remember," Brent ________.
   Katie looked away.
8. "But I'll never be like that again," Brent ________. "I love you, Katie, and I'm a changed man."
9. Katie didn't answer. She ________, "Can I believe him? I wish I knew!"

B. Look at the sentences in Part A. Add a noun or a pronoun after the verb where possible. Include *to* if it is needed.

2. "I've traveled," Katie explained ^to him/Brent^. "I've gone to school."

3 Writing Quoted Speech: What Happened? What Will Happen?

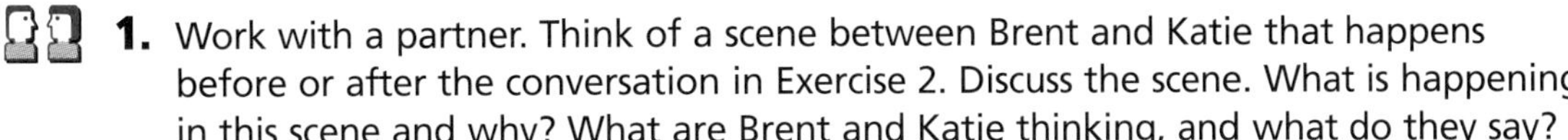

1. Work with a partner. Think of a scene between Brent and Katie that happens before or after the conversation in Exercise 2. Discuss the scene. What is happening in this scene and why? What are Brent and Katie thinking, and what do they say?

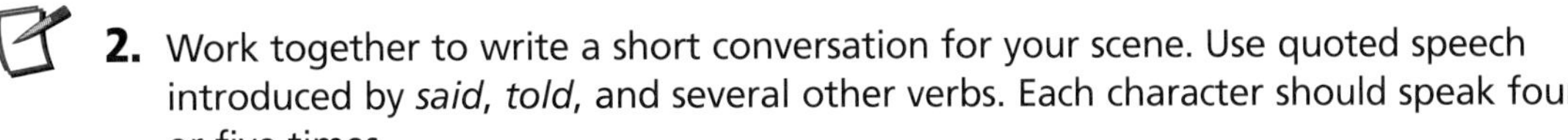

2. Work together to write a short conversation for your scene. Use quoted speech introduced by *said*, *told*, and several other verbs. Each character should speak four or five times.

GRAMMAR BRIEFING 2

Changes in Reported Speech; Verb Tense in Reported Speech

Changes in Reported Speech

FORM and FUNCTION

Overview

Reported speech usually occurs in a different situation from the speech it reports: The speaker, listener(s), time, and place might be different. Therefore, often some changes in wording are needed.	*Original speech: Josh to Liz, Monday, on the street:* I don't know if I can meet you at school on Wednesday. *Reported speech: Liz to Paul, Wednesday, at school:* Josh said that **he didn't know if he could meet me here today**.
These changes involve:	
• Verbs (see below).	don't know → didn't know
• Modals (see Grammar Briefing 3, page 410).	can → could
• Pronouns (see Grammar Briefing 4, page 412).	I → he; you → me
• Time and place expressions (see Grammar Briefing 4, page 412).	on Wednesday → today; at school → here

Verb Tense in Reported Speech*

FORM

A. Verb Tense with a Present Tense Introducing Verb

Sometimes the verb that introduces reported speech is a present tense verb. In this case, the verb tense does not change in reported speech.	He **is** very bored with school. John's parents **say** (that) he **is** very bored with school.

*Contractions can be used in reported speech (e.g., *John's parents say (that)* **he's** *very bored with school.*).

(continued on next page)

B. Verb Tense with a Past Tense Introducing Verb

1. Usually, the introducing verb is a past tense verb. In this case, the tense of the verbs in the reported speech often changes, as follows:

• Simple present → simple past.	She **writes** every day. → He said (that) she **wrote** every day.
• Present progressive → past progressive.	She **is writing** a letter. → He said (that) she **was writing** a letter.
• Present perfect → past perfect.	She **has written** many letters. → He said (that) she **had written** many letters.
• Present perfect progressive → past perfect progressive.	**She has been writing** many letters. → He said (that) she **had been writing** many letters.
• Simple past → past perfect.	I **wrote** a letter last week. → He said (that) she **had written** a letter last week.
• Past progressive → past perfect progressive.	She **was writing** a letter this morning. → He said (that) she **had been writing** a letter this morning.

2. However, there is **no** change if the verbs are:

• Past perfect verbs.	He **had traveled** to India before. → She said (that) he **had traveled** to India before.
• In unreal conditionals:	
Present unreal conditionals.	If Ted **loved** Mary, he **would marry** her. → She said (that) if Ted **loved** Mary, he **would marry** her.
Past unreal conditionals.	If Ted **had loved** Mary, he **would have married** her. → She said (that) if Ted **had loved** Mary, he **would have married** her.

C. Optional Changes in Verb Tense

The verb tense changes mentioned above are **optional** when the reported speech:

• Expresses a general truth.	The earth **revolves** around the sun. → The teacher said (that) the earth **revolved/revolves** around the sun. Hard work **pays off.** → My mom always said (that) hard work **paid/pays off.**
• Expresses a situation that is still true.	Bob **has** a new car. → She said (that) Bob **had/has** a new car.
• Is about future events.	Kirsten **is starting** college in the fall. → She said (that) Kirsten **was starting/is starting** college in the fall.

GRAMMAR PRACTICE 2

Changes in Reported Speech; Verb Tense in Reported Speech

Old Barkley and Mrs. Barkley

John Small

Niles and Victoria Pierson

Background Information for the Mystery Story in Exercises 4–9

On the evening of Monday, May 4, in the dining room of her country mansion, old Mrs. Pierson fell over dead, apparently from a heart attack. Present on the sad occasion were:

- **Old Barkley** and **Mrs. Barkley**, butler and housekeeper to Mrs. Pierson for nearly 50 years.
- **John Small**, house guest, a young man who ran many charities and had become a close friend of Mrs. Pierson's since he met her last year.

The occasion turned from sad to potentially ugly when the doctor examined the dead woman and said he feared that she'd been poisoned. He immediately contacted the police and **Professor Wendell**, a retired history professor whose hobby was solving crimes. He also contacted Mrs. Pierson's nephew, **Niles**, and Niles's wife, **Victoria**.

In working on Exercises 4–9, see if you can arrive at the solution with Professor Wendell. Look for clues and try not to get fooled by red herrings (false clues)!

butler = a male servant in charge of managing a house. *charity* = an organization to help people.

4 Changes in Verb Tense in Reported Speech: The Doctor and the Lawyer Speak

The following quotes are from Professor Wendell's interviews with Mrs. Pierson's doctor and lawyer. Finish changing them to reported speech by filling in the appropriate forms of the verbs. Make all changes, including those that are optional. Where a change is not possible, fill in the verb form given in the original speech.

1. *Doctor*: We have been having flu epidemics here every year, yet I don't remember Mrs. Pierson ever getting sick.

   The doctor said that they had been having flu epidemics there every year yet he didn't remember Mrs. Pierson ever getting sick.

2. *Doctor*: If everyone were that healthy, I would be out of a job.

   He said that if everyone ______________ that healthy, he ______________ out of a job.

3. *Doctor*: She'd been really sick only once—about three months ago, she was getting weaker over a period of several weeks, but then suddenly she recovered.

   He said that she ______________ really sick only once—about three months ago, she ______________ weaker over a period of several weeks but then suddenly she ______________.

4. *Doctor*: Someone poisoned her. I feel sure of it since her health was so good.

   He said that someone ______________ her—that he ______________ sure of it since her health ______________ so good.

5. *Lawyer*: I've been reviewing Mrs. Pierson's will, which she had recently changed.

   The lawyer said that he ______________ Mrs. Pierson's will, which she ______________ recently ______________.

6. *Lawyer*: If she hadn't changed her will, nearly all her money would have gone to her nephew, Niles, and his wife, Victoria.

   He said that if she ______________ her will, nearly all her money ______________ to her nephew, Niles, and his wife, Victoria.

7. *Lawyer*: In the new will, nearly all her money is going to her friend John Small.

   He said that in the new will nearly all her money ______________ to her friend John Small.

8. *Lawyer*: Under both wills, Mr. and Mrs. Barkley receive a cottage and a pension.

   He said that under both wills Mr. and Mrs. Barkley ______________ a cottage and a pension.

cottage = a small house. *pension* = money a person receives when retired.

5 **Optional Changes in Verb Tense:** The Money Angle

In the following statements, tense changes in the underlined verbs are optional. For each statement, decide why the change is optional. Choose one of the following reasons: *a general truth*; *situation still true*; *future event*.

	Original Speech	Reported Speech	
1.	*John Small*: I <u>am not</u> interested in the money for myself but for my charities.	John Small said that he <u>is not</u> interested in the money for himself.	situation still true
2.	*John Small*: Mrs. Pierson's faults? It <u>is</u> unkind for people to speak ill of the dead.	John Small said that it <u>is</u> unkind for people to speak ill of the dead.	______
3.	*Niles Pierson*: In hard times, people <u>spend</u> on necessities, not on things like charity.	Niles Pierson said that in hard times people <u>spend</u> on necessities.	______
4.	*Niles Pierson*: John Small <u>is starting</u> a new charity soon, when he gets Aunt's money.	Niles Pierson said that John Small <u>is starting</u> a new charity soon.	______
5.	*Niles Pierson*: I <u>run</u> a successful art gallery.	Niles Pierson said that he <u>runs</u> a successful art gallery.	______
6.	*Old Barkley*: Next week, we <u>move</u> into our new cottage.	Old Barkley said that next week they <u>move</u> into their new cottage.	______

speak ill of = say bad things about.

GRAMMAR BRIEFING 3

Modals in Reported Speech

FORM

A. Modals That Change Form in Reported Speech

When the verb introducing the reported speech is past tense, many modals change form. These include:

• *Can → could.*	He **can** try it. → She said (that) he **could** try it.
• *May → might.*	He **may** be there now. → She said (that) he **might** be there now.
• *Will → would.*	They **will** go to the theater next week. → She said (that) they **would** go to the theater next week.
• *Have to, must → had to.*	He **must/has to** know the answer. → She said (that) he **had to** know the answer.
• Phrasal modals with *be*, for example: *Am/is/are going to → was/were going to. Am/is/are able to → was/were able to.*	They **are going to** buy a car. → She said (that) they **were going to** buy a car

B. Modals That Do Not Change Form in Reported Speech

Modals that do not change form include:

• *Could, might, should, would, ought to,* and *had better.*	It **might** be too late. → She said (that) it **might** be too late.
• The perfect modals (e.g., *could have, may have, might have, must have, should have, would have*).	They **should have** bought it. → She said (that) they **should have** bought it.

C. Optional Changes in Modals

As with changes in verb tense, the changes in modals are optional when the reported speech:

• Expresses a general truth.	You **have to** have a well-balanced diet to be healthy. → She said (that) you **had to/have to** have a well-balanced diet to be healthy.
• Expresses a situation that is still true.	Megan **can** play the piano well. → She said (that) Megan **could/can** play the piano well.
• Is about the future.	They **will** go to the theater next week. → She said (that) they **will/would** go to the theater next week. They **are going to** buy a car. → She said (that) they **were going to/are going to** buy a car.

GRAMMAR PRACTICE 3

Modals in Reported Speech

6 Changes in Modals in Reported Speech: More Clues Emerge

Finish changing the speech to reported speech by filling in each modal + verb. Make all possible changes. Where a change is not possible, fill in as in the original speech.

1. *Mrs. Barkley*: Finally my husband and I will relax a bit, because people ought to relax when they're old.

   Mrs. Barkley said that finally her husband and she would relax ________ a bit because people ought to relax ________ when they were old.

2. *John Small*: I can't talk now because I have to meet with the director of the orphanage.

   John Small said that he ________________ then because he ________________ with the director of the orphanage.

3. *Police Inspector*: Someone must have poisoned Mrs. Pierson.

   The police inspector said that someone ________________________ Mrs. Pierson.

4. *Police Inspector*: Anyone could be the murderer, so no one should leave.

   He said that anyone ________________ the murderer, so no one ________________.

5. *Lawyer*: As a young man, Niles did some things he shouldn't have done—mainly gambling.

   The lawyer said that, as a young man, Niles had done some things he ________________.

6. *Lawyer*: But now he's quite wonderful. He must be disappointed about his aunt's will, but he didn't complain.

   He said that he ________________ disappointed about his aunt's will but he hadn't complained.

7. *Niles Pierson*: I may talk to a lawyer about the will—but then again I might not since I am able to live well on money from my art gallery.

   Niles Pierson said that he ________________ to a lawyer about the will but that he ________________ not since he ________________ well on money from his art gallery.

GRAMMAR BRIEFING 4

Pronouns and Time and Place Expressions in Reported Speech

Pronouns in Reported Speech

FORM

A. Changes in Subject, Object, and Reflexive Pronouns and Possessives

Reported speech often requires changes in:

- Subject, object, and reflexive pronouns.
- Possesive pronouns and possessive determiners.

The changes occur when the speaker(s) and/or listener(s) are not those of the original speech.

Original speech:
Abby: **I**'m not going to do **your** work for **you**.
Phil: **I**'ll do it **myself**.

Reported by Phil: Abby said (that) **she** wasn't going to do **my** work for **me**. I said (that) **I**'d do it **myself**.

Reported by Ben: Abby told Phil (that) **she** wasn't going to do **his** work for **him**. He said (that) **he**'d do it **himself**.

B. Changes in Demonstratives

Demonstratives often change, especially for objects that were nearby during the original speech but are not nearby during the reported speech.

I've read **this** (book). → She said (that) she'd read **that** book.

I've read **those** (books). → She said (that) she'd read **those** books.

Time and Place Expressions in Reported Speech

FORM

A. Changes in Time Expressions

1. Time expressions often change when the time of the original and reported speech differ.

Original speech, Sunday: My sister is coming **today** to stay with me for a while.

The next week: Sara said (that) her sister was coming **last Sunday** to stay with her for a while.

2. Common changes include:
   - *Now → then.*
   - *Today → that day, then.*
   - *Tomorrow → the next day.*
   - *Yesterday → the day before.*
   - *Next week → the following week.*

It's starting **now.** → He said (that) it was starting **then.**

I saw her **yesterday**. → He said (that) he had seen her **the day before**.

(continued on next page)

A. Changes in Time Expressions (continued)

3. There are many different possibilities, depending on when the reported speech occurs.	*Monday*: The exam is **two weeks from today.** *Later that day*: The teacher said (that) the exam is **two weeks from today.** *The next day*: The teacher said (that) the exam is **two weeks from yesterday.** *One week later*: The teacher said (that) the exam is **next Monday.**

B. Changes in Place Expressions

Place expressions often change when the place of the original and reported speech differ. Common changes include: • *Here* → *there* (*at school, in Chicago, etc.*). • *There* → *here* (*at school, in Chicago, etc.*).	I'll meet you **here.** → She said (that) she would meet me **there/in her office.** I'll be **there** soon. → She said (that) she would be **here/at school** soon.

GRAMMAR PRACTICE 4

Pronouns and Time and Place Expressions in Reported Speech

7 Changes in Pronouns in Reported Speech: Poisoned Grape Juice?

Professor Wendell's assistant has conducted some interviews and is reporting to the professor. Complete the speech as reported by the assistant to the professor by filling in the pronouns. Where no change is needed, fill in the pronoun from the original speech.

1. *Wendell's assistant*: I would like to hear about anything you or your husband remember only Mrs. Pierson eating or drinking.

   I told Mrs. Barkley that ___I___ would like to hear about anything ___she___ or ___her___ husband remembered only Mrs. Pierson eating or drinking.

2. *Mrs. Barkley*: Oh! Mrs. Pierson never had dinner without her special organic grape juice from Switzerland, and she never let us or anyone else touch a drop.

   Mrs. Barkley said that Mrs. Pierson had never had dinner without ________ special organic grape juice from Switzerland and ________ had never let ________ or anyone else touch a drop.

3. *Mrs. Barkley*: So, when Mrs. Pierson asked me, I poured it for her myself from this very same bottle that I am showing you.

   Mrs. Barkley told me that when Mrs. Pierson asked ______________, ______________ had poured ______________ for ______________ ______________ from ______________ very same bottle that ______________ was showing ______________.

4. *Old Barkley*: You mean when Mrs. Pierson *ordered* you—she wasn't very polite to us; we put up with a lot from her.

   Mr. Barkley told his wife that ______________ meant when Mrs. Pierson had *ordered* ______________—that ______________ hadn't been very polite to ______________ and ______________ had put up with a lot from ______________.

5. *Mrs. Barkley*: I got a new bottle that night from a locked pantry that can be opened only with my key.

   Mrs. Barkley said that ______________ had gotten a new bottle ______________ night from a locked pantry that could be opened only with ______________ key.

6. *Mrs. Barkley*: Oh, no! You'd better call the professor. You need to tell him something important: The new bottle of grape juice had already been opened.

   Mrs. Barkley cried out to me that ______________ had better call ______________ and that ______________ needed to tell ______________ something important: The new bottle of grape juice had already been opened.

8 Changes in Time and Place Words in Reported Speech: Getting at the When and Where of It

The assistant is reporting to Professor Wendell about other interviews. Read the information about the times and places of this report and the interviews. Then complete the reported speech by filling in time and place words. Make appropriate changes (some words can be changed in several ways). If no change is needed, fill in the words as they appear in the original speech.

Item 1: The assistant interviewed John Small on **Tuesday, May 6**, at the **country mansion**. He is reporting this interview to Professor Wendell on **Wednesday, May 7**, in the **city**.

1. *John Small*: I was here all last weekend and then returned last night for dinner.

   John Small said that he had been <u>there</u> all <u>last weekend</u> and then had returned <u>Monday night</u> for dinner.

Items 2–4: The assistant interviewed Victoria Pierson on **Tuesday, May 6**, at the **country mansion**. He is reporting this interview to Professor Wendell on **Wednesday, May 7**, in the **city**.

2. *Victoria Pierson*: My husband and I were here for the weekend and then returned to the city Sunday night after dinner.

   Victoria Pierson said that she and her husband had been ________________ for the weekend and then had returned ________________ ________________ after dinner.

3. *Victoria Pierson*: We came back this morning as soon as we heard she had died.

   Victoria Pierson said that they had come back ________________________________ as soon as they'd heard she had died.

4. *Victoria Pierson*: Niles had to leave this evening because he has some important meeting about the gallery tomorrow, but I've stayed until now.

   She said that Niles had had to leave ________________________________ because he had some important meeting about the gallery ________________________ but that she had stayed until ________________________________.

Item 5: The assistant interviewed Niles Pierson **just now**, on **Wednesday, May 7**, in the **city**. He is reporting this interview to Professor Wendell on **Wednesday, May 7**, in the **city**.

5. *Niles*: I have a meeting in a few minutes, so I can't talk now, but everything seemed fine there Sunday evening, although when I came back from my walk they'd been looking for a thief.

   Niles said that he has a meeting in a few minutes so he can't talk ________________ but that everything had seemed fine ________________ ________________________.

9 Changes That Occur in Reported Speech: Putting It All Together

A. Rewrite the sentences as speech that is reported by someone else at a later time in a different place. Make all possible changes.

1. *Professor Wendell*: It may be important for us to learn more about the man in the garden.

   Professor Wendell said that it might be important for them to learn more about the man in the garden.

2. *Mrs. Barkley*: After dinner Victoria Pierson was helping me put things away in the pantry.

   Mrs. Barkley said that ____

   ____.

3. *Victoria Pierson*: Suddenly I saw someone creeping behind the bushes and I screamed.

   Victoria Pierson said that ____

   ____.

4. *Mrs. Barkley*: I ran into the garden, but I wasn't able to get a good look at him.

   Mrs. Barkley said that ____

   ____.

5. *Old Barkley*: Later that evening we looked through the house, but nothing seemed to be missing.

   Old Barkley said that ____

   ____.

6. *Police Officer (to Police Inspector, showing him a small bottle)*: We've just now found a bottle of nitroglycerin.

   The police officer told the police inspector that ______________________________

   ____.

7. *Police Inspector*: If a person takes too much nitroglycerin, it can cause death.

   The police inspector said that ______________________________________

   ____.

8. *Police Officer*: We found it in the trash can in the bedroom that Mr. Small has been using.

   The police officer said that ______________________________________

   ____.

B. 1. Who murdered Mrs. Pierson? Work in a small group. Look for clues in Exercises 4–9. You might want to take notes on a piece of paper. Discuss why and how the various characters might have murdered Mrs. Pierson. Use reported speech to talk about the evidence.

Example: The Barkleys might have murdered Mrs. Pierson. Mr. Barkley said that they had put up with a lot from Mrs. Pierson and that she wasn't very polite to them.

2. As a group, decide who you think murdered Mrs. Pierson. Write down your solution and explanation, and tell the class what you decided. Then turn to page A-4 for Professor Wendell's solution.

10 Relationship Between Original and Reported Speech: What Exactly Did They Say?

Listen to each conversation twice. The second speaker uses reported speech. Decide what the original speaker said. Circle *a* or *b*.

1. (a.) Marcia said, "He's doing fine."
   b. Marcia said, "He was doing fine."
2. a. Shana's sister said, "Shana is going to move back here in the fall."
   b. Shana's sister said, "Shana was going to move back here in the fall."

3. a. Brad said, "We might sell all the tickets."
   b. Brad said, "We might have sold all the tickets."
4. a. Lee said, "I'll be here tonight."
   b. Lee said, "I'll be there tomorrow night."
5. a. Heather said, "I don't want to speak to her anymore."
   b. Heather said, "She doesn't want to speak to me anymore."
6. a. Maria said, "I teach Spanish."
   b. Maria said, "I taught Spanish."
7. a. Ilya said, "I'll lend it to you."
   b. Ilya said, "I would lend it to you."
8. a. Paul said, "If I started my own business, I would hire you."
   b. Paul said, "If I had started my own business, I would have hired you."

GRAMMAR BRIEFING 5

Reported Questions, Commands, and Requests

Reported Questions

FORM and FUNCTION

A. Clauses for *Wh-* and *Yes/No* Reported Questions

1. Like statements, questions are reported in noun clauses. All the changes for reported speech discussed in Grammar Briefings 2–4 apply to reported questions.	Were **you here last night**? → She asked **if/whether I had been there Friday night.** (noun clause)
2. To report *wh-* questions, use *wh-* noun clauses.* (See Chapter 20, Grammar Briefing 3, page 394.)	When does the next train come? → He asked **when the next train comes.** What are you reading? → He asked **what I was reading.**
3. To report *yes/no* questions use *if/whether* noun clauses.* (See Chapter 20, Grammar Briefing 4, page 397.)	Is the train here yet? → He asked **if/whether the train was here yet.** Is your book good? → He asked **if/whether my book was good.**

*Remember! *Wh-* and *if/whether* noun clauses have statement word order.

(continued on next page)

B. Verbs to Introduce Reported Questions

1. Reported questions are usually introduced by *ask*. *Ask* may be followed by a noun phrase.	Where are you going? → He **asked** (**me**) where I was going.
2. The expression *want to know* can also be used to introduce reported questions. *Wonder* can be used, too, especially for thoughts.	He **wanted to know** where I was going. He **wondered** where I was going.

Reported Commands and Requests

FORM and FUNCTION

A. Overview of Reported Commands and Requests

Commands and requests are reported using **infinitives**, not noun clauses. Reported commands and requests have the same changes in pronouns and time and place expressions as other reported speech (see Grammar Briefing 4, page 412).	*Command*: Sit down! → He said **to sit down.** *Request*: Could **you** help **me tomorrow**? → He asked **me** to help **him today**.

B. Reported Commands

1. Reported commands are introduced by *tell* + noun phrase, *say*, or *ask* + noun phrase.	She **told us** / **said** / **asked us** to go.
2. If the command is a negative, put *not* before the *to* of the infinitive.	**Don't go** yet. → She told us **not to go** yet.

C. Reported Requests

1. Reported requests are introduced by *ask* + noun phrase.	Could you give me a ride? → He **asked us** to give him a ride.
2. You can also report a request in an *if/whether* noun clause with a modal.	He asked (us) **if** we **could** give him a ride.

GRAMMAR PRACTICE 5

Reported Questions, Commands, and Requests

11 Reported Questions: Brainstorming

The students in Mrs. Blair's English class met in groups to brainstorm questions for a paper about reading. Carrie is reporting to the class about her group's questions. Rewrite the speech as questions reported by Carrie. Make all possible changes.

1. *Angela*: What kinds of books do people like to read? (ask)
   Angela asked what kinds of books people liked to read.
2. Paul: Do more men or women buy books? (want to know)
   ____
   ____
3. *Tim*: How many books does the average person in the United States read each year? (want to know)
   ____
   ____
4. *Carrie*: Can reading books change people's lives? (wonder)
   ____
   ____
5. *Tanya*: Have people been reading fewer books because of TV and the Internet? (wonder)
   ____
   ____
6. *Paul*: What reasons do people give for reading books? (ask)
   ____
   ____
7. *Angela*: Will children who read a lot continue to read a lot when they are adults? (wonder)
   ____
   ____
8. *Carrie*: What can be done to encourage people to read more? (ask)
   ____
   ____

brainstorm = come up with ideas, especially in a group.

Go to the *Grammar Links* Website to find out more about reading habits.

12 Reported Commands and Requests: She Told Us to Write

David is in Carrie's group but was absent yesterday, so Carrie is telling him what happened. Rewrite the speech as commands and requests reported by Carrie. Include the original listener if given in parentheses. Rewrite requests in two ways. Make all possible changes.

1. *Mrs. Blair* (to Carrie): Could you tell David about everything we discussed today? (ask)

   Mrs. Blair asked me to tell you about everything we discussed yesterday.

   Mrs. Blair asked me if I could tell you about everything we discussed yesterday.
2. *Mrs. Blair* (to class): Write a paper on a topic related to reading books. (tell)

   Mrs. Blair told us to write a paper on a topic related to reading books.
3. *Mrs. Blair* (to class): First think about questions you have about reading. (tell)
4. *Mrs. Blair* (to class): Could you help me get everyone started by sharing your questions with each other? (ask)
5. *Mrs. Blair*: Use the questions for ideas about topics. (say)
6. *Mrs. Blair* (to class): Don't use just your own ideas for this paper. (tell)
7. *Mrs. Blair*: Work on the paper in groups. (say)
8. *Tanya and Paul* (to Carrie): Could you and David do some research for the paper? (ask)
9. *Tanya and Paul* (to Carrie): Will you and David also edit the final paper? (ask)
10. *Mrs. Blair* (to class): Don't write more than five pages because I don't want to have too much reading to do. (tell)

13 Using Noun Clauses and Reported Speech: A Survey About Reading

A. Work with a partner. Ask your partner the following questions, and write down your partner's answers.

1. Do you read more often for information, more often for pleasure, or equally for both reasons?
2. Do you read more often in English or in another language?
3. What have you been reading lately (fiction books, textbooks and other nonfiction books, newspapers, magazines, comic books, other)?
4. Where and when do you read (on the bus? in the library? on weekends? in the evening? before going to bed? other?)?
5. When you were a child, did you read more or less than you do now?
6. Would you like to spend more time reading? Why or why not?

B. Join with two other pairs. Report on some of the questions you asked and on your partner's answers. Use some of the following verbs: *ask, add, admit, answer, comment, explain, mention, say, tell, think*.

Example: I asked Betty whether she reads more often for information or for pleasure. She said she reads more for information. She explained that she has been reading lots of magazine articles about taking care of babies. . . .

Discuss the questions and answers as a group. Were people's answers similar or different?

C. Write a paragraph about the reading habits of people you surveyed. You can either write about the people in your group or use the questions to survey other people. Tell about what, why, when, and how much people read. Use noun clauses with reported speech.

Example: The people I surveyed have very different reading habits. Some people said that they read a lot. Other people said that they didn't read much or that they just read things for work or school. One woman said that she wanted to read more but never had enough time. . . .

See the *Grammar Links* Website for a complete model paragraph for this assignment.

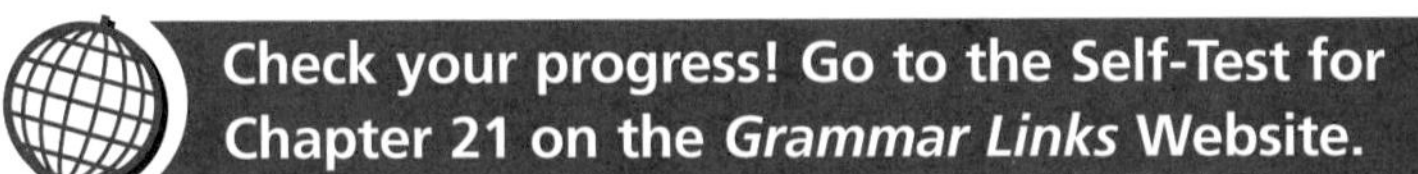

Check your progress! Go to the Self-Test for Chapter 21 on the *Grammar Links* Website.

Wrap-up Activities

1 The Business of Romance Fiction: EDITING

Correct the 12 errors in the passage. There are errors in noun clauses and in quoted and reported speech. Some errors can be corrected in more than one way. The first error is corrected for you.

For my assignment, I decided to interview Alexa Smith, president of Forever Yours Publishers. I wondered ~~that~~ whether I could get an interview with her, because I know that she's very busy. I was surprised at that her secretary said there would be no problem.

As soon as I met Ms. Smith, I told to her how much I enjoy reading Forever Yours romances. I added that I had a whole bookcase of them and asked if this was unusual. She answered that some women bought every Forever Yours romance that was published. Then she told me to don't be shy about asking my questions.

I started by asking Ms. Smith how did she decide which books to publish. Computer analyses could be useful seemed obvious to me, so I asked her whether she used computers. Ms. Smith replied that she preferred to use Madge. She explained me that Madge was a secretary who always guessed right about if a book would be a success.

I asked her whether she read manuscripts by first-time writers. She told me that she has just looked at one. It began like this: "Oh, Uncle, if you had come into my life years ago, I wouldn't have been alone." Maggie said. According to Ms. Smith, after that first line she wasn't sure if to read any more. But she pointed out that some inexperienced writers had become very successful. For this reason, she always tells her workers that they had to read each manuscript. After this, Ms. Smith ended the interview by giving me a copy of the latest Forever Yours romance.

2 A ________ Story: SPEAKING/WRITING

Step 1 Work with a partner. Read the paragraphs and think about what kind of story they might be the beginning of. Use noun clauses in discussing your ideas.

Step 2 Complete the sentences with quoted speech, reported speech, and other noun clauses, as appropriate. Then read your paragraphs to the class.

All night long, I'd been unable to sleep because I was thinking about ____. I was worried ____. Now the phone was ringing, and I knew ________________________________. I picked it up. As I'd expected, it was Craig. I wondered ________________________________.

"____?" I asked.

"____," he answered.

________________________________ was obvious to me. Craig said that it was urgent ________________________________. And he told me not ________________________________. Trying hard to control my voice, I asked him ________________________________, but he had hung up. For the first time, I realized ________________________________. I could only hope ________________________________.

3 Reporting a Scene: WRITING

Step 1 Watch a TV show or a video. You can watch a movie or any kind of show in which people are talking—a comedy, a drama, a talk show, etc. While you are watching the movie or show, choose a scene or a part of a scene that is about three to five minutes long to tell the class about using reported speech. Take notes on what the people say. Don't write everything down—just a few things that are important—and don't try to write down the exact words. If you are watching a video, you can watch the scene again.

Step 2 When the show is finished, use your notes to write a paragraph. In your first two or three sentences, tell what the show was about. Then use reported speech to tell about the scene.

Example: In the movie I saw, a man wanted to marry a woman he didn't love. She was plain and clumsy, but she had a lot of money. In one scene, she spilled coffee all over the rug and said that she was sorry. He said that it didn't matter because only she mattered. He added that he had something to ask her. He wanted to ask her to marry him, but he couldn't quite manage to. So he asked her what time it was. Then he asked her if she'd like more coffee. Finally, he asked her if she would marry him. She answered that she would.

4 Write Your Own Story: SPEAKING/WRITING

Step 1 Work in a small group. Write a one-page story—a romance, science-fiction, horror, or mystery story or any other kind of story. You can use one of the beginnings below or make up your own beginning. Plan and discuss your story carefully before you start writing. Who are your characters? What happens and what will they do? How will the story end?

Step 2 Write your story. Include *that, wh-,* and *if/whether* noun clauses, quoted speech (start a new paragraph each time a different character speaks), and reported speech. When you have written your story, read it to the class.

A.

The big house on the hill had been empty for longer than anyone could remember. It was overgrown with plants, and its broken shutters banged in the wind. The people in town all avoided the house. They said it had a terrible secret. But no one seemed to know what that secret was. One day in late summer, my brother and I decided to find out. . . .

B.

We were driving home from a movie late one night when we saw it. Edgar saw it first and pointed it out to us. Al brought the car to a screeching stop.

"It's just a weird plane," I said. "It's just some plane from the Air Force base."

But I knew that wasn't true. As we watched, the strangely lit disk became larger and brighter. With a whirring noise, it touched down in the cornfield. . . .

C.

Miss Watson looked like a sweet old lady. But everyone knew that she was a great detective—capable of outwitting the most brilliant criminal minds. Mrs. Astor called her as soon as she discovered that someone had replaced her priceless jewels with clever fakes.

"The insurance men said they'll pay, but I don't care about money," Mrs. Astor said. "You must help me get my jewels back."

"I'll do my best, dear," Miss Watson replied, and she hopped on a bus to Mrs. Astor's place. . . .

D.

It was Friday night, and Ana was home again. Ana wondered why she was always stuck at home every weekend. She didn't really feel like reading or watching TV. She wished that her phone would ring and someone would ask her out. Ana thought about that new boy, Kurt.

"But he'll figure out who the popular kids are," Ana thought. "And he'll hang out with them."

Just then, the phone rang. . . .

See the *Grammar Links* Website for a complete model story.

Unit **Eleven**

Adverb Clauses; Connecting Ideas

TOPIC FOCUS

Advertising and Consumer Behavior

UNIT OBJECTIVES

- **subordinating conjunctions**
  (*Before* I buy a computer, I'm going to get some advice.)
- **adverb clauses**
  (*Before I buy a computer*, I'm going to get some advice.)
- **coordinating conjunctions**
  (Some commercials are entertaining, *but* this one is annoying.)
- **transitions**
  (The company wanted to know people's opinions. *Therefore*, it conducted a survey.)

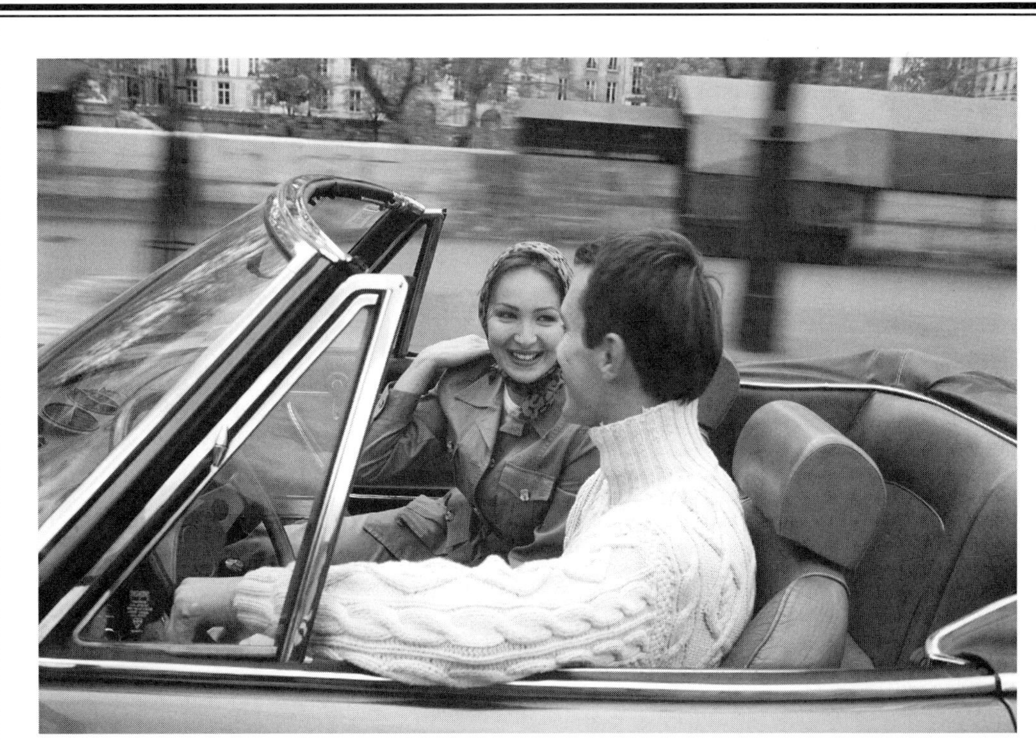

This car will change your life.

Grammar in Action

Reading and Listening: Watch Ads

Read and listen to these advertisements.

A

Ruben Valas is an artist. He has never followed the crowd. He never will.

Ruben chose the Individualist **because** it expresses his unique personal style.

Ruben's passion for creating new art forms never leaves him. **After** he spends the day painting in his studio, he moves on to composing experimental music.

Although Ruben's life is complex, his watch is simple.

The Individualist is simply the most innovative and stylish timepiece in the world.

B

Joyce Bailey explores the deepest oceans, **and** she climbs the highest mountains.

Joyce needs a durable, accurate watch, **so** she wears the Adventurer.

Joyce's days are filled with the most extreme physical and mental challenges. In the evening, she writes books about her explorations and figures out new worlds to explore.

Joyce's life is complex, **but** her watch is simple.

The Adventurer is simply the toughest and most accurate timepiece in the world.

C

Edgar Ross is an investment banker. **Furthermore**, he is a director of one of the largest companies in the world.

Edgar wants a watch that reflects the importance of his position. **Therefore**, he wears the Prestige.

Edgar's typical day is a whirlwind of meetings and decision making. **Afterward**, in the evening, he usually attends a charity event.

Edgar's life is complex. His watch, **however**, is simple.

The Prestige is simply the most elegant and precise timepiece in the world.

passion = strong enthusiasm. *experimental* = having a new or unusual form. *innovative* = newly introduced and different. *timepiece* = watch. *durable* = strong and long-lasting. *whirlwind* = busy rush. *charity event* = party given to raise money to help people.

Think About Grammar

A. Connectors connect ideas. Types of connectors include **subordinating conjunctions** (as in advertisement A), **coordinating conjunctions** (as in B), and **transitions** (as in C).

Look at these sentences from the advertisements. Write the ideas that each boldfaced connector connects. Answer the question that follows.

Ruben chose the Individualist **because** it expresses his unique personal style. (subordinating connector)

Ruben chose the Individualist. ____ It expresses his unique personal style.

Joyce needs a durable, accurate watch, **so** she wears the Adventurer. (coordinating connector)

____

____

Edgar wants a watch that reflects the importance of his position. **Therefore**, he wears the Prestige. (transition)

____

____

Which kind of connector is connecting ideas that are expressed in separate sentences: the coordinating connector, the subordinating connector, or the transition?

____

B. Connectors express different types of relationships between ideas—for example, of addition, reason, contrast, and time. Each type of relationship can be expressed by connectors of different types: subordinating connectors, coordinating connectors, and transitions.

Look at the boldfaced connectors in the advertisements. Use them to complete the sentences.

1. **Addition connectors** show that an idea adds more, similar information. Examples of addition connectors are and ________ and ________.
2. **Reason connectors** and **result connectors** show that one idea gives the reason for or the result of another idea. Examples of reason and result connectors are ________ , ________ , and ________.
3. **Contrast or opposition connectors** show that two ideas are different or opposites in some way. Examples of contrast or opposition connectors are ________, ________, and ________.
4. **Time connectors** show the time relationship between two ideas or events. Examples of time connectors are ________ and ________.

Chapter 22

Adverb Clauses

Introductory Task: A Questionnaire on Advertising and Your Buying Behavior

A. Mark the box that indicates your level of agreement with each of the following statements.

1. Since I see and hear so many advertisements, I don't pay much attention to them.

   ❑ Strongly agree ❑ Somewhat agree ❑ Disagree

2. I often decide to buy a product because I've seen an advertisement for it.

   ❑ Strongly agree ❑ Somewhat agree ❑ Disagree

3. Although a few television commercials are memorable, I usually forget most of them in a short time.

   ❑ Strongly agree ❑ Somewhat agree ❑ Disagree

4. When a celebrity (e.g., a sports or television star) is in a commercial for a product, I am more likely to want to buy that product.

   ❑ Strongly agree ❑ Somewhat agree ❑ Disagree

5. When a new product comes out, I usually don't try it right away. I wait until other people have tried it and ask them for advice.

   ❑ Strongly agree ❑ Somewhat agree ❑ Disagrec

6. I buy some products because they give people prestige.

   ❑ Strongly agree ❑ Somewhat agree ❑ Disagree

prestige = qualities that bring admiration or honor.

B. Work in a small group. Compare your responses to the statements in Part A. Did anyone else in the group give responses similar to yours?

C. In your group, discuss your reactions to television commercials. Which ones do you like? Which do you hate? Which ones are entertaining? Which ones are annoying? Which ones are especially informative, persuasive, or memorable? Why? In your discussion, use sentences with *because*.

Example: I like that fast-food commercial with the little dog because the dog is really cute.
OR I hate car dealers' commercials because the announcers talk so loud and fast.

GRAMMAR BRIEFING 1

Adverb Clauses

FORM and FUNCTION

A. Sentences with Adverb Clauses

MAIN CLAUSE	ADVERB CLAUSE			
	SUBORDINATING CONJUCTION	SUBJECT	VERB	
Sara had to leave	**because**	**her class**	**was starting**	**in a few minutes.**

1. An adverb clause must occur in a sentence with a main clause. It cannot stand alone.

   main clause / adverb clause
   He stays late **because he is the manager**.
   NOT: He stays late. ~~Because he is the manager.~~

2. An adverb clause begins with a subordinating conjunction (e.g., *although, because, if, when*).

   Call me **if** you need me.
   He visits us **while** he's in town.

3. Like all clauses, an adverb clause has a subject and a verb.

   subject / verb
   They finished before **they went** to lunch.

4. Most adverb clauses can come before or after the main clause. Use a comma between clauses when the adverb clause comes first.

   We will start the meeting **when he comes.**
   When he comes, we will start the meeting.

B. Use of Adverb Clauses

Adverbs clauses function like adverbs. They modify the verb in the main clause, or they modify the entire main clause. They answer questions like *when* and *why.*

They worked on the project **before he arrived.** (tells when they worked)

She was late **because the traffic was bad.** (tells why she was late)

GRAMMAR PRACTICE 1

Adverb Clauses

1 Identifying Adverb Clauses: The Research Behind the Advertising

The following passage contains six adverb clauses, including the example. Read the passage. Underline each adverb clause and circle its subordinating conjunction. (Remember: A clause has a subject and a verb.)

Before they try to sell a product, advertisers need to know which group of consumers would be most likely to buy it. Advertisers call these consumers the "target market" for the product. The target market for a product may be very large (e.g., the market for snack foods) or relatively small (e.g., the market for luxury cars). Because they want to advertise effectively, advertisers do a great deal of research on the consumers in the target market. They try to find out about the consumers' habits, interests, opinions, and buying behavior.

Advertisers use various techniques to get information from and about consumers. When consumers buy a product, they are often asked to fill out a questionnaire. They are asked to comment on products or advertisements in telephone surveys or in group interviews. Advertisers also interview or observe consumers while they are shopping. Although consumers may not be aware of it, advertisers gather data about their Internet shopping habits, too. After advertisers have collected all this information, they analyze it. Then they make decisions about products and advertising.

consumer = person who buys and uses a product. *data* = pieces of information.

GRAMMAR BRIEFING 2

Types of Adverb Clauses I

FORM and FUNCTION

A. Adverb Clauses of Time

1. Adverb clauses of time tell when the action or state in the main clause occurs.
   (See Chapter 2, Grammar Briefing 3, page 31, and Chapter 5, Grammar Briefing 2, page 86, for tenses in time clauses.)

   He moved to California **after he graduated from college**.

2. Subordinating conjunctions used in time clauses include *after*, *before*, *since*, *when*, *until*, *while*, and:
   - *As*, which means "when, while, at the same time."
     I looked up **as** he was coming into the room.
   - *As long as*, which means "during an entire period of time."
     I've known him **as long as** I can remember.
   - *As soon as*, which means "right after."
     We rushed over **as soon as** we heard the news.
   - *Once*, which means "(right) after."
     Once you explained the problem to me, I understood.
   - *Whenever*, which means "at any or all times."
     Call me **whenever** you need me.

B. Adverb Clauses of Condition

Adverb clauses of condition give the condition for the result in the main clause.
(For sentences with these clauses, see Unit 9.)

If you advertise your car in the newspaper, you'll sell it in no time.

C. Adverb Clauses of Reason

1. Adverb clauses of reason express a cause for the action or state in the main clause.

   Let's take a taxi **since we're in a hurry**. (Being in a hurry is a cause for taking a taxi.)

2. Subordinating conjunctions used include *because*, *since*, and *as*. All have the same meaning, but *because* and *since* are more common than *as*.

   Because/Since/As apartments cost a lot to rent, I'll have to find some roommates.

GRAMMAR PRACTICE 2

Types of Adverb Clauses I

2 Adverb Clauses of Time: New Products and Consumer Behavior

A. Use the subordinating conjunction in parentheses to combine the pairs of sentences in brackets into one sentence containing an adverb clause of time. Use the sentences in the order in which they are given. Use commas where needed.

352 Market Research Chapter 22

Innovators (2.5%) ↓ Early adopters (13.5%) } Opinion leaders
↓
Other consumers (68%)
↓
Laggards (16%)

1. [People began doing market research in the 1920s. Advertisers have learned a great deal about how trends spread through a group.] (since)

   Since people began doing market research in the 1920s, advertisers have learned a great deal about how trends spread through a group.

2. [A new product is introduced. Only a few people begin using it.] (when)

   ____

3. Researchers refer to these interested and adventurous people as "innovators." [Innovators try the new product. They hear that it is available.] (as soon as)

   ____

4. [Innovators adopt a new product. Some other people will try it.] (once)

   ____

5. Researchers refer to these people as the "early adopters" of the product. [The innovators and early adopters accept the product. They become "opinion leaders" for other people.] (after)

   ____

6. [Other consumers try the product. They usually ask an opinion leader for information and advice about it.] (before)

   ____

Chapter 22 Market Research 353

7. Researchers refer to people who remain uninterested in the product as "laggards." [Laggards may never adopt the product. They live.] (as long as)

____

____

8. Innovators and early adopters often pay attention to advertising for certain new products. [Advertisers introduce new products. They want these opinion leaders to notice the products.] (whenever)

____

____

9. Opinion leaders have more influence on other consumers than advertising does. [Advertisers must think about these opinion leaders. They are planning their advertising strategies.] (as)

____

____

10. If opinion leaders do not accept a product, it probably won't be successful. For example, in Norway, opinion leaders had a negative reaction to microwave ovens. [Microwave ovens were introduced. Only a few Norwegians have started using them.] (since)

____

____

B. The time that it takes for a consumer to try a new product depends on the type of product—that is, a person might be an early adopter for sports equipment or music CDs but a laggard for electronic equipment or new clothing styles.

1. Use your ideas about your buying behavior to complete the following sentences.

1. Before I buy clothes, I usually look at what others in my group are wearing.
2. I didn't buy ______________ until ______________________________.
3. I will buy ______________ as soon as ______________________________.
4. Once someone else has ______________, I ______________________________.
5. My friends ______________________________ whenever they ______________.
6. I've never bought ______________ as long as I ______________________________.
7. As I ______________________________, I get ideas about ______________.

2. Work in a small group. Compare the sentences you wrote. Did anyone write similar sentences?

To learn more about market research and consumer behavior, click on the *Grammar Links* Website.

3 Adverb Clauses of Reason: The Opinions You Trust

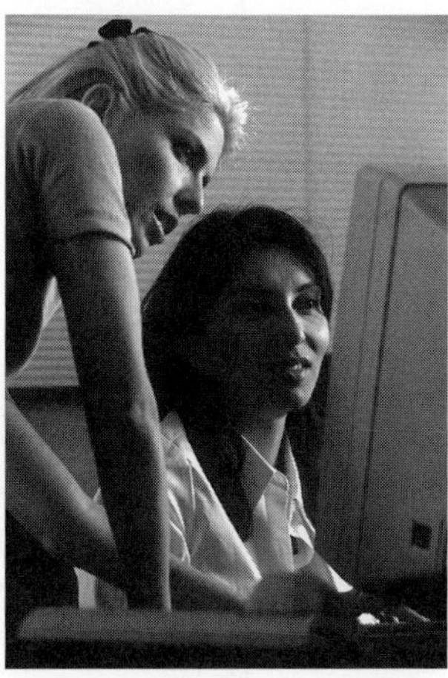

A. Use the subordinating conjunction in parentheses to combine each pair of sentences in two different orders. Use commas where needed.

1. I needed a computer for my school work. I'd been looking at computer ads. (because)

   I'd been looking at computer ads because I needed a computer for my school work.

   Because I needed a computer for my school work, I'd been looking at computer ads.

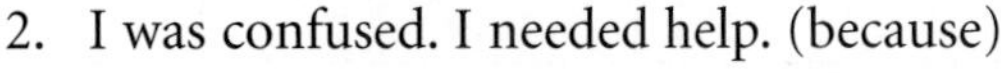

2. I was confused. I needed help. (because)

   ____

   ____

3. I asked a friend for advice. Computers are so expensive. (since)

   ____

   ____

4. Lots of her friends trust her opinion. She is an expert. (as)

   ____

   ____

B. Use your own ideas about the opinions you trust to complete the sentences.

1. Because I wanted ____________________, I ____________________.
2. I asked ____________________ since ____________________.
3. As my friend ____________________, I ____________________.

4 Using Adverb Clauses of Time and Reason: Enter the Contest!

A. Imagine that you bought one of the watches—the Individualist, the Adventurer, or the Prestige—shown in the advertisements on page 426. Now the advertiser is having a contest. Contestants must write a paragraph about their watch; the best paragraphs will be used in future ads. Write a paragraph about your watch and why you like it. In your paragraph, use at least two adverb clauses of time and two adverb clauses of reason.

Example: Since I wanted a sports watch, I decided to buy the Adventurer. I've been very satisfied with it because it has everything I want in a watch. For one thing, it's accurate. As long as I'm wearing it, I don't need to worry about being late. Also, because it's so stylish, all my friends admire it. As soon as they see it, they want one just like it. . . .

See the *Grammar Links* Website for a complete model paragraph for this assignment.

B. Read your paragraph to the class. Which paragraphs do you think the advertiser will want to use in future advertisements? Why? Use adverb clauses of reason in your discussion.

GRAMMAR BRIEFING 3

Types of Adverb Clauses II

FORM and FUNCTION

A. Adverb Clauses of Contrast and Opposition

1. Adverb clauses of contrast and opposition express content that:	
• Contrasts with the content of the main clause.	**While some people like coffee**, others like tea. (contrast between two groups of people)
• Makes the content of the main clause surprising or unexpected.	They closed the business **even though it was doing well**. (The fact of doing well makes the closing surprising.)
2. Subordinating conjunctions used in clauses of contrast and opposition include *while* and *although*, *though*, and *even though*.	**While** I don't agree with you, I'm not going to interfere. **Although/Though/Even though** she wasn't prepared, she took the exam.
3. Clauses with *although*, *though*, and *even though* can occur before or after the main clause.	**Even though** I just ate, I'm hungry. I'm hungry **even though** I just ate.
Clauses with *while* can always come before the main clause. They can come after the main clause only when the adverb clause contrasts with the main clause (**not** when it makes the main clause surprising or unexpected). Use a comma between the clauses even when a clause with *while* comes after the main clause.	**While** some hate the movie, others like it. = Some like the movie, **while** others hate it. (adverb clause contrasts with main clause) **While** I wasn't very interested in the movie, I decided to see it. **NOT**: I decided to see the movie, ~~while I wasn't very interested in it~~. (adverb clause makes main clause surprising)

(continued on next page)

B. Adverb Clauses of Purpose

1. Adverb clauses of purpose express the purpose of the action in the main clause.	Let's take a taxi **so we can save time.** (Saving time is the result we want to get by taking a taxi.)
2. *So* (*that*) is used as a subordinating conjunction.	Do your work now **so/so that** we can go to a movie this evening.
3. The main clause comes before the adverb clause of purpose.	He's coming over **so that we can talk.** **NOT:** ~~So that we can talk,~~ he's coming over.
4. Adverb clauses of purpose usually include modals:	
• *Can* or *will*, if the main clause has a present tense verb.	I get up at six o'clock every morning so (that) I **can/will** get to work on time.
• *Could* or *would*, if the main clause has a past tense verb.	I got up at six o'clock this morning so (that) I **could/would** get to work on time.

GRAMMAR HOTSPOT!

Some subordinating conjunctions are used in more than one type of adverb clause. These include *as*, *since*, and *while*.	Lots of people shop at that store **since** its prices are so good. (reason) I've been shopping there **since** I moved to the neighborhood. (time)

GRAMMAR PRACTICE 3

Types of Adverb Clauses II

5 Adverb Clauses of Contrast and Opposition: Escape to the Mall

Use the subordinating conjunction in parentheses to combine each pair of sentences in two different orders. Use commas where needed.

1. We didn't need to buy anything. We went to the shopping mall. (although)

   We went to the shopping mall although we didn't need to buy anything.

   Although we didn't need to buy anything, we went to the shopping mall.

2. He had a lot of homework to do. He came to the mall with us. (although)

____

____

3. We bought snacks at the food court. We had had a big lunch. (even though)

____

____

4. The mall was noisy and crowded. We had a good time. (though)

____

____

6 Using *While* to Show Contrast: Information About Consumers

A. Complete each sentence and then write it in another way.

1. While some people like shopping, others hate it.
   Some people like shopping, while others hate it. OR While some people hate shopping, others like it. OR Some people hate shopping, while others like it.

2. Some people prefer to eat dinner at home, while others prefer to eat dinner _______________ _______________.

   ____

3. Females account for 51.2 percent of the population, while _______________ account for 48.8 percent.

   ____

4. While it takes a short time to decide which brand of toothpaste to buy, it takes _______________ which brand of car to buy.

   ____

   ____

5. While very few people had home computers in the 1970s, _______________ now.

   ____

   ____

B. Use your own ideas about any topic to complete these sentences.

1. Some _______________, while others _______________.
2. While many _______________, a few _______________.

7 Reason Versus Contrast and Opposition: Brand Loyalty

A. Complete each sentence with the correct subordinating conjunction.

Mrs. Meyer is loyal to Dentafresh toothpaste ___because___ (1 because / even though) she likes its flavor. She will buy Dentafresh ______________ (2 because / even though) it's more expensive than the other brands of toothpaste. Another shopper, Mrs. Rossi, isn't loyal to any brand of toothpaste. She bought Glisten yesterday ______________ (3 since / although) her husband doesn't like it. Mrs. Rossi bought Glisten ______________ (4 since / although) it cost less than the other brands of toothpaste.

Mr. Eaton always buys Roma Roast coffee ______________ (5 as / while) he's had good experiences with it. Today his supermarket is out of Roma Roast. ______________ (6 As / While) there are many other brands of coffee at his supermarket, Mr. Eaton won't buy any of them. Mr. Eaton is going to buy Roma Roast ______________ (7 because / even though) he has to drive five miles to another store to get it. Mr. Eaton is very loyal to Roma Roast.

> *brand* = an identifying name on a product. *brand loyalty* = a consumer's tendency to keep buying a certain brand of a product.

B. Use your own ideas about different products and brands to complete the sentences.

1. Though ______________________ is expensive, I ______________________.
2. Because ______________________ is expensive, I ______________________.
3. I usually buy ______________________ because ______________________.
4. I usually buy ______________________ even though ______________________.
5. I don't like ______________________ because ______________________.
6. I don't like ______________________ although ______________________.

8 Adverb Clauses of Purpose: The Psychology of Buying

A. Use *so (that)* to combine each pair of sentences into one sentence with an adverb clause of purpose. Use *can* or *could* for ability. Otherwise, use *will* or *would*. Delete words as necessary.

1. We buy products. We want to be able to fulfill our various needs and desires.
   We buy products so (that) we can fulfill our various needs and desires.
2. Consumers buy food. They want to be able to satisfy a basic survival need.
   ____
   ____
3. People buy some products. They want to stay safe and healthy.
   ____
   ____
4. Scott and Martha bought a car seat. They wanted to be able to protect their baby from injury in an accident.
   ____
   ____
5. People buy some things. They want other people to accept or admire them.
   ____
   ____
6. Jay drove a luxury car. He wanted other people to know that he had achieved financial success.
   ____
   ____
7. Dolores always wore an unusual style of clothing. She wanted to be able to express her individuality.
   ____
   ____

fulfill = satisfy. *individuality* = the qualities that make someone different from others.

B. 1. Use your own ideas to complete the sentences for a market research survey.

1. I wear certain styles of clothing so that ______________________________.
2. I ______________________________ so that I will be healthy.
3. I ______________________________ so that I could ______________________________.
4. I ______________________________ so that other people wouldn't ______________________________.
5. Recently, I bought ______________________________ so that ______________________________.
6. People need ______________________________ so that ______________________________.

2. Work in a small group. Compare your sentences. Are your ideas similar to or different from those of others in your group?

Check out the *Grammar Links* Website to learn more about consumer psychology and influences on buying behavior.

9 Using Adverb Clauses: The Influences on Your Buying Behavior

A. Work in small groups.

1. Choose four of the following kinds of products: toothpaste, shampoo, cola or other soft drinks, coffee or tea, snack chips, fast food, film, jeans, shoes, gasoline, and long-distance telephone service.

2. For each of the four, discuss these questions: Who or what influences your choice of brands? Are you influenced more by advertising or by other factors, such as the opinions of family members or friends, past experience with brands, or price? Why? Use adverb clauses in explaining the influences on your buying behavior. You can use any appropriate subordinating conjunctions, including these:

when	because	although	so (that)	whenever
before	since	even though	while	as

Example: *Whenever I shop for new shoes, my friends influence me a lot. I always buy the ones they like because I trust their opinions about styles.* OR *I don't look for low prices when I buy shoes. Even though I don't have a lot of money, I buy expensive shoes.*

B. Write three short paragraphs describing the influences on your buying behavior for three of the kinds of products listed in Part A. Use each of the following types of adverb clauses at least twice: time, reason, contrast or opposition, and purpose.

Example: Price is the main influence on my choice of gasoline. Although I buy a lot of gasoline for my car, I don't pay attention to ads for it. I buy HiPro as it's cheaper than the other brands. Since all the brands are similar, it doesn't make any difference. OR Advertising is the main influence on my choice of film. I've used QPV film since I saw an ad for it a couple of years ago. Because the ad gave information about the improved quality of the color, I was interested in trying it. OR My family is the main influence on my choice of fast food. While I like chicken, my sister likes hamburgers. I go to Lottaburger so that my sister will be happy.

See the *Grammar Links* Website for additional model paragraphs for this assignment.

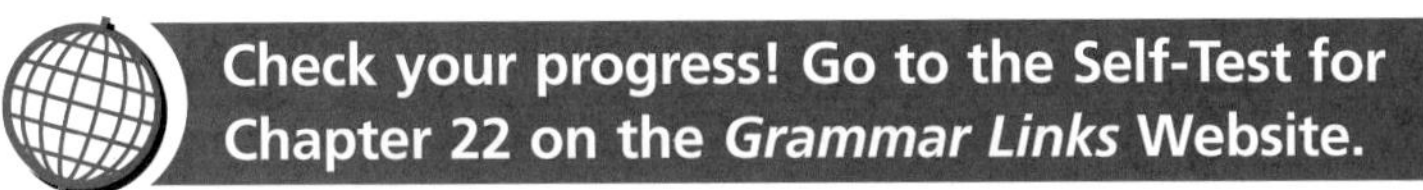

Check your progress! Go to the Self-Test for
Chapter 22 on the Grammar Links Website.

Chapter 23

Connecting Ideas

Introductory Task: Is It Fair?

Pixie Puffs are an exciting and magical part of a good breakfast!

A. Two people are participating in a panel discussion about issues in advertising. Listen once for the main ideas. Then listen again and fill in the missing connectors. You will use some connectors more than once.

and	besides	but	first	furthermore	however
nevertheless	nonetheless	or	so	then	

A: That commercial for Pixie Puffs cereal fascinates children, but (1) it makes me angry. Pixie Puffs are mostly sugar! They cause tooth decay, ________ (2) they make children fat. ________ (3), that's not the image the ad presents. ________ (4), it shows healthy, active children eating Pixie Puffs. ________ (5) it uses animated "magical" characters, ________ (6) children associate the cereal with a fantasy world. Advertising to young children really shouldn't be allowed.

B: I agree that advertisers are real experts at tempting ______(7)______ persuading children. ______(8)______, I think that advertisers have the right to promote their products to children. ______(9)______, television networks can't provide programs for children without the money they get from selling advertising.

A: That may be true, ______(10)______ advertising to young children isn't really fair. They don't have the experience ______(11)______ the knowledge to make informed decisions about products. ______(12)______, they can't always distinguish the commercials from the programs ______(13)______ fantasy from reality.

B: I realize that commercials can cause problems. ______(14)______, I think children need to watch them so that they can learn to resist the persuasive techniques used in advertising.

image = a picture; a symbol that represents an idea. *associate* = bring together in one's mind or imagination. *distinguish* = recognize something as different.

B. As a class, talk about the discussion. Do you agree with speaker A or speaker B? Can you think of other points for or against advertising to children?

GRAMMAR BRIEFING 1

Coordinating Conjunctions

FORM

A. Using Coordinating Conjunctions to Connect Main Clauses

MAIN CLAUSE	COORDINATING CONJUNCTION	MAIN CLAUSE
I cook the meals,	**and**	my roommate does the dishes.

1. The coordinating conjunctions include *and*, *but*, *or*, *so*, and *yet*.* All can be used to connect main clauses.

   **For*, which means "because," and *nor*, which means "and not," are also coordinating conjunctions.

   My job is fun, **but** it doesn't pay well.

   We could go to a movie, **or** we could just stay home.

2. Put a comma before the coordinating conjunction.

   I needed some new clothes**,** **so** I went shopping.

(continued on next page)

B. Using Coordinating Conjunctions to Connect Words or Phrases

1. *And*, *but*, *or*, and *yet* can connect words.	He is tall **and** good-looking. (adjectives) Do you want juice **or** water? (nouns)
They can also connect phrases. Do not use a comma when connecting two words or phrases.	We need a carton of eggs **and** a loaf of bread. (noun phrases) Our football team won its first game **but** lost the next five games. (verb phrases) My parents are thinking of going skiing **or** taking a cruise. (gerund phrases)
2. *And* and *or* can connect more than two words or phrases. Put a comma between each of the words or phrases.	Tiffany**,** Suzanne**, and** Andrew will be at the meeting. She's probably doing her homework**,** talking to a friend**, or** watching TV.
3. The content connected must be parallel. That is, it must belong to the same grammatical category (i.e., adjective, adverb, noun phrase, verb phrase, infinitive phrase, gerund phrase, etc.).	I like **studying hard during the week** and **having a good time on the weekend**. (gerund phrase + gerund phrase) **NOT**: I like ~~to study hard during the week~~ and ~~having a good time on the weekend~~. (infinitive phrase + gerund phrase)

FUNCTION

A. Signaling Addition

1. *And* shows that information is being added.	You must write two papers, **and** you must take a final exam. Buy juice **and** milk.
2. *Or* shows that information is being added as an alternative.	You can write two papers, **or** you can take a final exam. He is walking the dog **or** playing soccer.

B. Signaling Result

So signals that the content in the second clause is a result of the content in the first clause.	We started working early, **so** we got a lot done.

(continued on next page)

C. Signaling Contrast and Opposition

But and *yet* signal that the information that follows:

• Contrasts with previous information in the sentence.	Most students are having difficulty with the material, **but/yet** some find it really easy. He likes English **but/yet** doesn't like math.
• Makes previous information surprising or unexpected.	The students find the class difficult, **but/yet** they really enjoy it. English is hard **but/yet** fun.

But is more common than *yet.*

GRAMMAR HOTSPOT!

1. Do not connect two main clauses with a comma unless you include a coordinating conjunction. Connecting two main clauses with only a comma is an error called a *comma splice.*	My friends went with me, and we had a great time. **NOT**: My friends went with ~~me, we~~ had a great time.
2. Subjects joined by *and* have plural verbs. If subjects are joined by *or*, the verb agrees with the subject nearest to it.	Alison **and** Latisha **are** home now. My sister **or** my parents **are** home now. My parents **or** my sister **is** home now.

GRAMMAR PRACTICE 1

Coordinating Conjunctions

1 Coordinating Conjunctions—Meaning: Children's Wants and Needs

Circle the correct choice to complete each sentence.

1. You can have a Krunchy Kake (or) / and a Twisper bar. You can't have both.
2. First, eat your spinach or / and your carrots. You need to eat both of them.
3. I'll pour you some milk, and / or I'll pour you some orange juice. Which one do you prefer?
4. Krunchy Kakes are mostly sugar, so / but I don't want my children to eat them.
5. Twisper candy isn't good for children, so / but they like it.
6. The ads for Twisper bars are very appealing, so / but my children beg me for them.
7. I want my children to eat healthy food, so / yet I sometimes let them have Krunchy Kakes or Twisper bars.

2 Combining Ideas with Coordinating Conjunctions; Subjects Joined with *And, Or*: Cartoons and Superheroes Sell Toys

Use the conjunction in parentheses to combine the sentences. Use the subjects in the order given.

1. The cartoons are on TV now. Another children's show is on TV now.
   a. (or) The cartoons or another children's show is on TV now.
   b. (and) ______
2. Robby has seen the ads for those toys. Jenna has seen the ads for those toys.
   a. (and) ______
   b. (or) ______
3. A cartoon character was in the commercial. A superhero was in the commercial.
   a. (or) ______
   b. (and) ______
4. Their grandparents are going to buy those toys for them. Their aunt is going to buy those toys for them.
   a. (and) ______
   b. (or) ______

3 Punctuating Sentences with or Without Coordinating Conjunctions: Image Advertising

Use commas and periods where necessary to punctuate the following sentences. Make letters capital where necessary, but do not add words. If no changes are needed, write *NC*.

1. We buy some products to fulfill our basic needs for food, clothing, and shelter. ~~o~~Other products fulfill our need for safety and security.
2. A consumer's decision to buy a product may be based on logic or on emotions. NC
3. Advertisers know this so they often use images or music to appeal to consumers' emotions.
4. Sometimes commercials don't show the product at all they show positive images that advertisers want consumers to associate with the product.
5. Images of freedom youthfulness and friendship are common in American commercials.
6. Consumers want to protect their family members and to show their love for them.
7. The car seems to be traveling through a terrible storm but the family inside it is safe.
8. The woman in the ad is wearing a diamond necklace but no other jewelry.
9. Hector loves his wife very much and he would like to give her a diamond necklace.

10. Car commercials often show wild driving scenes advertisers know that consumers want fun adventure and excitement in their lives.

11. Naomi isn't really an adventurous person yet she bought a fast sports car.

> *image advertising* = advertising that is designed to make a product seem unique and to give consumers a good feeling about the product and the people who use it. *security* = freedom from risk or danger. *logic* = clear reasoning. *positive* = good, desirable. *youthfulness* = quality of being young.

4 Parallel Structures: The Messages the Images Send

Correct the errors in parallel structure in the following sentences. If a sentence contains no errors, write *NC*. Some errors can be corrected in more than one way.

1. You can be popular, glamorous, and ~~success~~ successful.
2. Attractive and intelligent people choose this bank and use its services.
3. When you serve these snacks at your parties, your life will be full of pleasure, happy, and friendship.
4. With these tapes, anyone can learn to speak Spanish quickly, correctly, and fluently.
5. As soon as a man buys this car, he begins having exciting adventures and to attract beautiful women.
6. They will know that his car is elegant, powerful, and it costs a lot.

 For links to information about advertising, go to the *Grammar Links* Website.

GRAMMAR BRIEFING 2

Connecting Main Clauses That Have the Same Verb Phrase

FORM

A. Using . . . *Too* or *So* . . . with Affirmative Main Clauses

MAIN CLAUSE	*AND*	SUBJECT	VERB	*TOO*
I'm going away this weekend,	**and**	my roommate	**is,**	**too.**

MAIN CLAUSE	*AND*	*SO*	VERB	SUBJECT
I'm going away this weekend,	**and**	**so**	**is**	my roommate.

1. If affirmative main clauses connected by *and* have the same verb phrase, the second verb phrase can be shortened with . . . *too* or *so* . . . :

   - Subject + verb + *too.*

     I **can come to the party**, and Jessie can come to the party. → I can come to the party, and **Jessie can, too.**

   - *So* + verb + subject.

     I **can come to the party**, and Jessie can come to the party. → I can come to the party, and **so can Jessie.**

2. For the verb, use:

   - The (first) auxiliary verb (modal, *have*, *be*).

     Your daughter **has** been calling you, and your husband **has**, too. OR Your daughter **has** been calling you, and so **has** your husband.

   - Main verb *be*, if there is no auxiliary verb.

     I **was** at the party, and Jessie **was**, too. OR I **was** at the party, and so **was** Jessie.

   - *Do* in all other cases.

     Mark **brought** a dessert, and Ashley **did**, too. OR Mark **brought** a dessert, and so **did** Ashley.

(continued on next page)

B. Using . . . *Not Either* or *Neither* . . . with Negative Main Clauses

MAIN CLAUSE	*AND*	SUBJECT	VERB	*NOT EITHER*
I will not be here this weekend,	**and**	my roommate	**will**	**not**, **either**.

MAIN CLAUSE	*AND*	*NEITHER*	VERB	SUBJECT
I will not be here this weekend,	**and**	**neither**	**will**	my roommate.

1. If negative main clauses connected by *and* have the same verb phrase, the second verb phrase can be shortened with . . . *not either* or *neither* . . . :

   - Subject + verb + *not* + *either*.

     The bus **doesn't go there**, and the train **doesn't go there**. → The bus doesn't go there, and **the train doesn't, either**.

   - *Neither* + verb + subject.

     The bus **doesn't go there**, and the train **doesn't go there**. → The bus doesn't go there, and **neither does the train**.

2. The rules for the verb in the second clause are the same as for sentences with *too* or *so*.

   I **haven't** seen the movie, and Ben **hasn't**, either/neither **has** Ben. (auxiliary)

   They**'re not** ready to leave yet, and we **aren't**, either/neither **are** we. (main verb *be*)

   I **didn't see** anything happen, and they **didn't**, either/neither **did** they. (*do*)

GRAMMAR PRACTICE 2

Connecting Main Clauses That Have the Same Verb Phrase

5 Connecting Main Clauses: What Are Your Reactions? I

A. Underline the two verb phrases in each sentence. If the verb phrases are different, mark the sentence *NC* for *no change*. If the verb phrases are the same, shorten the second main clause in two ways.

1. The Space-Lex ads are creative, and they've made me aware of a useful product. NC
2. Their TV commercial is informative, and their print ad is informative.

   Their TV commercial is informative, and their print ad is, too.
   Their TV commercial is informative, and so is their print ad.

3. I've seen the Burger Heaven commercial, and my children have seen the Burger Heaven commercial.
4. My children see a lot of fast-food commercials, and I'm not happy about that.

5. French fries aren't good for them, and sodas aren't good for them.
6. Barry likes the sports car ad, and Diego likes the sports car ad.
7. The fast driving looks exciting, and the scenery is amazing.
8. Laura can't remember that ad, and Wendell can't remember that ad.
9. I saw the new sneaker ads, and Heather saw the new sneaker ads.
10. The music didn't impress us, and the basketball players didn't impress us.
11. Alvin thinks the commercials on TV are better than the programs, and I think Alvin has watched every one of them.

B. 1. Work with a partner. Discuss specific ads or kinds of ads that both of you have either seen or heard about. Which ones do you both have the same reactions to? Make a list of six ads or kinds of ads that you both react to in the same way.

2. Join another pair. Each pair tells their shared reactions to the other pair using shortened verb phrases.

Example: *I enjoyed the Super Bowl commercials, and Lin did, too.*
I don't like pop-up ads on the Internet, and neither does Greg.

6 Using Coordinating Conjunctions: What Are Your Reactions? II

Think of an advertisement—for example, a TV commercial, a print ad, an outdoor ad, or an ad on the Internet—that you like or dislike very much. Write a paragraph about it. Describe the ad and tell what you think is good or bad about it. Use several different coordinating conjunctions and at least one sentence with connected main clauses that have the same verb phrase.

Example: *There are several commercials that I like, but the one I like most is for jeans. The people in the ad are all wearing white shirts and jeans, and they're dancing. The music is from the 1950s, and the style of dancing is, too. . . . This commercial is entertaining, so it's fun to watch.*

See the *Grammar Links* Website for a complete model paragraph for this assignment.

GRAMMAR BRIEFING 3

Transitions I

FORM

MAIN CLAUSE	TRANSITION	MAIN CLAUSE
We can finish the work sooner;	**however,**	we will have to charge you more.
We can finish the work sooner.	**However,**	we will have to charge you more.

1. There are many transitions, including *also, for example, however, in addition,* and *therefore.* They can be used to connect main clauses in a single sentence or in separate sentences.

   The apartment is too small; **in addition,** it's too expensive.

   The apartment is too small. **In addition,** it's too expensive.

2. If the transition connects main clauses in a single sentence, use a semicolon before it and a comma after it.

   It's fun to have a roommate; **also,** you can save money if you have a roommate.

3. If the transition connects main clauses in separate sentences, use a comma after it.

   We wanted to advertise on TV. **However,** TV advertising costs too much.

4. Many transitions can also occur in the middle or at the end of a clause. However, the beginning is the most common position. Transitions in any position are separated from the rest of the clause by a comma or commas.

   Different words are sometimes used in different parts of the United States. **For example,** carbonated drinks may be called *soda* or *pop.* OR . . . Carbonated drinks may be called *soda* or *pop,* **for example.**

GRAMMAR **HOT**SPOT!

Main clauses in a single sentence must be separated by a semicolon unless a coordinating conjunction is used:

- If you connect main clauses in a sentence with a transition, use a semicolon before the transition.

  I liked the school**; however,** I decided not to go there.
  NOT: I liked the school~~, however,~~ I decided not to go there.

- Use a comma only when main clauses are connected with coordinating conjunctions.

  I liked the school**, but** I decided not to go there.

GRAMMAR PRACTICE 3

Transitions I

7 Punctuating Sentences Connected by Transitions: All Image and No Product?

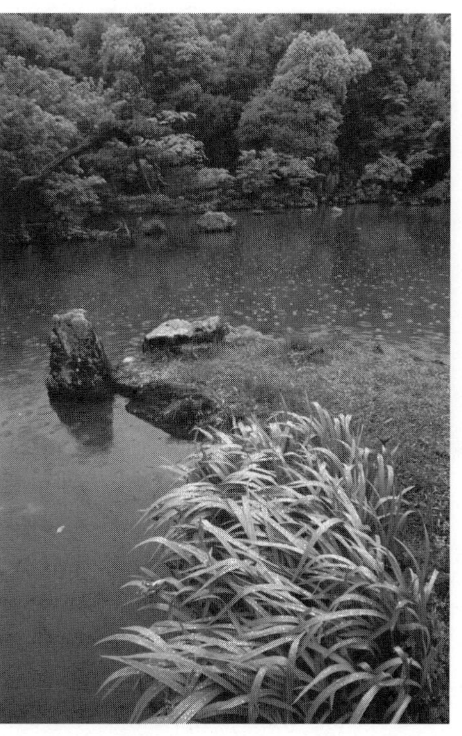

Punctuate the following items. Each one can be punctuated in two ways. Use a semicolon in three items and a period in three items. Add capital letters where necessary.

1. Advertisers say that image advertising may not "sell" a product however it does influence consumers' emotional response to the product.

   Advertisers say that image advertising may not "sell" a product. However, it does influence consumers' emotional response to the product. OR Advertisers say that image advertising may not "sell" a product; however, it does influence consumers' emotional response to the product.

2. The manufacturer of Infiniti automobiles hoped to create excitement and curiosity about them the advertising agency decided therefore to follow an unusual approach in introducing the cars to consumers.
3. They wanted consumers to associate Infinitis with nature also they wanted consumers to equate the cars with peace of mind and serenity.
4. The commercials consisted of lovely natural scenes in addition they featured an announcer quietly discussing the harmony that exists between nature and man.
5. The commercials showed rocks and trees and rain falling on ponds they didn't show the cars at all however.
6. The announcer talked about the simplicity of nature many people consequently were confused about what was being advertised.
7. The advertisers were convinced that the "no product" commercials were a great success because millions of people were curious about their meaning however the manufacturer decided to hire a new agency.

advertising agency = a company that plans and designs advertising. *equate* = consider to be the same. *peace of mind* = freedom from worry. *serenity* = quality of being calm and peaceful. *harmony* = pleasing, agreeable relationship.

GRAMMAR BRIEFING 4

Transitions II

FUNCTION

A. Signaling Addition

Transitions including *also*, *besides*, *in addition*, and *furthermore* show that information is being added.	The food in the cafeteria is good; **also/besides/ in addition/furthermore**, it's cheap.

B. Expressing Time Relationships

Many transitions express how events are related in time, including:	
• *Before* (*that*), *after that*, and *afterward*.	The students went on a trip; **after that/afterward**, they wrote a report about the trip.
• *Meanwhile*, meaning "at the same time" or "in the time between two events."	I was doing a search on the Internet; **meanwhile**, Jack was making calls. We came back after being away for four years; **meanwhile**, everything had changed.
• *First*, *second*, and so on, for the events in a sequence. *Next* and *then* can also be used. *Finally* can be used for the last event in a sequence.	**First**, we're going to study adverb clauses. **Then/Next**, we'll study coordinating conjunctions. **Finally**, we'll look at transitions.

C. Signaling Result

Various transitions are used to signal that the content in the clause that follows the transition is the result of the content in the previous clause. These transitions include *therefore*, *consequently*, and *as a result*.	People are working longer hours; **therefore/ consequently/as a result**, they have less time for leisure activities.

D. Signaling Contrast and Opposition

However, *nevertheless*, and *nonetheless* are among the transitions used to signal that the content in the following clause:	
• Contrasts with the previous content.	Some stores in the mall are doing well; **however/nevertheless**, others are in trouble.
• Makes the previous content surprising or unexpected.	This store is doing well; **however/nonetheless**, the owner has decided to close it.

(continued on next page)

E. Signaling an Example

For example and the less common *for instance* signal that the content in a clause is an example of something stated in the previous clause.	More students are studying languages. **For example**, enrollments in Chinese and Japanese are growing.

GRAMMAR **HOT**SPOT!

Be careful! Do not use two words that express the same idea to connect clauses.	**Although** it's cold, I didn't wear a coat. OR It's cold. **However,** I didn't wear a coat. OR It's cold, **but** I didn't wear a coat. **NOT**: Although it's cold, ~~but~~ I didn't wear a coat. OR It's cold, but I didn't wear a coat, ~~however~~.

GRAMMAR PRACTICE 4

Transitions II

8 Addition Transitions: Valuable Information?

A. Connect the ideas in the following paragraph by inserting addition transitions at the beginning of the two sentences where they are appropriate. You can use any two addition transitions (*also, furthermore, in addition, besides*).

Many people have criticisms of advertising. They say that it causes dissatisfaction among people who can't afford the products that it promotes. They say that advertising leads to materialism in our culture. It does this by encouraging people to want and buy more things. However, other people point out the benefits of advertising. It informs consumers about services such as health care and educational programs. Advertising gives consumers information about prices and about new products that they might need or want. These kinds of information can be valuable for consumers. Although I can understand both points of view, I believe that advertising has the potential to do more good than harm.

materialism = the tendency to be too interested in money and possessions.

B. Work with a partner. Write two sentences in response to each of the following instructions. Connect the second sentence to the first with an addition connector. Use each of the following at least once: *also, besides, furthermore,* and *in addition*.

1. Tell two things that people should do to be prepared for a natural disaster.

   Before a severe storm strikes, you should make sure that you have plenty of canned food. Also, it's a good idea to check the batteries in your flashlight and radio.

2. Tell two things that are excellent about the community where you live.
3. Give two reasons why reading fiction is a better form of entertainment than watching television.
4. Give two reasons why teenagers should not drop out of high school.
5. Tell two advantages of being able to speak more than one language.
6. Give two reasons why people should exercise regularly.

9 Time Transitions: At Work at an Ad Agency

A. Use the time connectors given to connect the ideas. Use each connector once. More than one answer is possible.

First	Finally	Next	Then

This is the agenda for our meeting today. Jack is going to describe the process he used to carry out the market research for a new client. The client is happy with the results, so we can all benefit from Jack's information. Helene is going to give us a progress report on her project. We'll look at and discuss the artwork for the new Space-Lex ads. Those are the ads that Nora and Perry have been working on. We're going to brainstorm ideas for the next Burger Heaven commercials.

B. Write a paragraph about what happened at the ad agency. The first sentence has been written for you. Use the rest of the events in the order they are given in the schedule. Use each transition once. Various answers are possible.

Schedule of Events

10:00—Ms. Ryan, a new client, arrives from Chicago. (Before 10:00, Jack prepares a report for Ms. Ryan.)
11:00—Yuri does research; Nora works on the art for Space-Lex ads.
1:30—Perry writes the text for a print ad.
3:00—Helene designs questionnaires for a consumer survey.
5:00—Everyone gathers for a meeting.

after that	afterward	before that	finally	meanwhile	next

Ms. Ryan, a new client, arrived from Chicago. . . .

C. Think of a several-step process that you often follow—for example, getting ready to go to school or cooking dinner. Write a paragraph about it. Use at least four time connectors to show the order of the steps.

Example: This is the process that I go through when it's my turn to cook dinner. First, I look at cookbooks and choose a recipe. After that, I . . .

10 Result Transitions; Contrast and Opposition Transitions: The Images Versus Reality

Rewrite each sentence using the transition given. Punctuate carefully.

A. 1. This soft drink contains special ingredients, so it gives you energy.

(therefore) This soft drink contains special ingredients. Therefore, it gives you energy.
OR This soft drink contains special ingredients; therefore, it gives you energy.

2. One of the "special ingredients" is sugar, so the soft drink causes tooth decay.

(consequently) __________

3. People who use this product have lost weight, so it can make you lose weight.

(therefore) __________

4. Those people ate less and exercised more, so they lost weight.

(as a result) __________

5. Michael Jordan wears these shoes, so you can succeed in sports by wearing these shoes.

(therefore) __________

6. Michael Jordan worked very hard, so he succeeded in sports.

(consequently) __________

B. 1. Dr. Miller is a real doctor, but that man is an actor.

(however) Dr. Miller is a real doctor. However, that man is an actor. OR
Dr. Miller is a real doctor; however, that man is an actor.

2. He isn't a doctor, but he plays the part of one in advertisements.

(however) __________

3. The actress has never used that product, but she recommends using it in the ad.

(nonetheless) __________

4. The men in those ads weren't really dentists, but many people believed that they were.

   (however) ____

   ____

5. Using actors to play the parts of "real" people can be misleading, but advertisers continue to do it.

   (nevertheless) ____

   ____

11 **Result Versus Contrast and Opposition Transitions:** Telling the Difference

Complete the sentences with content that is appropriate to the previous sentence + transition.

1. a. Ed didn't have enough money to pay his bills. Nevertheless, he bought another car.
   b. Ed didn't have enough money to pay his bills. Consequently, he got a second job.
2. a. Howard had more money than he needed. Therefore, ____.
   b. Howard had more money than he needed. Nonetheless, ____.
3. a. Amanda is a kind and generous person. As a result, ____.
   b. Amanda is a kind and generous person. However, ____.
4. a. Melissa doesn't have many friends. Consequently, ____.
   b. Melissa doesn't have many friends. Nevertheless, ____.
5. a. Travis would like for people to admire him. However, ____.
   b. Travis would like for people to admire him. Therefore, ____.

12 **Example Transitions:** Can You Support These Ideas?

Follow each of the ideas with an idea of your own that gives an example. Use *for example* and *for instance*.

1. Advertisers show commercials during the programs that members of their target markets are likely to be watching.

   For example, fast-food restaurants are often advertised during children's programs.

2. Sometimes it seems as though advertising is everywhere. ______________________________

____

3. If I could control television advertising, I would make some changes. ______________________________

____

4. I have positive feelings about some advertisements. ______________________________

____

5. However, my reaction to some advertisements is negative. ______________________________

____

13 Transitions—Function: Issues in Advertising

Listen to the lecture once for the main ideas. Then listen again and circle the letter of the choice that expresses the meaning that you hear.

1. The lecturer says that advertising has negative aspects. This is
   (a.) in contrast to the fact that advertising has some benefits for consumers.
   b. a result of the fact that advertising is controversial.
2. After the lecturer talks about defenses of advertising, he will
   a. talk about criticisms of advertising.
   b. answer questions.
3. The lecturer says that a major criticism of advertising is that there is simply too much of it. This is
   a. a reason why advertising is everywhere.
   b. a result of the fact that advertising is everywhere.
4. The lecturer says that advertising can deceive or mislead people. This is
   a. a result of the nature of advertising.
   b. an example of specific criticisms of advertising.
5. The lecturer says that false claims are rare in advertisements today. This is
   a. in contrast to the fact that many years ago it was common for advertisements to make false claims.
   b. additional information about the kinds of claims that advertisements make.
6. The lecturer says that advertisers often use actors to play the parts of "real" people in television commercials. This is
   a. in contrast to the ways in which advertisers continue to deceive or mislead consumers.
   b. an example of the ways in which advertisers continue to deceive or mislead consumers.
7. The lecturer says that advertisers respond to the criticism that advertising leads to materialism by asserting that children learn materialism from their parents and friends. This is
   a. in contrast to arguments with which advertisers defend their industry.
   b. an example of an argument with which advertisers defend their industry.

8. The lecturer says that advertisers point to studies showing that advertising stimulates price competition and lowers the prices that consumers pay for products. This is
   a. additional information about the value of advertising to consumers.
   b. in contrast to the value of advertising to consumers.
9. The lecturer gives information about opticians and prices for eyeglasses. This information is
   a. in contrast to studies that have shown that advertising can lower prices for consumers.
   b. an example of how advertising can lower prices for consumers.
10. The lecturer says that most people probably would prefer to have less advertising in their lives. This is
   a. in contrast to the fact that both critics and defenders of advertising have important arguments to make.
   b. a result of the arguments about advertising.

For more information about issues in advertising, go to the *Grammar Links* Website.

14 Using Connectors: Your Turn Now

The two kinds of products that are most frequently advertised to children are toys and "junk food," including highly sweetened breakfast cereal, fast food, soft drinks, candy, and other snacks. Do you think that the advertising of one or both of these kinds of products to children should be restricted in some way or prohibited? Why or why not? (The discussion *Is It Fair?* in the Introductory Task on page 442 can help you with ideas on this topic.)

Write a paragraph that explains your opinion on this topic. Use a variety of connectors to show the relationship of your ideas. Use at least three of the following types of transitions: addition, time, result, contrast and opposition, and example. Also, use at least two coordinating conjunctions to connect main clauses.

Example: There are many commercials for junk food products on children's television programs. These products may be harmful to children's health, so some people believe that commercials for them should not be allowed. However, I believe that there are good reasons for allowing these commercials to be shown to children. First, . . .

See the *Grammar Links* Website for a complete model paragraph for this assignment.

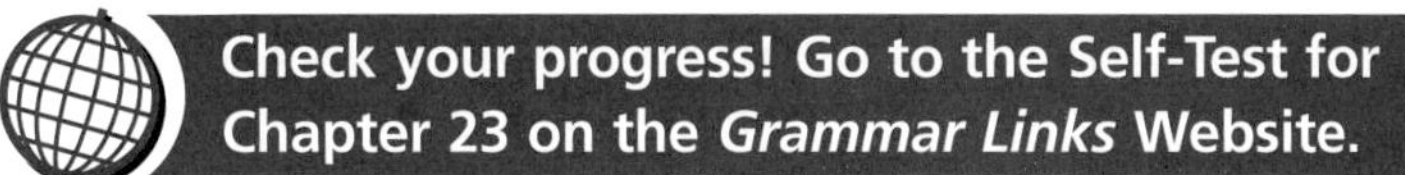

Check your progress! Go to the Self-Test for
Chapter 23 on the Grammar Links Website.

Unit **Eleven**

Wrap-up Activities

1 New Coke: EDITING

Correct the 12 errors in the following passage. There are errors in connectors and in parallel structures and punctuation with connectors. Some errors can be corrected in more than one way. The first error is corrected for you.

184 Marketing—Case Study

The story of New Coke began in the early 1980s. When Pepsi began using the rock star Michael Jackson in commercials, sales of Pepsi rose rapidly. Young people were turning away from Coke; therefore, the president of Coca-Cola Company decided that Coke needed a new image. He instructed the chemists at Coca-Cola to develop a new recipe for Coke, they produced New Coke. It had a sweeter, less fizzy taste than old Coke. After they developed the new product the company spent $4 million and two years on consumer research. In taste tests, consumers preferred the new taste over the original by 61 to 39 percent. The company was sure that New Coke would be successful. Because its flavor was so popular in the tests.

In 1985, Coca-Cola announced that old Coke would soon be replaced by New Coke. Trouble began, as soon as this announcement was made. Consumers wanted to buy old Coke while they still could. However, they began to buy all the old Coke that they could find. Coca-Cola spent over $10 million on advertisements to introduce New Coke. Nonetheless people remained loyal to old Coke. They hated the flavor of New Coke, furthermore many of them were emotionally upset about the change. Thousands of people wrote letters to the company. One letter said, "My wife doesn't like New Coke, and neither don't I. It's too sweet and flat. We liked drinking old Coke and to feel its tingle in our throats. If you don't bring back old Coke, we'll sue you in court for taking away a beloved symbol of America." Another man wrote and performed a protest song to express his strong feelings. Although the company had spent millions on research and advertising, but they hadn't taken into account people's emotional attachment to old Coke. Millions of consumers were very angry so the company announced that it would bring back old Coke as Coke Classic. No one was disappointed. Today you won't find New Coke anywhere, and Coca-Cola has no plans to change "the real thing" again.

2 A Print Advertisement: WRITING

Work with a partner.

Step 1 Choose a product—either a real one or one that you "invent." Discuss the following: Which consumers are in the target market for the product? What are their wants and needs? What will persuade them to buy the product? What kind of magazine should you advertise the product in?

Step 2 Write a one- or two-paragraph ad for the product for a magazine. Make the product sound desirable, and make the ad informative and persuasive. Illustrate your ad with a drawing if you'd like. Use a variety of connectors to link the ideas in the advertisement, including at least four of the following:

a subordinating conjunction for expressing contrast or opposition (*although*, *while*, etc.)

a subordinating conjunction for expressing time (*after*, *once*, etc.)

a subordinating conjunction for expressing reason (*because* or *since*)

a coordinating conjunction (*and*, *but*, *so*, etc.)

a transition (*in addition*, *for instance*, etc.)

Example: **Because you've worked hard all year, you deserve a long vacation at the Oasis Resort. At the Oasis you will relax on sunny beaches and eat delicious seafood. In addition, you'll enjoy dancing to live music under the stars every night. The fun starts as soon as you arrive. . . .**

3 A Television Commercial: SPEAKING

Work in a small group.

Step 1 Choose a real or an imaginary product. Discuss the following: Which consumers are in the target market for the product? What are their wants and needs? What will persuade them to buy the product? What kind of television program should a commercial for the product be shown on?

Step 2 Write the script for a one- to two-minute commercial for the product. Use your imagination. If you want, make the commercial humorous. There should be a part for each person in the group in it. Use at least one of each of the following in the script:

an adverb clause of time (e.g., *Allegri softens your hands as it cleans your pots and pans.*)

an adverb clause of purpose (e.g., *Let's take Mom to Burger Heaven so that she can have a rest from cooking.*)

a coordinating conjunction (e.g., *Bambi tissues are soft but strong.*)

a transition (e.g., *The Steamatic cooks rice perfectly. In addition, it can be used to prepare delicious puddings.*)

Step 3 Perform your commercial for the class.

4 An Essay: WRITING

Step 1 Work in a small group. Brainstorm for ideas on the following topic:

The Benefits and Problems of Advertising

First, think of as many benefits of advertising as you can. Then think of as many problems it causes as you can. (The lecture, *Issues in Advertising*, for Exercise 13 on page 468 can help you with ideas on this topic.)

Step 2 On your own, write a list of the benefits and of the problems. Decide whether, in your opinion, the benefits or the problems of advertising are greater.

Step 3 Write a four-paragraph essay on the topic. The first paragraph should introduce the topic.

Example: Advertising has benefits for consumers. However, it causes certain problems. Which are greater—the benefits or the problems?

The second paragraph should discuss benefits of advertising. The third paragraph should discuss problems. The concluding paragraph should tell whether you think advertising has more benefits or more problems and why. Use a variety of connectors to link your ideas, including at least five transitions.

See the *Grammar Links* Website for a model essay for this assignment.

Exercise Pages

UNIT 2 ■ Chapter 3

Introductory Task: Quiz: What Is Your Time Type?

Scoring for Quiz

16–18 points = a very "fast" person (tends to be extremely aware of time and speed)

12–15 points = a "fast" person (tends to be somewhat concerned about time and speed)

9–11 points = a "slow" person (tends not to be concerned about time or speed)

6–8 points = a very "slow" person (tends to be extremely relaxed about time and speed)

6 Using Present Perfect Progressive: What Have People Been Doing? II

For Student B.

College Campus

10 Future Time with Simple Present: An Outdoor Vacation—Yellowstone National Park

Information for Student B.

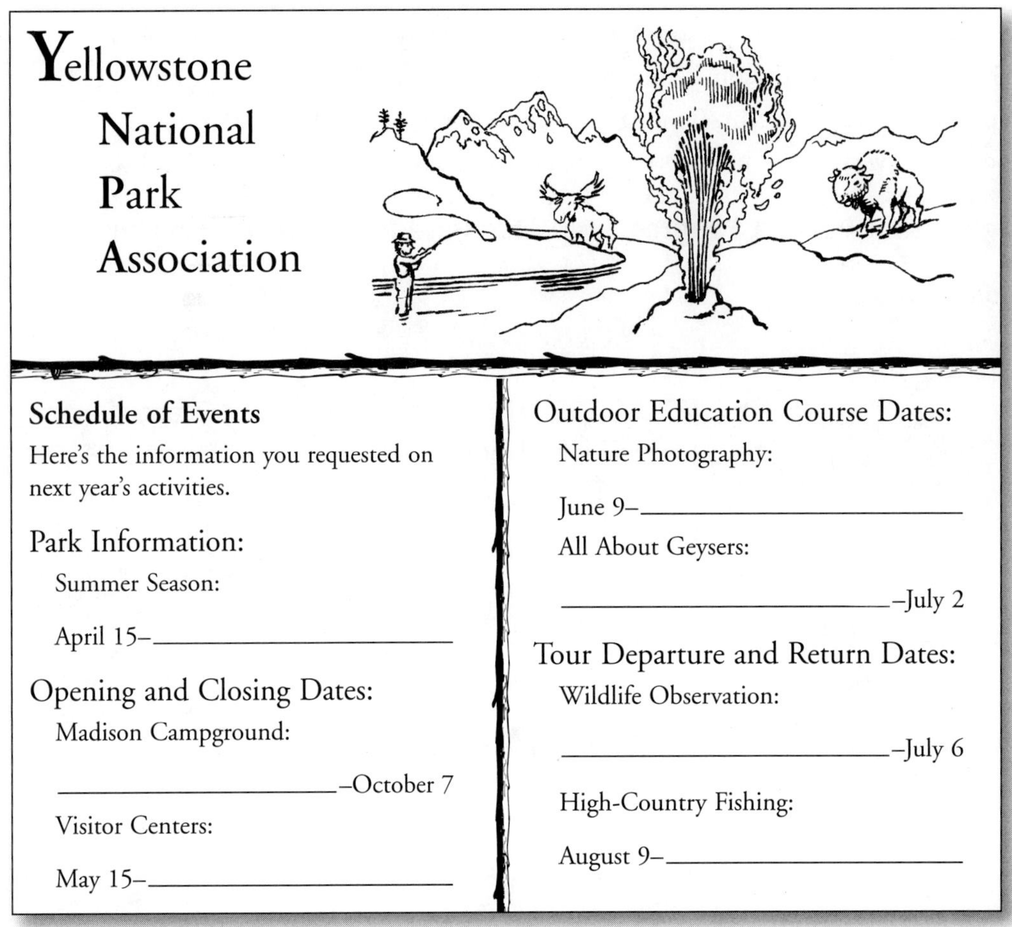

Yellowstone National Park Association

Schedule of Events

Here's the information you requested on next year's activities.

Park Information:

Summer Season:

April 15–____________________

Opening and Closing Dates:

Madison Campground:

____________________–October 7

Visitor Centers:

May 15–____________________

Outdoor Education Course Dates:

Nature Photography:

June 9–____________________

All About Geysers:

____________________–July 2

Tour Departure and Return Dates:

Wildlife Observation:

____________________–July 6

High-Country Fishing:

August 9–____________________

12 Listening to Tag Questions: Christopher Columbus

Part B: Information About Columbus

Columbus set out on his first voyage in 1492. He and his crew were not the first Europeans to arrive in North America. The Vikings had landed on the northern coast of the continent around the year 1000. Columbus made a contract, or agreement, with the king and queen of Spain to pay for his expedition, but he was an Italian, not a Spaniard. Before he arrived in America, no one in Europe knew that North and South America existed. Columbus believed that he could sail west from Europe directly to Asia. Columbus made a total of four voyages to America. He landed on several islands off the coast of North America, and he reached the coasts of Central and South America on two of his voyages. But he never landed on the coast of North America. Columbus believed that Cuba was Japan, and he never realized that he hadn't reached Asia. For this reason, he didn't give the land a new name. A German mapmaker named it America after

Amerigo Vespucci, who explored the coast of South America. Columbus's contract made him viceroy and governor of all the lands he discovered and gave him 10 percent of the profits from his discoveries. At first he became rich, but later he had troubles and lost his titles and all his money.

viceroy = person who represents the king.

UNIT 3 ■ Wrap-up

4 Ask the Oracle

Instructions for the oracle: Copy each answer in the following list on a small slip of paper. Put the slips into an empty container, such as a box or jar. After each question is asked, draw out an answer (without peeking) and read it aloud. After each answer, return the slip of paper to the container and mix it in with the rest.

The oracle's answers:

1. Yes, definitely.
2. No, definitely not.
3. It's certain.
4. It isn't certain.
5. It's possible.
6. It's probable.
7. The answer isn't clear yet.
8. It will happen.
9. It won't happen.
10. The chances are good.

5 Acting Out the Verbs

Lists of Phrasal Verbs for Skits

Telephoning the travel agent:
call back, call up, hang up, look up, take down, talk over

At the hotel desk:
add up, check in, check out, hand over, settle in, show up

In a restaurant:
fill up, pass around, run out of, take back, think over, sit down

Dressing for an expedition:
have on, pick out, put on, take off, try on, wear out

On a tour:
find out, finish up, look over, point out, speak up, start off

UNIT 5 ■ Chapter 10

Introductory Task: The Birth-Order Theory of Personality Development—A Test

According to the birth-order theory, firstborns tend to be practical and follow rules, while laterborns are more likely to be creative and willing to bend or break rules. If you circled **a** four or more times, you show the personality characteristics of a firstborn child; if you circled **b** four or more times, you show the characteristics of a laterborn child. (An only child usually has characteristics similar to those of a firstborn.)

Now turn back to page 192 and go on to Part B of the task.

UNIT 8 ■ Chapter 16

Introductory Task: Sports Trivia

1. b	5. h
2. a	6. g
3. d	7. f
4. e	8. c

4 Passive Sentences with Verbs in Different Tenses—Questions and Answers: Stadiums

Invesco Field at Mile High

1. 2001
2. football and soccer
3. yes
4. to monitor the water needed for the grass and heat the field in winter
5. by selling seats from the old Mile High Stadium

The Skydome

1. 1989
2. football, baseball, basketball, other events
3. no; on artificial grass called "Astroturf"
4. with three panels that take 20 minutes to open or close
5. eight miles of zippers

UNIT 8 ■ Chapter 17

Introductory Task: The Things Fans Do

Answers: All the statements are true!

UNIT 10 ■ Chapter 21

4–9

Professor Wendell's solution: The police inspector was about to arrest John Small for the murder of Mrs. Pierson. He said that Small had poisoned her to obtain money that he otherwise might not have gotten for many years. Professor Wendell stepped in and told the inspector that he was making a serious mistake. He said that the real murderers had been Mr. and Mrs. Niles Pierson. He explained that Niles Pierson had been in serious financial difficulty: Hard times meant that people were spending less on luxuries like art. Pierson had tried to raise money by gambling and had wound up deeply in debt. Several months before the murder, Pierson had begun to slowly poison his aunt. He thought that it would look like she had died of an illness and that he would inherit her money. Suddenly, however, she had written a new will, leaving her money to John Small. Feeling desperate after Mr. Torrance had told him that there was nothing he could do about the new will, Pierson had come up with another plan. He would poison his aunt in a more obvious way and make it look as if Small had been the murderer. If Small were found guilty and sent to jail, Pierson would inherit the money after all, and his troubles would be at an end. He got his wife to help him, and on Sunday night, he pretended to be an intruder in the garden, and when everyone left the house, his wife was able to slip the poison in a new bottle of Mrs. Pierson's special Swiss organic grape juice. On Monday, when Niles Pierson and his wife were miles away, old Mrs. Pierson drank the poisoned juice and died.

Appendixes

APPENDIX 1

Spelling Rules for the Third Person Singular Form of the Simple Present Tense

1. Most verbs: Add *-s.*	work → works	play → plays
2. Verbs that end in *ch, sh, s, x,* or *z*: Add *-es.*	teach → teaches	miss → misses
3. Verbs that end in a consonant + *y*: Drop *y.* Add *-ies.*	try → tries	
4. The third person singular forms of *do, go,* and *have* are irregular.	does, goes, has	

APPENDIX 2

Pronunciation Rules for the Third Person Singular Form of the Simple Present Tense

The *-s* ending is pronounced as:

• /s/ after the voiceless sounds /p/, /t/, /k/, and /f/.	stops	gets	takes	laughs
• /z/ after the voiced sounds /b/, /d/, /g/, /v/, /*th*/, /m/, /n/, /ng/, /l/, /r/, and all vowel sounds.	robs	gives	remains	hears
	adds	bathes	sings	agrees
	begs	seems	tells	knows

• /ĭz/ after the sounds /s/, /z/, /sh/, /zh/, /ch/, /j/, and /ks/.	passes	catches
	freezes	judges (ge = /j/)
	rushes	relaxes (x = /ks/)
	massages (ge = /zh/)	

APPENDIX 3

Spelling Rules for the *-ing* Form of the Verb

1. Most verbs: Base form of verb + *-ing*.	work → work**ing**	play → play**ing**
2. Verbs that end in *e*: Drop *e*. Add *-ing*.	write → wri**ting**	live → li**ving**
3. Verbs that end in *ie*: Change *ie* to *y*. Add *-ing*.	**tie** → **tying**	**lie** → **lying**
4. Verbs that end in consonant + vowel + consonant: Double the final consonant. Add *-ing*.	**run** → run**ning**	**begin** → begin**ning**
BUT: Do not double the final consonant when:		
• The last syllable is not stressed.	**lís**ten → listen**ing**	**háp**pen → happen**ing**
• The final consonant is *w* or *x*.	allow → allow**ing**	fix → fix**ing**

APPENDIX 4

Adverbs of Frequency

1. Adverbs of frequency tell how often something happens—from all of the time to none of the time:

AFFIRMATIVE	
always, constantly, continually	We **always** eat breakfast.
almost always	
usually, generally, normally	
frequently, often	
sometimes	
occasionally	
NEGATIVE*	
seldom, rarely, hardly ever	
almost never	I **almost never** go to bed before midnight.
never	

*Negative adverbs of frequency are not used in sentences with *not.*

(continued on next page)

Adverbs of Frequency (continued)

2. Adverbs of frequency usually occur:

• Before main verbs (except *be*).	We **often go** on vacation in the summer.
• After *be*.*	They **are rarely** home in the evenings.
• After the first auxiliary.*	I **will never** forget how nice they were. We **weren't usually** allowed to leave.
• After the subject in questions.	Does **he ever** take the bus? Are **your parents always** so nice?
• Before negatives (except *always* and *ever*, which usually come after the negative).	He **often didn't** get home until late at night. Our friends **usually aren't** late. They **won't ever** call here again!

*Adverbs can also precede *be* and a first auxiliary, especially for emphasis (e.g., *We **usually weren't** allowed to leave*).

3. Some adverbs of frequency can often occur at the beginning and/or end of the sentence. These include *frequently*, *generally*, *normally*, *occasionally*, *often*, *sometimes*, and *usually*.	**Sometimes** we need to take a break. We need to take a break **sometimes**. **Often** he works late. He works late **often**.

APPENDIX 5

Spelling Rules for the *-ed* Form of the Verb

1. Most verbs: Add *-ed*.	work → work**ed**	play → play**ed**
2. Verbs that end in *e*: Add *-d*.	live → live**d**	decide → decide**d**
3. Verbs that end in a consonant + *y*: Change *y* to *i*. Add *-ed*.	**try** → **tried**	
4. Verbs that end in consonant + vowel + consonant: Double the final consonant. Add *-ed*.	**stop** → sto**pped**	per**mit** → permi**tted**
BUT: Do not double the final consonant when:		
• The last syllable is not stressed.	**lís**ten → listen**ed**	**háp**pen → happen**ed**
• The last consonant is *w* or *x*.	allo**w** → allow**ed**	bo**x** → box**ed**

APPENDIX 6

Pronunciation Rules for the *-ed* Form of the Verb

The *-ed* ending is pronounced as:

- /t/ after the voiceless sounds /p/, /k/, /f/, /s/, /sh/, /ch/, and /ks/.

clapped	wished
talked	watched
laughed	waxed
passed	

- /d/ after the voiced sounds /b/, /g/, /v/, /*th*/, /z/, /zh/, /j/, /m/, /n/, /ng/, /l/, /r/, and all vowel sounds.

robbed	remained
begged	banged
waved	called
bathed	ordered
surprised	played
massaged (ge = /zh/)	enjoyed
judged (ge = /j/)	cried
seemed	

- /ĭd/ after the sounds /t/ and /d/.

started	needed

APPENDIX 7

Irregular Verbs

BASE FORM	PAST	PAST PARTICIPLE	BASE FORM	PAST	PAST PARTICIPLE
be	was, were	been	broadcast	broadcast	broadcast
beat	beat	beaten	build	built	built
become	became	become	burn	burned/burnt	burned/burnt
begin	began	begun	burst	burst	burst
bend	bent	bent	buy	bought	bought
bet	bet	bet	catch	caught	caught
bind	bound	bound	choose	chose	chosen
bite	bit	bitten	come	came	come
bleed	bled	bled	cost	cost	cost
blow	blew	blown	creep	crept	crept
break	broke	broken	cut	cut	cut
bring	brought	brought	deal	dealt	dealt

(continued on next page)

Irregular Verbs (continued)

BASE FORM	PAST	PAST PARTICIPLE	BASE FORM	PAST	PAST PARTICIPLE
dig	dug	dug	know	knew	known
dive	dived/dove	dived	lay	laid	laid
do	did	done	lead	led	led
draw	drew	drawn	leap	leaped/leapt	leaped/leapt
dream	dreamed/dreamt	dreamed/dreamt	learn	learned/learnt	learned/learnt
drink	drank	drunk	leave	left	left
drive	drove	driven	lend	lent	lent
eat	ate	eaten	let	let	let
fall	fell	fallen	lie	lay	lain
feed	fed	fed	light	lit/lighted	lit/lighted
feel	felt	felt	lose	lost	lost
fight	fought	fought	make	made	made
find	found	found	mean	meant	meant
fit	fit	fit	meet	met	met
flee	fled	fled	mistake	mistook	mistaken
fly	flew	flown	pay	paid	paid
forbid	forbade	forbidden	prove	proved	proved/proven
forecast	forecast/forecasted	forecast/forecasted	put	put	put
forget	forgot	forgotten	quit	quit	quit
forgive	forgave	forgiven	read	read	read
freeze	froze	frozen	rid	rid	rid
get	got	gotten	ride	rode	ridden
give	gave	given	ring	rang	rung
go	went	gone	rise	rose	risen
grind	ground	ground	run	ran	run
grow	grew	grown	say	said	said
hang	hung	hung	see	saw	seen
have	had	had	seek	sought	sought
hear	heard	heard	sell	sold	sold
hide	hid	hidden	send	sent	sent
hit	hit	hit	set	set	set
hold	held	held	sew	sewed	sewed/sewn
hurt	hurt	hurt	shake	shook	shaken
keep	kept	kept	shave	shaved	shaved/shaven

(continued on next page)

Irregular Verbs (continued)

BASE FORM	PAST	PAST PARTICIPLE
shine	shined/shone	shined/shone
shoot	shot	shot
show	showed	showed/shown
shut	shut	shut
sing	sang	sung
sink	sank	sunk
sit	sat	sat
sleep	slept	slept
slide	slid	slid
speak	spoke	spoken
speed	sped	sped
spend	spent	spent
spin	spun	spun
split	split	split
spread	spread	spread
spring	sprang	sprung
stand	stood	stood
steal	stole	stolen
stick	stuck	stuck
sting	stung	stung
strike	struck	struck
swear	swore	sworn

BASE FORM	PAST	PAST PARTICIPLE
sweep	swept	swept
swell	swelled	swelled/swollen
swim	swam	swum
swing	swung	swung
take	took	taken
teach	taught	taught
tear	tore	torn
tell	told	told
think	thought	thought
throw	threw	thrown
understand	understood	understood
upset	upset	upset
wake	woke	woken
wear	wore	worn
weave	wove	woven
weep	wept	wept
wet	wet	wet
win	won	won
wind	wound	wound
withdraw	withdrew	withdrawn
write	wrote	written

APPENDIX 8

Common Phrasal Verbs and Their Meanings

Phrasal Verbs Without Objects

blow up	1. come into being or happen suddenly (as in weather) 2. express anger suddenly and forcefully
break down	fail to function
break up	1. come apart 2. come to an end

catch up	reach the same place as others who are ahead
check in	1. register 2. see or talk to somebody briefly
check out	leave (as a hotel)
come along	progress
come back	return
come out	result, end up, turn out

(continued on next page)

Common Phrasal Verbs and Their Meanings (continued)

Phrasal Verbs Without Objects (continued)

come over	visit
come up	appear or arise
drop out	leave an activity or group
get along	1. have a friendly relationship 2. manage with reasonable success
go back	return
go on	continue
grow up	become adult
head back	start to return
head out	leave a place
keep up	continue at the same level or pace
let out	end (for classes)
let up	slow down or stop
pay off	be successful
push on	continue despite difficulty
set in	begin to happen (for weather)

set off	start on a journey
settle in	move comfortably into
show up	appear
sit down	be seated
slow down	become slower
speak up	speak more loudly
stand out	1. be better or the best 2. be different
start off	begin a journey
start out	begin
take off	start (to fly or move); leave
turn in	go to bed
turn out	end or result
turn up	be found; arrive or appear, often unexpectedly
watch out	be careful
work out	1. exercise 2. succeed

Phrasal Verbs with Objects

add up	total (a bill)
blow up	1. explode 2. fill with air 3. make (a photograph) larger
break up	separate into smaller pieces
bring back	return with
bring down	cause somebody or something to lose power
bring in	earn profits or income
bring off	accomplish
bring on	cause something to appear or happen
bring out	produce or publish something
bring up	take care of and educate (a child)

build up	make stronger
burn down	destroy by fire
call back	return a telephone call
call off	cancel (a plan or an event)
call up	telephone
carry out	do as planned
check in	1. register someone (at a hotel, etc.) 2. return (as a book or equipment)
check out	1. find information about 2. take something and record what is being taken (as a book or equipment)
drive back	force to return
figure out	discover by thinking
fill up	make or become completely full
find out	discover (an answer)

(continued on next page)

Common Phrasal Verbs and Their Meanings (continued)

Phrasal Verbs with Objects (continued)

finish up	end (something)
get through	finish successfully
give up	stop doing (an activity)
hand over	give (something) to someone else
hang up	end a telephone conversation
have on	wear
hold up	stop or delay
keep back	1. discourage 2. keep from advancing
keep up	continue something at the same level
leave behind	abandon
let down	disappoint
look over	examine quickly
look up	search in a dictionary or other reference
make up	1. invent 2. replace; compensate
pass around	give to others in order to share
pass over	disregard
pick out	choose or select
pick up	get; collect
play down	make something seem unimportant
play up	make something seem more important
point out	tell
pull along	drag something
put down	insult
put off	delay; postpone
put on	1. host 2. dress (a part of) the body in something
put together	assemble
put up	1. provide (money); invest or pay in advance 2. assemble or build
run off	print or copy
run up	make an expense larger
set back	slow down progress
set off	1. make different from others 2. cause to explode 3. make angry
set up	1. assemble or build 2. create or establish
show off	display proudly
sign up	register someone for an activity; add (a name) to a list
stick out	continue to the end of something difficult
take back	return something
take down	write (pieces of) information
take off	1. remove 2. make (time) free
take on	accept responsibility for (e.g., a project)
take over	get control or ownership of
take up	begin an activity
talk over	discuss
think over	consider carefully
think up	create
tire out	cause to be exhausted
try on	put on (clothing) to test its fit
try out	test
turn down	1. make quieter 2. say no to (an invitation)
turn in	1. give to an authority 2. inform an authority about
turn off	stop from working
turn up	make louder
wear out	make unusable through long or heavy use
work out	solve (a problem)

APPENDIX 9

Common Verb–Preposition Combinations

agree with	confide in	know about	pay for	rely on	wait for
believe in	depend on	learn from	plan for	search for	write about
belong to	dream of	listen to	play with	succeed in	worry about
care about	forget about	live on	prepare for	suffer from	
care for	happen to	look after	prevent from	talk about	
check in	hear about	look for	protect from	talk to	
come from	hear of	look over	read about	think about	
concentrate on	hope for	pass over	recover from	think of	

APPENDIX 10

Common Phrasal Verb–Preposition Combinations and Their Meanings

catch up with	come up from behind and reach the same level
close in on	surround
come out against	1. oppose 2. end with a bad result
come up with	discover (an idea)
cut down on	use or have less
drop in on	visit unexpectedly
face up to	confront, meet bravely
get along with	enjoy the company of
get back from	return from
get down to	begin (work)
get through with	finish
give up on	admit defeat and stop trying
keep on at	continue

keep up with	go at the same speed as
look forward to	think of (a future event) with pleasure
meet up with	meet unexpectedly
miss out on	lose a chance for something
put up with	tolerate
run out of	use all the supply of
run up against	meet and have to deal with
stand up to	1. confront somebody or something 2. tolerate or endure harsh conditions
start out for	begin a journey toward a particular place
watch out for	be careful of

Some Proper Nouns with *The*

1. Names of countries and islands:

the Bahamas	the Falkland Islands	the Philippines/the Philippine Islands
the British Isles	the Hawaiian Islands	the United Arab Emirates
the Czech Republic	the Netherlands	the United Kingdom
the Dominican Republic	the People's Republic of China	the United States of America

2. Regions:

the East/West/North/South	the East/West Coast	the Midwest	the Near/Middle/Far East

3. Geographical features:

- Map features:

the Eastern/Western/Northern/Southern Hemisphere	the Occident/the Orient
the North/South Pole	the Tropic of Cancer/Capricorn

- Canals, channels, gulfs:

the Suez Canal	the English Channel	the Arabian Gulf	the Gulf of Mexico

- Deserts:

the Gobi (Desert)	the Mojave (Desert)	the Sahara (Desert)	the Sinai (Desert)

- Mountain ranges:

the Alps	the Caucasus (Mountains)
the Andes (Mountains)	the Himalaya Mountains (the Himalayas)
the Atlas Mountains	the Rocky Mountains (the Rockies)

- Oceans and seas:

the Arctic Ocean	the Indian Ocean	the Sea of Japan
the Atlantic (Ocean)	the Mediterranean (Sea)	the South China Sea
the Black Sea	the Pacific (Ocean)	
the Caribbean (Sea)	the Red Sea	

- Peninsulas:

the Iberian Peninsula	the Yucatan Peninsula

(continued on next page)

3. Geographical features: (continued)

- Rivers:

the Amazon (River)	the Mississippi (River)	the Rio Grande	the Thames (River)
the Congo (River)	the Nile (River)	the Seine (River)	the Tigris (River)

- Names with *of*:

the Bay of Naples	the Cape of Good Hope	the Strait of Gibraltar	the Strait of Magellan

4. Buildings and other structures:

the Brooklyn Bridge	the Museum of Modern Art	the Statue of Liberty
the Eiffel Tower	the Ritz-Carlton Hotel	the White House

5. Ships, trains, and airplanes:

the *Mayflower*	the *Titanic*	the *Orient Express*	the *Spirit of St. Louis*

6. Newspapers and periodicals:

the *New York Times*	the *Washington Post*	the *Atlantic Monthly*	the *Economist*

APPENDIX 12

Spelling Rules for Regular Plural Count Nouns

1. Most verbs: Add *-s.*	room → rooms	studio → studios
2. Nouns that end in *ch, sh, s, x,* or *z*: Add *-es.*	lunch → lunches	box → boxes
	brush → brushes	buzz → buzzes
	kiss → kisses	
If a noun ending in one *s* or *z* has one syllable or stress on the last syllable, double the *s* or *z.*	**bus** → busses	**quiz** → quizzes
3. Nouns ending in a consonant + *y*: Change *y* to *i.* Add *-es.*	story → stories	university → universities
4. Nouns ending in *f* or *fe*: Change *f* to *v.* Add *-es* or *-s.*	leaf → leaves	knife → knives
	Exceptions: belief → beliefs, chief → chiefs, roof → roofs	
5. A few nouns ending in a consonant + *o*: Add *-es.*	hero → heroes	potato → potatoes
	mosquito → mosquitoes	tomato → tomatoes

APPENDIX 13

Pronunciation Rules for Regular Plural Count Nouns

The *-s* ending is pronounced as:

• /s/ after the voiceless sounds /p/, /t/, /k/, /f/, and /th/.	cups	cuffs
	hats	paths
	books	
• /z/ after the voiced sounds /b/, /d/, /g/, /v/, /*th*/, /m/, /n/, /ng/, /l/, /r/, and all vowel sounds.	jobs	bones
	kids	things
	legs	bells
	knives	bears
	lathes	days
	dreams	potatoes
• /ĭz/ after the sounds /s/, /z/, /sh/, /zh/, /ch/, /j/, and /ks/.	classes	churches
	breezes	judges (ge = /j/)
	dishes	taxes (x = /ks/)
	massages (ge = /zh/)	

APPENDIX 14

Irregular Plural Count Nouns

1. Nouns that have different forms in the singular and plural:

SINGULAR	PLURAL	SINGULAR	PLURAL	SINGULAR	PLURAL	SINGULAR	PLURAL
child	children	goose	geese	mouse	mice	tooth	teeth
foot	feet	man	men	person	people	woman	women

2. Nouns that have the same form in the singular and plural:

SINGULAR	PLURAL	SINGULAR	PLURAL	SINGULAR	PLURAL
fish	fish	moose	moose	sheep	sheep
means	means	series	series	species	species

3. Nouns from Latin and Greek that have kept their original plural forms:

SINGULAR	PLURAL	SINGULAR	PLURAL
alumnus (alumna)	alumni (alumnae)	medium	media
analysis	analyses	memorandum	memoranda (memorandums)
basis	bases	parenthesis	parentheses
crisis	crises	phenomenon	phenomena
curriculum	curricula (curriculums)	stimulus	stimuli
datum	data	syllabus	syllabi (syllabuses)
hypothesis	hypotheses	thesis	theses

4. Nouns with no singular form:

cattle	police

5. Nouns with only a plural form:

belongings	clothes	congratulations	goods	groceries	tropics

6. Nouns for things in pairs with only a plural form:

jeans	pajamas	pants	scissors	shorts	(sun)glasses	tongs	trousers

APPENDIX 15

Common Noncount Nouns

1. Names of groups of similar items:

cash	equipment	furniture	jewelry	mail	stuff
change (i.e., money)	food	garbage	luggage	money	trash
clothing	fruit	homework	machinery	scenery	traffic

(These groups often have individual parts that can be counted, e.g., clothing is made up of dresses, shirts, coats, etc.)

2. Liquids:

coffee	gasoline	honey	juice	lotion	milk	oil	sauce	soup	tea	water

(continued on next page)

Common Noncount Nouns (continued)

3. Foods:

bacon	cabbage	chicken	food	lettuce	pie	seafood	vitamin
beef	cake	chocolate	garlic	meat	pizza	spaghetti	wheat
bread	candy	corn	hamburger	pasta	pork	spice	
broccoli	celery	fish	ice cream	pastry	rice	spinach	
butter	cheese	flour	jelly	pepper	salt	sugar	

4. Other solids:

aspirin	detergent	glass	hair	paper	silk	toothpaste
chalk	dirt	gold	ice	rope	silver	wood
cotton	film	grass	nylon	sand	soap	wool

5. Gases:

air	carbon dioxide	hydrogen	nitrogen	oxygen	smoke	steam

6. Natural phenomena:

cold	fire	hail	light	smog	sunshine	warmth
darkness	fog	heat	lightning	snow	temperature	weather
electricity	gravity	humidity	rain	space	thunder	wind

7. Abstract ideas:

advice	education	help	law	permission	tradition
art	energy	history	life	practice	travel
beauty	entertainment	honesty	love	pride	trouble
behavior	freedom	importance	luck	progress	truth
business	friendship	information	music	quiet	variety
competition	fun	insurance	news*	responsibility	violence
confidence	grammar	intelligence	noise	slang	vocabulary
courage	hatred	interest	opportunity	sleep	wealth
crime	happiness	knowledge	patience	space	work
democracy	health	laughter	peace	time	

8. Fields of study:

accounting	business	engineering	journalism	music	psychology	writing
art	chemistry	geography	literature	nutrition	science	
biology	economics	history	mathematics*	physics*	sociology	

*Some noncount nouns, such as *news*, *mathematics*, and *physics*, end in *s*. These nouns look plural, but they are not; they always take a singular verb.

Common Noncount Nouns (continued)

9. Activities

baseball	cards	dancing	running	skating	studying	traveling
basketball	conversation	golf	sailing	skiing	surfing	
bowling	cooking	hiking	shopping	snowboarding	swimming	
camping	cycling	reading	singing	soccer	tennis	

10. Languages:

Arabic	English	German	Japanese	Portuguese	Spanish	Turkish
Chinese	French	Indonesian	Korean	Russian	Thai	Urdu

APPENDIX 16

Pronouns

SINGULAR	SUBJECT	OBJECT	REFLEXIVE	POSSESSIVE DETERMINER	POSSESSIVE PRONOUN
First person	I	me	myself	my	mine
Second person	you	you	yourself	your	yours
Third person	he	him	himself	his	his
	she	her	herself	her	hers
	it	it	itself	its	its
PLURAL					
First person	we	us	ourselves	our	ours
Second person	you	you	yourselves	your	yours
Third person	they	them	themselves	their	theirs

APPENDIX 17

Common Adjective + Preposition Combinations That Are Followed by Gerunds

accustomed to	critical of	good at	responsible for	used to
afraid of	discouraged about	happy about	sad about	useful for
angry at/about	enthusiastic about	interested in	sorry about	worried about
ashamed of	familiar with	known for	successful in	
(in)capable of	famous for	nervous about	tired of	
certain of/about	fond of	perfect for	tolerant of	
concerned about	glad about	proud of	upset about	

APPENDIX 18

Some Verbs That Can Be Followed by Gerunds

acknowledge	complete	encourage*	forgive	mind	recollect	start*
admit	consider	endure	hate	miss	recommend	stop**
advise*	continue*	enjoy	imagine	permit*	regret*	suggest
allow*	defend	escape	include	postpone	remember**	support
anticipate	defer	excuse	involve	practice	report	tolerate
appreciate	delay	explain	justify	prefer*	require*	try**
avoid	deny	feel like	keep	prevent	resent	understand
begin*	detest	finish	like*	prohibit	resist	urge*
can't help	discuss	forbid*	love*	quit	resume	
celebrate	dislike	forget**	mention	recall	risk	

*Verbs that can take either a gerund or an infinitive.
**Verbs that can take either a gerund or an infinitive but with a difference in meaning.

APPENDIX 19

Some Verbs That Can Be Followed by Infinitives

1. Verb + infinitive:

agree	claim	don't/didn't care	manage	refuse	try**
aim	consent	fail	mean	remember**	wait
appear	continue*	forget**	offer	seem	
attempt	decide	hesitate	plan	start*	
begin*	decline	hope	pledge	stop**	
can't/couldn't afford	demand	intend	pretend	struggle	
can't/couldn't wait	deserve	learn	promise	tend	

2. Verb + noun phrase + infinitive:

advise*	command	forbid*	invite	persuade	teach	urge*
allow*	convince	force	order	remind	tell	warn
cause	encourage*	hire	permit*	require*	trust	

3. Verb + (noun phrase) + infinitive:

ask	choose	expect	hate*	love*	need	prefer	want	would like
beg	dare	get	like*	know	pay	prepare	wish	

*Verbs that can take either a gerund or an infinitive.
**Verbs that can take either a gerund or an infinitive but with a difference in meaning.

Grammar Glossary

active sentence A sentence that is not in passive form; often, the subject is the performer of the action of the verb.

Millions of people watch the World Cup.

adjective A type of noun modifier; often describes a noun.

He drinks **strong, black** coffee.

adjective clause (also called *relative clause*) A clause that modifies a noun.

A scientist **who studies personality** has developed a new theory.

adverb A word that describes or otherwise modifies a verb, an adjective, another adverb, or a sentence.

They worked **quickly** and **carefully** on the project.

adverb clause A clause that functions like an adverb, modifying the main clause verb or the main clause.

Because they want their product to sell, companies do market research.

adverb of frequency An adverb that tells how often an action occurs.

"Night owls" **usually** do their best work at night.

agent The performer of the action of the verb. In a passive sentence, the agent, if included, is in a *by* phrase.

The goalie stopped the ball.
The ball was stopped by **the goalie.**

article The words *a/an* and *the*, which are used to introduce or identify a noun.

a cook **an** orange
the menu **the** recipes

auxiliary verb A verb that is used with a main verb to make questions and negative sentences and to help make tenses and express meaning (*do, be, have*, and modals).

Are you working?
We **did**n't finish the exam.

She **has** traveled a lot.
They **should** get out more.

base form of a verb (also called *the simple form of a verb*) A verb without *to* in front of it or any endings.

play **work** **be** **do**

causative verb A verb (e.g., *have, let, make*) used to mean to cause or allow someone to do something.

John **had** us buy the concert tickets.

clause A group of related words that has a subject and a verb.

Before he leaves, . . .
We're back!
. . . because it sells well.

collective noun A noun that refers to a group.

committee **family**
audience **team**

common noun A noun that does not name a particular person, place, or thing.

cat **coffee** **students**
buildings **loyalty**

conditional sentence A sentence that contains a condition clause and a result clause and expresses a relationship between the condition and result.

If a storm comes up, you should go inside.

connector A word that shows how ideas are related.

because **but**
also **nevertheless**

■ **coordinating conjunction** A word—*and, but, or, nor, so, for, yet*—that connects clauses and, in some cases, also phrases or words.

We wrote the proposal, **and** they accepted it.
I tried **but** didn't succeed.

■ **count noun** A noun that can be counted.

a **restaurant** two **restaurants**
an **apple** three **apples**

■ **definite article** *The*; used to identify nouns that refer to something specific and are known to both the speaker and listener.

The chef in this restaurant wrote a best-selling cookbook.

■ **demonstrative** *This, that, these, those*; demonstratives can be pronouns or determiners.

That is really good.
These days, dining out is popular.

■ **determiner** A word that comes before a common noun; determiners can be articles, quantifiers, demonstratives, and possessives.

the salad **many** desserts
this table **your** order

■ **future** *Will/be going to* + base form of the verb; used to talk about future events; sometimes also expressed with simple present, present progressive, *be about to*, and modals such as *can* and *may*.

The weather **will be** nice tomorrow.
They**'re going to see** a movie tonight.

■ **future perfect** *Will/be going to* + *have* + past participle; tense used to talk about an action or state that will occur before a future action, state, or time.

I **will have finished** my work by then.

■ **future perfect progressive** (also called *future perfect continuous*) *Will/be going to* + *have* + *been* + verb + *-ing*; tense used to talk about an action that will continue to a future action, state, or time.

They **will have been traveling** for many days when they get there.

■ **future progressive** (also called *future continuous*) *Will/be going to* + *be* + verb + *-ing*; tense used to talk about actions that will be in progress in the future.

He **is going to be flying** to Hawaii next week.

■ **gerund** Formed from verb + *-ing*; often functions as a noun.

We enjoy **dancing** and **singing**.

■ **indefinite article** *A/an*; used to introduce a noun that doesn't refer to something specific or that the speaker and listener don't both know.

a banana **an** author

■ **indefinite pronoun** A pronoun that is used to talk about unspecified people or things or about people or things in general.

Is **anybody** out there?

■ **infinitive** Formed from *to* + base form of the verb; often functions as a noun.

We wanted **to go** to the circus.
To climb Mount Everest is our dream.

■ **intensifier** A word that is used before an adjective or adverb to strengthen the meaning of the adjective or adverb.

That restaurant is **very** expensive.
We got our food **quite** quickly.

■ **intransitive verb** A verb that does not take an object.

We **stood** in line for football tickets.

■ **main clause** (also called *independent clause*) A clause that is, or could be, a complete sentence.

We arrived late.
When we got there, **he had to leave**.

■ **main verb** The verb in a sentence in the simple present or simple past and, in sentences in other tenses, the verb that carries the primary verbal meaning (i.e., not an auxiliary verb).

We **traveled** to Japan.
We had **gone** there once before.

- **modal** An auxiliary verb that expresses ideas related to degrees of certainty, social functions, and/or ability.

  She **might** be at home.
  They **must** leave soon.
  We **can** sing well.

- **modifier** A word, phrase, or clause that describes and gives more information about another word, phrase, or clause.

  You look **happy**.
  The man **in white** is the chef.

- **noncount noun** A noun that cannot be counted.

  rain **sand** **happiness**
  physics **swimming**

- **noun** A word that names a person, place, or thing.

  Albert Einstein **ocean** **table**

- **noun clause** A clause that functions like a noun.

  We think **that they will get married and live happily ever after**.

- **noun phrase** A noun and its determiners and modifiers, if any.

  We ate at **that very charming new restaurant**.

- **object** A noun, pronoun, or noun phrase that receives the action of the verb.

  Paul called **us**.
  The chef prepared **a delicious meal**.

- **object of a preposition** A noun, pronoun, or noun phrase that comes after a preposition.

  for **Mary** to **them**
  with **my best friend's mother**

- **particle** An adverb that is part of a phrasal verb.

  They set **out** late.

- **passive causative** A structure, with *get/have* + object + past participle, that expresses the idea that someone "causes" someone else to perform a service.

  The players **had** their uniforms **cleaned**.

- **passive sentence** A sentence that has *be* followed by the past participle of the main verb; the subject of the sentence is the receiver of the action of the verb.

  The World Cup is watched by millions of people.

- **past perfect** *Had* + past participle; tense used to talk about past actions or states that occurred before another past action, state, or time.

  I **had read** the book before I saw the movie.

- **past perfect progressive** (also called *past perfect continuous*) *Had* + *been* + present participle; tense used to talk about an action that began before and continued to another past action, state, or time.

  They **had been working** for hours when he arrived.

- **past progressive** (also called *past continuous*) *Was/Were* + present participle; tense used to talk about an action in progress in the past.

  He **was sleeping** when the phone rang.

- **phrasal verb** A verb + adverb (particle); its meaning is different from the meaning of the verb + the meaning of the particle.

  They **kept on** despite the difficulties.
  She **called** him **up**.

- **phrasal verb with preposition** (also called a *three-word verb*) The combination of a phrasal verb + a preposition.

  We **ran out of** time.

- **phrase** A group of related words that does not contain both a subject and a verb.

  on the street **the people upstairs**
  had already gone

- **possessive** A word or structure that shows ownership; may be a determiner, noun, pronoun, or phrase.

  our homework **David's** house
  It's **theirs.** the corner **of the table**

- **preposition** A function word such as *at, from, in,* or *to* that takes a noun, pronoun, or noun phrase as an object to form a prepositional phrase; often helps express meanings related to time, location, or direction.

  in the classroom **around** the same time
  with my friends

- **prepositional phrase** A preposition plus a noun, pronoun, or noun phrase.

  in the classroom **around the same time**
  with my friends

- **present perfect** *Have* + past participle; tense used to talk about actions or states that occurred at an unspecified time in the past or, with a time expression of duration, to talk about actions or states that began in the past and continue to the present.

  They **have written** a book.
  They **have lived** there for many years.

- **present perfect progressive** (also called *present perfect continuous*) *Have* + *been* + present participle; tense used to talk about actions that began in the past and continue to the present; it often emphasizes that the action is ongoing.

  They **have been cleaning** all morning.

- **present progressive** (also called *present continuous*) *Am/Is/Are* + present participle; tense used to talk about actions in progress at this moment or through a period of time including the present.

  Look! It**'s snowing.**
  He **is studying** in the United States this year.

- **pronoun** A word that replaces a noun or noun phrase that has already been mentioned or that is clear from context.

  I need to talk to **you.**
  Al is looking at **himself** in the mirror.

- **proper noun** A noun that names a particular person, place, or thing.

  Molly Brown **Denver, Colorado**
  the *Titanic*

- **quantifier** A word or phrase that indicates the quantity of a noun.

  some potatoes **a few** choices
  not much oil

- **quoted speech** A way of reporting speech that uses the exact words of the speaker.

  "I'll love you forever!" he promised.

- **reciprocal pronoun** A pronoun (*each other* or *one another*) that is used when two or more people or things give and receive the same feelings or actions.

  They stared at **each other** from across the restaurant.

- **reflexive pronoun** A pronoun that is used instead of an object pronoun when the object refers to the same person or thing as the subject of the sentence.

  They bought **themselves** a new car.

- **relative pronoun** A pronoun that begins an adjective clause.

  The author **who** wrote the book gave a speech.
  I like the book **that** we saw in the store.

- **reported speech** A way of reporting speech that does not use the speaker's exact words.

  He told her **that he would love her forever.**

- **simple past** Verb + *-ed*; tense used to talk about actions and states that began and ended in the past.

  We **walked** to school.
  He **looked** healthy.

- **simple present** Verb (+ *-s*); tense used to talk about habitual or repeated actions in the present and about things that are generally accepted as true.

  I **work** in a restaurant.
  Water **freezes** at 32°F.

- **stative passive** *-ed* adjective following *be* or *get*; unlike true passives, expresses states rather than actions.

  The door **is closed**.
  We **got excited** about the team.

- **subject** The noun, pronoun, or noun phrase that comes before the verb in a statement and that generally is what the statement is about.

  Kate went to the restaurant.
  The woman in the white hat ordered coffee.

- **subject complement** A noun, pronoun, noun phrase, or adjective that renames, identifies, or describes the subject of a sentence.

  He is **a superb chef**.
  They looked like **professionals**.

- **subordinate clause** (also called *dependent clause*) A clause that cannot stand alone but must be used with a main clause.

  When we met, we discussed the ad campaign.

- **subordinating conjunction** A word (*when, where, because, although, if,* etc.) that begins an adverb clause.

  Although they advertised the product, it didn't sell well.

- **tag question** A statement with a short question ("tag") added at the end.

  You haven't been to London, **have you?**
  He lives here, **doesn't he?**

- **time clause** A clause that begins with a time word like *when, while, before,* or *after*.

  After this class ends, I'm going home.
  They came **while she was working**.

- **transition** A word (*also, however, in addition, therefore,* etc.) that connects main clauses, sentences, or larger units, such as paragraphs.

  The clients were pleased. **Therefore**, they accepted our design.

- **transitive verb** A verb that takes an object in an active sentence.

  The golfer **hit** the ball.

- **verb** A word that shows an action or state.

  do **come** **be** **have**

- **verb–preposition combination** A combination formed by certain verbs and certain prepositions.

  We **looked for** the cat.
  They **heard from** him.

- **verb with stative meaning** A verb that refers to a state, not an action.

  She **has known** him for years.
  He **is** a good lawyer.

- ***wh-* question** (also called *information question*) A question that begins with a *wh-* word (*who, what, where, when, why, how,* etc.) and asks for information.

  Who will win the game?
  How far did you travel last night?

- ***yes/no* question** A question that can be answered with *yes* or *no*.

  Do you like chocolate?
  Was he at the game?

- **[0] article** (called the "zero" article) used instead of *a/an* with indefinite plural count nouns and noncount nouns.

  I bought **[0]** bananas at the store.
  I put **[0]** fruit in the pie.

Index

C

D

E

F

Q

R

U

V

W

Y

Z